HELLENIC PHILOSOPHY

Hellenic Philosophy
Origin and Character

CHRISTOS C. EVANGELIOU
Towson University, USA

ASHGATE

Published by
Ashgate Publishing Limited
Gower House
Croft Road
Aldershot
Hampshire GU11 3HR
England

Ashgate Publishing Company
Suite 420
101 Cherry Street
Burlington, VT 05401-4405
USA

Ashgate website: http://www.ashgate.com

British Library Cataloguing in Publication Data

Evangeliou, Christos
   Hellenic philosophy : origin and character
   1.Philosophy, Ancient
   I.Title
   180

Library of Congress Cataloging-in-Publication Data

Evangeliou, Christos.
   Hellenic philosophy : origin and character / Christos C. Evangeliou.
      p. cm.
   Includes bibliographical references and index.
   ISBN 0-7546-5847-3 (hardcover : alk. paper)
   1. Philosophy, Ancient. I. Title.
   B171.E88 2006
   1800150dc22

2006011546

ISBN-13: 978-0-7546-5847-4
ISBN-10: 0-7546-5847-3

Printed and bound in Great Britain by MPG Books Ltd. Bodmin, Cornwall.

I have a vivid memory of the first impression that this work on the origin of Philosophy had upon me. It really was an absolute eye-opener that completely shifted the intellectual paradigm that I had been raised with; by the same token, it made absolute good sense and had so much supporting evidence, that it is now very difficult to read the great giants in our field on these topics. ... [It] gives a radically new account of the origins of Hellenic philosophy ... and proceeds to indict the great majority of modern philosophers for their intellectual servitude to religion or science. I can't think of any real competitors with the range or intellectual focus of this book.

Professor Phillip Mitsis,
New York University, USA

Hellenic Philosophy: Origin and Character *is an original and provocative book. It may be counted as a masterpiece in recent publications of philosophic books. It demands to change our viewpoint in regard to so-called "*Greek *philosophy" and "*European *philosophy," both of which are products of European prejudices against the true character of* Hellenic *philosophy. Evangeliou's argumentation is powerful and lucid. The book is timely in this global era and highly recommended, especially as an antidote to religious fanaticism.*

Professor Hideya Yamakawa,
St. Andrew's University, Osaka, Japan

Professor Evangeliou's bold and provocative treatment of the major movements in the history of philosophy deserves every reader's attention. His position is far-reaching as criticism and original as diagnosis of the misleading paths philosophy traveled after the Hellenic thinkers made their great contribution to the study of human reason and culture.

Professor John P. Anton,
University of South Florida, USA

This book is very welcomed and highly recommended. Drawing, in a sharp and bright way, the very specificity of Hellenic philosophy, it considers anew issues of significance in the philosophy of Plato and Aristotle, and in Neoplatonism. It would be of great interest to any scholar in the field, and of greater help to students in Philosophy and the Humanities, as well as the educated public which may wish to learn about the historical origin and the true character of ancient Hellenic philosophy.

Professor Catherine Collobert,
University of Ottawa, Canada

Professor Evangeliou's book on the origins of Hellenic philosophy is original and provocative. His challenges to traditional and current views are based on solid arguments and supported with references to primary ancient texts. This makes Hellenic Philosophy *a valuable source for scholars and students in the field.*

Professor K. Boudouris,
University of Athens, Greece

When he boldly placed Hellenic Philosophy *between Europe, Asia and Africa, Christos Evangeliou opened for us – the philosophers who philosophize from "Our" America, the so-called Latin America – the possibility of an authentic dialogue with the classical tradition, which belongs to all humanity and to each human being. Not happy with this opening, Evangeliou gives us something much greater, the historical truth that the origins of Hellenic Philosophy are to be found outside of Greece, as the great masters of Hellenic philosophy, Plato and Aristotle, had recognized. The deep roots of human wisdom* (sophia) *were sought by them in Africa. To accept this historical fact can dignify the dialogue between human beings from Europe, Asia, Africa, North and South America, "Our" America.*

Professor Horacio Cerutti-Guldberg,
UNAM, Mexico

Evangeliou's book is timely because it contributes to the ongoing debate on the conception of the history of Western philosophy. A growing number of thinkers are engaged in projects that challenge the prevailing orthodoxy in the construction and interpretation of this history ... The book will be useful to all those who teach and learn about the history of Hellenic philosophy and its relation to "Western philosophy." ... This kind of book belongs to every public and private library of educated persons. It is not only philosophically challenging, but also well argued and clearly written.

Professor John Murungi,
Towson University, USA

Hellenic Philosophy: Origin and Character *is a provocative book in many ways. I will confine myself to only one argument that it uses with its two horns ... According to this argument a close connection existed between philosophy and the other branches of Hellenic science, in the sense that they had an equal claim to wisdom. This statement does not apply to European "philosophy" because of the bifurcation of philosophy and science. But it cannot justify the second part of the argument either, regarding the relation of Hellenic philosophy and Egypt, because the concepts of science and of man for the Egyptians were practical and theocratic rather than theoretical and anthropocentric, as they were for the Ancient Hellenes.*

Professor Leonidas C. Bargeliotes,
University of Athens, Greece

Evangeliou's brilliant book makes some unorthodox assertions about the nature of Hellenic philosophy, in contrast with that of Christianized western philosophy. It refutes the European bias about the autochthonous origin of Greek Philosophy ... Philosophy demands unfettered inquiry. Faith *and* philosophy *cannot go together. The book is rich in content and definitely thought provoking. Indian readers will find it captivating. Nostalgia for the lost glory of Hellas is discernible in the book.*

Professor Lalit M. Bahuguna,
Central Institute of Hindi New Delhi, India

Contents

Prologue

This is a revised and expanded edition of the collection of essays, which was published in 1997 under the title, *The Hellenic Philosophy: Between Europe, Asia, and Africa*. The book has been out of print for two years and its warm reception by scholars and students (of ancient Hellenic philosophy especially, and of the history of philosophy generally), necessitated the new edition under the revised title, *Hellenic Philosophy: Origin and Character*. The change in the subtitle reflects better the extended content of the present book, which contains six essays. To the original four, two new essays have been added, which help to better determine the distinctly critical character of Hellenic philosophy, as was practiced by the ancient philosophers, especially Plato and Aristotle, and their followers. The Glossary and the Bibliography have been extended to accommodate the new essays. The Notes have been placed at the end of each chapter, to facilitate the reading and help the understanding of the thesis of the book better. Accents on Greek words follow the monotonic system.

The ordering of the essays has also been changed to reflect more accurately the historical origin and the critical development of Hellenic philosophy, from vague and indeterminate beginnings to its classical maturity and fruition in the minds, words, and works of the three great philosophers, Socrates, Plato, and Aristotle. Dignified nobility, respectful critique, and unfettered freedom of thought and freedom of expression clearly defined the character of classic Hellenic philosophy. This characteristic of freedom distinguished the Hellenic from other philosophies, especially the homonymous "philosophies," which were produced in Christian Europe during the long medieval period and in modern times.

I would like to take the opportunity to thank the good students and other scholars and friends, who read the book in its first edition with care and gave me their critical comments and thoughtful advice as to how it may become a better book in the future. It is hoped that the present revised and expanded edition of the book will fulfill their high expectations, to a certain extent at least.

Special thanks are due to the following friends and Professors of Philosophy for their support and encouragement over the years: George Anagnostopoulos, University of California at San Diego, USA; J.P. Anton, University of South Florida, USA; Linda Ardito, Dowling College, USA; Leonidas Bargeliotes, University of Athens, Greece; Konstantine Boudouris, University of Athens, Greece; Bulent Gozkan, Yeditepe University, Istanbul, Turkey; Lilia Castle, Chaminade University, Hawaii, USA; Bhuvan Chandel, ICPR, India; Horatio

Cerutti, UNAM, Mexico; Alexander Chumakov, University of Moscow, Russia; Catherine Collobert, University of Ottawa, Canada; Yiannis Dellis, University of Patras, Greece; Zhao Dunhua, Peking University, China; Myrto Dragona, University of Crete, Greece; John Finamore, University of Iowa, USA; Thomas Flynn, Emory University, USA; R. Baine Harris, Old Dominion University, USA; Satoshi Horie, Keio Gijuku University, Tokyo, Japan; Elleni Kalokairinou, University of Cyprus, Cyprus; Eleni Karampatzaki-Perdiki, University of Ioannina, Greece; Ioanna Kutsuradi, University of Ankara, Turkey; Tse-wan Kwan, The Chinese University of Hong Kong, China; Tasos Ladikos, University of Pretoria, South Africa; Fred Miller, Bowling Green State University, USA; Philip Mitsis, New York University, USA; Parviz Morevedge, Rutgers University, USA; Alexander Mourelatos, University of Texas at Austin, USA; Evangelos Moutsopoulos, University of Athens, Greece; John Murungi, Towson University, USA; Alexander Nehamas, Princeton University, USA; Robert Neville, Boston University, USA; Tasos Nikolaidis, University of Crete, Greece; Orsan Oymen, Yeditepe University, Istanbul, Turkey; John Philippoussis, Dawson College, Canada; Anthony Preus, Binghamton University, USA; Heather Reid, Morningside College, USA; Thomas Robinson, University of Toronto, Canada; Christofer Rowe, Durham University, UK; Mahmoud Sakr, University of Cairo, Egypt; Socrates Velivoyiatzis, University of Thessaloniki, Greece; Gery Santas, University of California at Irvine, USA; Hideya Yamakawa, St. Andrew's University, Japan; and Evaggelos Vallianatos, University of Maryland, USA.

Christos C. Evangeliou
Professor of Philosophy
Towson, Maryland, USA.

Introduction

This book is a collection of six essays on the origin, the character, and the historical influence of Hellenic philosophy, as well as its complex global relations to other non-Hellenic philosophies of Africa, Asia, and Europe. The essays are primarily historical and philosophical studies. However, they inevitably touch upon contemporary and politically sensitive issues, relating to the nature of Western culture and European "philosophy." The latter is understood as being different from Hellenic philosophy because historically it had unhealthy connections to modern "technocratic science" and to medieval "theocratic religions" of Christianity and Islam, which have shaped fundamentally the medieval, the modern, and even the "post-modern" European mind and ethos.

The collection opens with an essay on "The Origin of Hellenic Philosophy," which deals with the thorny question of the beginnings of Ancient Hellenic philosophy and its possible cultural connection with Egypt. A comparison of the expressed views of Hellenic philosophers, supported by solid evidence derived from Hellenic historians and poets, with the views of representative European historians of philosophy, such as Jaeger and Guthrie, clearly shows that the Ancient Hellenes were free of prejudices, which guided Modern Europeans. For example, unlike Modern Europeans, the Ancient Hellenes do not appear to have believed that philosophy, science, and civilization originated exclusively with them. Nor did the Hellenes, unlike the Modern Europeans, seem to have had a problem with regard to giving credit, when credit was due, to other peoples around them, especially to Egyptians, for their contributions to arts and sciences, and even to philosophy, as practiced by the Hellenes.

The supporting evidence for my thesis is derived primarily from the texts of Ancient Hellenic authors, historians, poets, and philosophers, especially Plato and Aristotle, whose works are the best preserved. They are generally recognized as the greatest philosophers among the many great Hellenic philosophers. Thus, a link is provided between the first essay and the other two essays in Part One, which deal respectively with the "alleged relations" between Plato and European philosophy, and between Aristotle and Western rationality. These claims are examined, criticized, and rejected because they distort the genuine character of Ancient Hellenic *philosophia* and its "passion," that is, the sequence of "abuses," which have plagued it in Christian Europe. It has suffered much in the hands and narrow minds of theologians, technocrats, and political ideologues during the centuries.

The second essay, "Plato and European Philosophy," focuses on a widely propagated European "myth" which claims that European "philosophy" is nothing but a "series of footnotes to Plato." This myth is exposed here for what it really is. By distinguishing two versions of Platonism, the Hellenic and the Christian, and by critically discussing a representative case, "Augustine vs. Porphyry," it is clearly shown that it was the Christian version, which influenced the medieval and the modern European mind for more than a millennium. It is also argued that this Christianized Platonism is incompatible with genuine Hellenic Platonism. Thus it is ironic that A.N. Whitehead, who popularized the hypothesis regarding European philosophy as "footnotes to Plato," is also the man who tried tactfully to recover its lost spirit, and to reconnect with genuine Platonic philosophy.

The third essay, "Aristotle and Western Rationality," also challenges another widely held misconception, to wit, the claim that Western culture is distinguished from other cultures by its rationality. The roots of this "rationality" are allegedly found in Aristotle's philosophy. But, by tracing Aristotle's method of dialectic through his major works, and by distinguishing the noetic or intuitive from the syllogistic aspect of his multifaceted thought, it is suggested that the case of Aristotle is not at all different from that of Plato. In terms of their respective relations with the European mind and ethos, the two cases of Hellenic philosophers are indistinguishable. It would seem, then, that the affinity of Hellenic philosophy, (which is represented by Plato and Aristotle here), with the geographically remote philosophies of India and China, is significantly greater than its supposed affinity with the "European philosophy." Yet, to the latter it has allegedly given birth, as European historians of philosophy dogmatically claim. With this assessment the author disagrees and will argue against it strongly.

The fourth essay, "Aristotle's Critique of the Platonic Polity," examines briefly a case of Hellenic criticism regarding the proper arrangement of the ideal *polis* (city-state). For specific and clearly articulated reasons, Aristotle did not accept Plato's proposal of radical "communism" of women, children, and property. This spirit (and method) of reasoned critique among friends is characteristic (not accidentally and not only) of Aristotle's philosophy and his respectful relation to his teacher. It also pervades the entire history of Hellenic philosophy and its millennial fruitful development by critical thinking, honest disagreement among philosophers, and free expression without fear.

The same point is exemplified also by the fifth essay, which centers on "Pletho's Critique of Aristotelian Novelties." Just as Aristotle respectfully disagreed with Plato, regarding the conception of the ideally best polity for the classical Hellenic *polis,* so Pletho, a Renaissance Platonist, criticized Aristotle on a number of points of philosophical import. Pletho had detailed reasons for preferring the more traditional and speculative Platonic doctrines to Aristotelian innovations regarding some cosmological, theological, ontological, psychological, aesthetic, and ethical matters. Thus, it is not surprising that his rigorous critique of the fashionable at that time Aristotelian philosophy was instrumental in effecting a revival of Platonism in the Italian Renaissance and beyond. Sadly, the brief Platonic revival was obscured by the fervor of Reformation that followed upon it.

The last essay, "The Character of Hellenic Philosophy," outlines another challenging thesis. This thesis will become the main theme and the focal point of a more thorough discussion, to which a separate book will be devoted in the future. As articulated here, my thesis contests certain uncritical assumptions which, for a long time, have uncritically guided the historiography of philosophy. Among such false assumptions the following are included: Firstly, Ancient Hellenic philosophy is taken to be, traditionally, the original part of Western or European "philosophy." In other words, European "philosophy" is considered incorrectly as the continuation of the free and bold spirit of Hellenic philosophy and its characteristic ethos. Secondly, it is assumed again falsely that "European philosophy," as it developed during the Middle Ages and in modern times, has made an overall improvement upon the legacy of Ancient Hellenic philosophy. My thesis is critical of each of these hasty claims, which are historically incorrect and philosophically unjustifiable. For, by the Hellenic definition of *philosophia*, understood as free inquiry, sharp critique, and unfettered reflection on both nature and culture, the so-called European "philosophy" becomes a clear case of "*homonymia*."

It is argued specifically that "European philosophy" has been deprived, for historical religious reasons, of that essential freedom of spirit, which is absolutely necessary for authentic philosophy to be born and flourish anywhere. While the Ancient Hellenic philosophers enjoyed such philosophic freedom (from Pythagoras and Parmenides to Plotinus and Porphyry, and to Proclus and Pletho), the so-called "European philosophers" for a millennium and a half had the great misfortune to serve, alternatively or simultaneously, three harsh and non-Hellenic masters. These alien forces can be identified respectively as dogmatic theology, scientific technology, and political ideology. Hence what is here called, perhaps poetically but accurately, "the passion of Hellenic philosophy," that is, the strange phenomenon of the various historical "metamorphoses" of Hellenic philosophy in Christian Europe, including Orthodox Greece. Philosophy has been the traditional *ancilla theologiae*, *ancilla scientiae*, and *ancilla ideologiae*, respectively. This is a broad and promising topic indeed waiting for its proper philosophical exploration.

The essays were originally written and presented at professional philosophy conferences and international symposia.[1] Over the years they have been reworked and expanded, especially in the endnotes, some of which are much longer than the usual footnotes to scholarly papers. The endnotes, therefore, should be read as carefully as the text of the essays, and with a sense of irony. For, in order to retain somewhat the tone of live presentation, some of the more interesting, more challenging and perhaps provocative comments have been placed in the notes for the more inquisitive minds.

However, the purpose of the notes, as well as the purpose of the essays, was not to provoke anybody but to enlighten everybody, or at least the eager students of philosophy, who seek the truth. In this case, they demand to know the historical truth regarding the origin and character of Hellenic philosophy and its "passion" in Europe.

Note

1. Shorter versions of the views presented in these essays were published previously in the following journals respectively: *Skepsis* 4 (1993): 41-76; *Dionysius* 13 (1989): 51-70; *Journal of Indian Council of Philosophical Research* 12 (1995): 49-78; *Philosophia 25* (1995-6): 200-213; *Skepsis* 8 (1997): 146-170; and *Alexandria* 4 (1997): 289-303. I thank the editors of these journals for the permission to revise and use the articles for this version of the book too.

PART 1
Origin and Maturity of Hellenic Philosophy

Chapter 1

The Origin of Hellenic Philosophy

Introduction

Alexander the Great built several great cities along the way from Pella, his birthplace in Hellenic Macedonia, to Punjab in Northern India, which marked the eastward limit of his campaign against the Persian Empire. Even before Alexander's time, the Persians had reached the shores of Eastern Mediterranean and had conquered many peoples including the two friendly nations, the Hellenes of Asia Minor and the Egyptians. In desperation, they had expected that Ammon (or Zeus) would send them a liberator. In Alexander the Great, they found such a god-sent leader, liberator and benefactor. The most magnificent of the cities bearing Alexander's name flourished on the banks of the Nile in Northern or Lower Egypt.[1]

Alexandria of the Nile was destined to function as the great melting pot where a cultural trinity, constituted by the spirit of Hellas (or Europe), Egypt (or Africa),[2] and Near East (or Asia) met, mated and fused together for the first time in recorded history.[3] As a result of that felicitous meeting of three diverse cultural traditions, a prolific fertilization of the spirit was accomplished in Alexandria. For it was there, in Alexandria of the Nile, where Platonism was reborn and renewed under the new names of Christian, Jewish, Gnostic, Hermetic, and Hellenic Platonism.[4] It would seem, in this light, that Plato, who had inherited from the Pythagorean tradition (through Socrates and Archytas respectively)[5] a double debt,[6] was able to pay off the debt, with the accumulated interest in the interval of centuries of Hellenic philosophy.[7]

At the present, however, I would like to concentrate on the roots rather than the branches, blossoms, and fruits of the tree of Platonism and of Hellenic Philosophy generally, in Egypt and in Northern Africa.[8] But even to speak of a possible Egyptian connection in Ancient Hellenic philosophy (or science and religion for that matter) is considered "anathema" by the prevailing scholarly opinion in the West. For the conventional European historiography, as practiced systematically in the last two centuries, claims rather dogmatically that the scientific method has set clearly marked and well-defined boundaries for the discipline of Hellenic philosophy, covering the period from Thales to Aristotle only.[9]

Accordingly, what the Hellenic genius had created before Thales of Miletus (6th BC) is conveniently assigned to "mythical account" (*mythos*) as opposed to "rational account" (*logos*), which is considered as trademark of pure "rationality" in philosophy and science.[10] What the Hellenic genius created after Aristotle of Stagira (384-322 BC) is often considered as decadent and set aside. However, what the same Hellenic genius created during the short period from Thales to Aristotle (6th-4th BC), in an effort to explain the origin of the orderly cosmos and to effect the political reorganization of human life in the Hellenic *polis*, is praised as Hellenic "rationality" at its finest moment.[11]

The implication of this interpretation is that the scientific and philosophic spirit was a rather short-lived Hellenic invention. For, we are told that the inquiring mind was born in the lovely land of Hellenic Ionia in Asia Minor, and was strengthened by the bright light of the Mediterranean sun. It was bathed in the clean blue waters of the Aegean Sea, being nurtured by the tolerant laws of the Hellenic free city-states, with their vigilant protection of the freedom of thought and speech. And it suddenly died out when Alexander the Great (the student of the last great Hellenic philosopher, Aristotle) put an end to the political liberties of those enviable free city-states at the battle of Chaeronea in 338 BC.[12]

The free spirit of scientific inquiry and philosophical speculation hibernated after that tragedy, so the story goes, for nearly two millennia, until the seventeenth century. Then, suddenly, the same philosophic and scientific spirit was revived in Northern Europe causing the great discoveries and technological achievements of modern times. On these achievements the Europeans, (especially the British, the French, the Dutch, and the German), have based over the years not only their economic and strategic power, but also their inordinate claims to cultural superiority, political hegemony and, for centuries, global colonization. Americans seem to follow them blindly, in this blind alley.

In this conventional light, then, it would seem that the Ancient Hellenes are acknowledged as the true teachers of a higher civilization. For Modern Europeans, they alone have set the standards of methodical inquiry into the nature of things and of political organization of human affairs, which can make life worth living for any intelligent, ethically responsible, and politically mature person. In this European mythology, those "Glorious Greeks" are supposed to have descended from the North, of course, and to have been self-taught, when it comes to things of higher culture such as politics, poetics, art, science, and philosophy.[13]

That is the story constantly, commonly, and conventionally told about the Ancient Hellenes by Modern Europeans in the histories of so-called "Western philosophy."[14] Assuming that the story is meant to glorify the Hellenes, by frankly acknowledging their achievements and solid contributions to our common civilization, we should consider whether the story is also "historically sound." To do so briefly, it would be necessary to address the following pertinent questions: How did the Ancient Hellenes perceive themselves and their relations to other non-Hellenic peoples, who surrounded them in historical times? Did they see themselves as the "potential teachers" of the Northern Europeans? Or, rather, did they consider themselves as students who had much to learn from the non-Hellenic civilizations of the great rivers (the Nile, the Euphrates, and even the Indus), which lured Alexander and directed his amazing energy relentlessly, not westward, but eastward?

Well, I would like to suggest that the available literary evidence (from Homer and Herodotus to Plato, Aristotle, Isocrates, Plutarch, Porphyry, and beyond) would support the latter hypothesis only.[15] In their own eyes the Ancient Hellenes, at least the intellectually aware among them, were the newcomers on the historical scene, who desired to learn from those who already knew. And they did learn from others, especially the nearby and wise Egyptians, whom they admired as much as the Northern Europeans would later admire the Ancient Hellenes. This was to take place in the distant future, when Europeans would have learned to read and appreciate the Hellenic sciences, arts, poetry, and philosophy.[16]

So, even if we accept the claim that the Ancient Athenians entertained the strange notion that, in comparison with other Hellenic tribes, they were like the cicadas of the Attic soil (autochthonous and aboriginal), this notion would certainly refer to their bodily birth only. Politically understood, it might have advantaged them over others by emphasizing their antiquity.[17] But in the sphere of the spirit, that is, in the arts and sciences, philosophy and religion, political organization and law, all Hellenic tribes (Ionian, Aeolian, and Dorian) were conscious of their youthful lack of wisdom and refinement, when compared with the much older, richer, and more civilized Egyptians. Like children, the travelling and intelligent Hellenes were full of questions and in awe of the experienced and "learned Egyptians."[18] The wonderful works of Egyptian art and the wise words of Egyptian sages made a lasting impression on the impressionable Hellenic minds.[19]

Renowned Hellenic travelers and theorists, such as Solon of Athens, Thales of Miletus, Pythagoras of Samos, Democritus, Plato, Herodotus, and Eudoxus, to mention only the most notable, all had traveled extensively and, according to an Ancient Hellenic tradition, had visited Egypt too.[20] They were greeted abroad perhaps in the same manner as Solon was greeted by an old Egyptian sage saying to him: "Solon, you Greeks are never anything but children, and there is not an old man among you."[21] As we will see below, to the Ancient Hellenes, especially to the Hellenic philosophers, this Egyptian assertion was nothing but a self-evident truth. That Modern European historians of Ancient Hellenic Philosophy overlook the simple truth of this historical fact was a puzzle for me (as an ardent student of philosophy), which originally motivated and ultimately justified the genesis of this study.[22]

Apparently, then, if the Ancient Hellenes desired enlightenment, they had to look to the East and South, that is, the realm of the rising Sun and the warm Wind. They could not possibly have looked to the West and North which, in their imagination, were places associated with darkness, dampness, and death. If we wish, therefore, to identify the origins of fecund ideas of Hellenic philosophy relating to Pythagorean "number theory,"[23] to Socratic "care of the soul,"[24] or even to Platonic "ideal state," we should know where to look for their roots.[25]

Three Basic Questions

To bring this prolonged introduction to an end and come to the core of the matter under consideration, it should be stated from the outset that our discussion will be limited and focused on the following three basic and closely related questions only:

First, what did the poets, the historians, and especially the philosophers of Ancient Hellas, know about the Egyptians, their civilized life, and their possible relation to Hellenic culture?

Second, how did the Hellenic philosophers, especially Plato and Aristotle, conceive of the origin of philosophy as a cultural phenomenon and its possible connection with Egypt in the distant past?

Third, if it appears that the picture which the Ancient Hellenes had of themselves and the people around them, especially the Egyptians, does not cohere with the picture, which is presented by the Modern Europeans, then we will have a serious dilemma. For we will have to face the question: Which of the two presented views is more likely to be accurate, closer to historical truth, and preferable to unbiased students of philosophy, who are ardent lovers of wisdom and truth?

I shall argue, regarding the first question, that by the sixth century, when Hellenic philosophy conventionally began with Thales of Miletus, travel by sea was easy, from the Aegean islands and the Hellenic cities in Asia Minor to the Delta of the Nile. Furthermore, the language barrier had been considerably overcome by trained Egyptian interpreters at least a century earlier. More significantly, during the sixth and subsequent centuries, the two nations were brought closer to each other by the "common threat" of the powerful Persian Empire. At that crucial time, it was rapidly expanding westward at the expense of the allied nations, Egypt and Hellas. So they had to stand together to defend what was their common cultural ground and freedom.

Regarding the second question, I shall argue that the Hellenic philosophers (unlike Modern European historians of philosophy), could not have claimed and as a matter of fact did not claim, that philosophy, science, and civilization originated with them "solely." Their cyclical conception of time and history, and their broad conception of philosophy as "the wonderful art of wondering," would not have allowed them such a narrow and petty view.[26] Therefore, we will conclude that the Ancient Hellenes were much more open-minded on the question of "origins" than their apparent admirers, the Modern European thinkers.

I shall argue further, regarding the third question, and conclude with the observation that the two methods (the Ancient/Hellenic and the Modern/European) of approaching the "origin of philosophy" problem, and its relation to Ancient Hellenes and to Ancient Egyptians, yield results clearly incompatible. It would be, therefore, reasonable for us to accept the one, which seems closer to the truth and the least biased. That turns out to be the Ancient method, with its much clearer picture of the Ancient Hellenes and their honest, sensitive, and sensible multicultural relations, especially with Egypt.[27]

The Way from Hellas to the Nile

In Homer, the eldest eponymous poet and educator of all the historical Hellenes, we find references to African peoples.[28] For instance, making use of poetic license, Homer claims that, when the Olympian Gods were fed up with the follies and constant quarrels of the restless residents of Achaia (Ancient Hellas), they would depart from Hellenic Olympus[29] for Ethiopia and the African mountains where they would enjoy peace. Thus, we read in the opening scene of the *Odyssey*, that absent from the meeting of the Gods, which would determine the fate of Odysseus and his long homecoming, was Poseidon, the great God of the sea and adversary of the Homeric hero, for the following reason:

> Poseidon, however, was now gone on a visit to the distant Ethiopians, the farthest outposts of mankind, half of whom live where the Sun goes down, and half where he rises. He had gone to accept a sacrifice of bulls and rams, and there he sat and enjoyed the pleasures of the feast.[30]

Later on in the story, when Odysseus had already reached Ithaca in disguise, he told the loyal Eumaeus of the adventure of a Cretan Prince, who had gathered a company and sailed for nearby Egypt:

> On the fifth day we reached the great river of Egypt, and there in the Nile I brought my curved ships to. And now I ordered my good men to stay by the ships on guard while I sent out some scouts to reconnoitre from the heights. But these ran amuck and in a trice, carried away by their own violence, they plundered some of the fine Egyptian farms, bore off women and children and killed the men. The hue and cry soon reached the city, and the townsfolk, roused by the alarm, turned out at dawn. The whole place was filled with infantry and chariots and the glint of arms. Zeus the Thunderer struck abject panic into my party. Not a man had the spirit to stand up to the enemy, for we were threatened on all sides. They ended by cutting down a large part of my force and carrying off the survivors to work for them as slaves. As for myself, a sudden inspiration saved me—though I still wish I had faced my destiny and fallen there in Egypt ... I passed seven years in the country and made a fortune out of the Egyptians, who were liberal with me, one and all. But in the course of the eighth, I fell in with a rascally Phoenician, a thieving knave who had already done a deal of mischief in the world. I was prevailed upon by this specious rogue to join him in a voyage to Phoenicia, where he had a house and estate; and there I stayed with him for a whole twelvemonth. But when the days and months had mounted up, and the second year began its round of seasons, he put me on board for Libya, on the pretext of wanting my help with the cargo he was carrying, but really in order that he might sell me for a handsome sum when he got there. Full of suspicion but having no choice I followed him on board. With a good

stiff breeze from the north the ship took the central route and ran down the lee side of Crete. But Zeus had their end in store for them.[31]

This is a revealing story. To the audience of Homer, the fine farms of the Egyptians, the easy way of getting there, their generosity and nobility, in comparison with the thieving Phoenician and the greedy Cretan, must have been all too familiar. However, the disguised as a Cretan Prince Odysseus was not the only Homeric hero who allegedly visited Egypt. More persistent is the legend that Helen, the beautiful daughter of Zeus and the poetic cause of the Trojan War, had spent some romantic and memorable moments in that distant land, as a guest of the King and Queen of Egypt. The visit occurred either in her escape with Paris from Sparta or, more likely, in her return from Troy to Sparta in the ship of Menelaus.[32] In either case Helen, as poetically portrayed by Homer, had fond memories of her alleged visit to Egypt. She had presumably received precious gifts from her Egyptian royal friends and, more to the point, she had picked up some pieces of precious "Egyptian wisdom," regarding medicine and potent drugs. Consider the following episode as an example of such medical knowledge:

> Helen, meanwhile, the child of Zeus, had a happy thought. Into the bowl in which their wine was mixed, she slipped a drug that had the power of robbing grief and anger of their sting and banishing all painful memories. No one that swallowed this dissolved in wine could shed a single tear that day, even for the death of his mother and father, or if they put his own son to the sword and he were there to see it done. This powerful anodyne was one of many useful drugs, which had been given to the daughter of Zeus by an Egyptian lady, Polydamna, the wife of Thon. For the fertile soil of Egypt is most rich in herbs, many of which are wholesome in solution, though many are poisonous. And in medical knowledge the Egyptian leaves the rest of the world behind. He is a true son of Paieon the Healer.[33]

We should heed the last remarks of Homer, in praise of Egyptian "medical knowledge," because it will help us later to properly evaluate the view held by certain Modern Europeans scholars concerning the origins of science, including medicine, and philosophy. Homer may have been the first eponymous poet of Hellas to make poetic use of Helen's legendary visit to Egypt, but he was by no means the last. For besides Homer, Euripides poetically exploited Helen's visit to Egypt and her dealing with potent drugs in a hilarious tragicomedy, which bears her beautiful name, *Helen:*[34]

> These are the waters of the Nile, stream of sweet nymphs.
> The river, fed with melting of pale snows, and not
> with rain, rises to flood the flats of Egypt. Here
> Proteus, while yet he lived, was lord over the land,
> at home in Pharos, king in Egypt; and his bride
> was Psamathe, one of the daughters of the deep,
> wife once of Aeacus, later sundered from him ...

Nor is my own country obscure. It is a place
called Sparta, and my father was Tyndareus: though
they tell a story about how Zeus took on himself
the shape of a flying swan, with eagle in pursuit,
and came on wings to Leda my mother, and so won
the act of love by treachery. It may be so.
They called me Helen. Let me tell you all the truth
of what has happened to me. The three goddesses came
to remote Ida, and to Paris, for him to judge
their loveliness, and beauty was the cause ...
Because of me, beside the waters of Scamander, lives
were lost in numbers; and the ever patient I
am cursed by all and thought to have betrayed my lord
and for the Hellenes lit the flame of a great war.
Why do I go on living, then? Yet I have heard
from the god Hermes that I yet shall make my home
in the famous plain of Sparta with my lord, and he
shall know I never went to Ilium, had no thought
of bed with any man. Here, while yet Proteus looked
upon this sun we see, I was safe from marriage. Now ...
Thus, though I wear the name of guilt in Greece, yet here
I keep my body uncontaminated by disgrace ...[35]

But it is time for us now to turn from the poets and their creative imagination to historians and their "matter of fact" and sober reasoning about the world of politics, diplomacy, and war. Not surprisingly, we find in the two greatest historians of Hellas, Herodotus and Thucydides, only admiration and praise for the civilized Egyptians and what they had to teach the Ancient Hellenes, who were their only allies against the common enemy, the powerful Persian Empire.[36] A few passages from their works will clearly show the close historical relations between the Hellenes and the Egyptians from the seventh century onward.[37] That is, one hundred years before the conventional beginning of Hellenic philosophy in the sixth century BC with Thales.[38] For Herodotus, the cooperation of the Ionian Greeks and the Egyptians began in the time of the reign of Psamitichus I, as a result of a raid similar to the one described above:

Psamitichus I gained control of the whole country from Sais by the help of Ionian and Carian sea-raiders who were by bad weather to land on the Egyptian coast ... He [granted them two pieces of land in the Delta and much gold and silver] even went so far as to put some Egyptian boys in their charge to be taught Greek; and their learning of the language was the origin of the class of Egyptian interpreters. The tracts of land where the Ionians and Carians settled, and where they lived for many years, lie a little distance seaward from Bubastis, on the Pelusian mouth of the Nile. Amasis subsequently turned them out and brought them to Memphis, to protect him from his own people. They were the first foreigners to live in Egypt, and after their original settlement there, the Greeks began regular intercourse with the Egyptians so that we have accurate knowledge of Egyptian History of the time of Psamitichus onward.[39]

Under King Amasis (568-526 BC), identified by Herodotus as "a friend of the Hellenes,"[40] the relations between the Hellenes and the Egyptians became even more cordial as the threat of the Persian menace moved westwards and came closer to them both.[41] The King went so far as to marry Ladice, a Princess of Cyrene (a Hellenic *polis* in Northern Africa).[42] But after Amasis' death, Egypt was conquered by the Persian King Cambyses and became a province of his immense Empire.[43] So did the Ionian Greek city-states less than a generation later in 494 BC. The famed battles of Marathon and Salamis saved the freedom of the Hellenes in mainland Hellas, while it raised the hopes of the Egyptians for regaining their lost freedom. Thus, inspired by Inaros, son of the above-mentioned Psamitichus, the Egyptians rebelled against the Persian tyranny. They asked their friends and freedom loving Hellenes, especially the Athenians, for help. The response was positive and prompt. Thucydides describes the event in the following manner:

> After taking over power himself, Inaros called in the Athenians to help him ... They came to Egypt and sailed from the sea up the Nile. They gained control of the river and of the two thirds of Memphis, and then attempted to subdue the remaining third, which was called the White Castle and inside which were the Persians and Medes who had escaped and those Egyptians who had not joined the revolt ... Meanwhile the Athenian and the allied force in Egypt was still engaged and suffered all the chances and changes of war. At first the Athenians were masters of Egypt, and the king sent to Sparta a Persian named Megabazus with money to bribe the Spartans to invade Attica and so force the Athenians to recall their fleet from Egypt ... Here [at the Medesian mouth] the Athenians were under attack from the land by the Persians and from the sea by the Phoenician fleet. Most of the ships were lost, though a few managed to escape. This was the end of the great expedition against Egypt made by the Athenians and their allies. (I, 96-99)[44]

Historically speaking, then, it is well documented that the Hellenes and their Egyptian allies, facing a common danger in the Persian expansion, developed close cultural bonds and relations. This began in the seventh century and continued until, three centuries later, a great son of Hellas, Alexander the Great, succeeded in uniting the Hellenes and in leading them victoriously against the Persians. He dissolved the Persian Empire and liberated both the Hellenes of Asia Minor and the Egyptians, who welcomed him as their savior sent by the Gods, calling him the son of Ammon (a synonym of Zeus).[45] Apparently with the intention of stressing the common cultural bonds between the two friendly nations,[46] Alexander built the Alexandria on the Nile. This Hellenistc *polis* was destined to become the great melting pot that fused together many cultures, especially the Hellenic and the Egyptian cultures for a millennium.[47]

A new world-order was born from Alexander's victories, known as the Hellenistic era (in distinction to Hellenic). One of the great political and cultural centers of the new era was the city of Alexandria, with its racial mixture and great cultural diversity. In this way the world was prepared for the birth of a cosmopolitan religion. It is no accident that Christianity (Eastern Orthodox Christianity especially, with its rich ritual, mystical spirituality, and a sophisticated Trinitarian Theology) was born and matured mainly in Alexandria. But in the same great city were also born some of the most potent Christian heresies. By challenging the authority of the Christian Church and its Orthodoxy, these heresies prepared the way for the coming of a new heretical religion, the strictly monotheistic and even more militant Islam.[48]

This being the case, it would seem that the scholars who doubt the possibility that some Hellenic philosophers (Thales, Pythagoras, Democritus, Plato, Eudoxus, and so on) could have visited Egypt and learned something there, as the ancient Hellenic tradition insists that they did,[49] do not stand on firm ground. Nor do those fare any better who, for whatever reasons, seem to want to downplay the possible influence that the civilized Egyptians might have had on the intelligent Hellenes, who paid then a visit and asked many questions, as Herodotus did later on and reported extensively on his experience.[50] Language could not have been a serious barrier because, by that time, the separate class of interpreters was numerous and ubiquitous, as we saw.[51]

In this sense, the great Egyptian god Thon or Theuth[52] had been generous to his people since, according to the Platonic Socrates: "He it was that invented number and calculation, geometry and astronomy, not to speak of draughts and dice, and above all writing."[53] Let this, then, suffice about the historical and poetic evidence regarding the multiple connections of ancient *Hellas* with *Aigyptos*.

The Origin of Hellenic Philosophy

Wonder and curiosity, love of learning and critical questioning, and above all leisure for free intellectual pursuits and amicable discourse are characteristics associated with genuine *philosophia,* as practiced and understood by the Ancient Hellenes. Plato and Aristotle, whose works mark the apex of Hellenic philosophy and, more importantly, whose writings have been preserved, agree on this essential point, although they respectfully disagree on other points of philosophic doctrine. For them, human wonder (*thaumazein*) is "the origin of philosophy" and the art of philosophizing.[54]

Accordingly, the beginning of what the Hellenes would consider as philosophy can go as far back as the appearance of *Homo Sapiens* on Mother Earth. For in order to satisfy an inborn curiosity and a very deep desire for enlightenment, human beings began to philosophize, that is, to acquire knowledge by questioning, distinguishing, comparing, and classifying things according to certain criteria. This knowledge was not only practical and useful, as it would have to be at the beginning, but also theoretical and for its own sake as time went on. But, for this kind of activity to be fruitful or even possible, a leisurely type of existence must have been secured for at least some people. They could, then, be allowed and even encouraged to spend time in thinking and discussing the problems of the natural cosmos and of human life in settled and politically organized communities.[55]

I will, therefore, allow first Plato and then Aristotle to speak for themselves on the question of origin/s of philosophy, the preconditions of its coming into being and its flourishing, and more significantly the possibility of its practice outside of Hellas, before the sixth century BC. To begin with, then, let us consider a dialogue between Socrates and his friend Theaetetus, which addresses clearly the first of these questions:

> I could give you countless other examples, if you are to accept these. For I think you follow me Theaetetus; I fancy, at any rate, such puzzles are not altogether strange to you.
> No, indeed it is extraordinary how they set me wondering whatever they can mean. Sometimes I get quite dizzy with thinking of them.
> That shows that Theodorus was not wrong in his estimate of your nature. This sense of wonder is the mark of the philosopher. Philosophy indeed has no other origin, and he was a good genealogist who made Iris the daughter of Thaumas ... Then just take a look around and make sure that none of the uninitiated overhears us. I mean by uninitiated the people who believe that nothing is real save what they can grasp with their hands and do not admit that actions and processes or anything invisible can count as real.
> They sound like a very hard and repellent sort of people.
> It is true they are remarkably crude. The others, into whose secrets I am going to initiate you, are much more refined and subtle. Their first principle, on which all that we said just now depends, is that the universe really is motion and nothing else.[56]

Thaumas or Thamus, mentioned by the Platonic Socrates here, is the same Egyptian king, to whom the wise Theuth (identified with the Hellenic Hermes) presented the invented arts and sciences, including the art of writing. Theuth/Hermes considered these arts as a remedy to memory and an inexhaustible source of wisdom for man. The King disagreed. To refresh our recollection, let us quote from *Phaedrus*:

> Socrates: Very well. The story is that in the region of Naucratis in Egypt there dwelt one of the old gods of the country, the god to whom the bird called Ibis is sacred, his own name being Theuth. He it was that invented number and calculation, geometry and astronomy, not to speak of draughts and dice, and above all writing. Now the king of the whole country at that time was Thamus, who dwelt in the great city of Upper Egypt, which the Greeks call Egyptian Thebes, while Thamus they call Ammon. To him came Theuth and revealed his arts, saying that they ought to be passed on to the Egyptians in general. Thamus asked what was the use of them all, and when Theuth explained, he condemned what he thought the bad points and praised what he thought the good. On

each art, we are told, Thamus had plenty of views both for and against; it would take too long to give them in detail. But when it came to writing Theuth said, "Here, O king, is a branch of learning that will make the people of Egypt wiser and improve their memories; my discovery provides a recipe for memory and wisdom." But the king answered and said, "O man full of arts, to one it is given to create the things of art, and to another to judge what measure of harm and of profit they have for those that shall employ them."[57]

One may wish to compare this story to that of the *Philebus*, where the Platonic Socrates again applies the theory of "the limit and the unlimited" to number and sound, stressing the importance of the "intermediate." Again he refers, significantly, to the Egyptians through their wise Theuth or Hermes:

Socrates: I will do so, but first a small additional point to what I have been saying. When you have got your "one" you remember, whatever it may be, you must not immediately turn your eyes to the unlimited, but to a number; now the same applies when it is the unlimited that you are compelled to start with. You must not immediately turn your eyes to the one, but must discern this or that number embracing the multitude, whatever it may be; reaching the one must be the last step of all. We might take our letters again to illustrate what I mean now.

Protarchus: How so?

Socrates: The unlimited variety of sound was once discerned by some god, or perhaps godlike man; you know the story that there was some such person in Egypt called Theuth. He it was who originally discerned the existence, in that unlimited variety, of the vowels—not "vowel" in the singular but "vowels" in the plural—and then of other things which, though they could not be called articulate sounds, yet were noises of a kind. There were a number of them too, not just one, and a third class he discriminated what we now call the mutes.[58]

These interesting comments on the "one" and the "many" coming so brilliantly from the mind of the Platonic Socrates can easily entice us into deep Parmenidean meditations. But, let us interrupt, at this point, the Socratic dialogue and turn to Aristotle's more sober way of making essentially the same point, that "human wonder" (*thaumazein*, same root as in *Thaumas*, the Egyptian King/God) is the origin of philosophy, the love of wisdom. What may be a surprise to some is that Aristotle clearly connects this "wonder" and the prerequisite "leisure" with Egypt:

That philosophy is not a science of production is clear even from the history of the earliest philosophers. For it is owing to their wonder that men both now begin and at first began to philosophize; they wondered originally at the obvious difficulties, then advanced little by little and stated difficulties about the greatest matters, for example, about the phenomena of the moon and those of the sun and of the stars, and about the genesis of the universe. And a man who is puzzled and wonders thinks himself ignorant (whence even the lover of myth is in a sense a lover of wisdom, for the myth is composed of wonders).[59]

And again:

> But as more arts were invented, and some were directed to the necessities of life, others to recreation, the inventors of the latter were naturally always regarded as wiser, because their branches of knowledge did not aim at utility. Hence when all such inventions were already established, the sciences which do not aim to give pleasure or at necessities of life were discovered, and first in the places where men first began to have leisure. This is why the mathematical arts were founded in Egypt; for there the priestly caste was allowed to be at leisure.[60]

This is a remarkable text. Aristotle's judgment is sound and clearly stated here.[61] Furthermore, it corroborates Plato's view that the arts of writing, number, and music were inventions of the wise Egyptian Theuth for the benefit of mankind.[62] It would be helpful, therefore, for a more integrated view of the matter, if we were to move now away from metaphysical considerations and toward more practical affairs, such as the best organization of the state.

Not surprisingly both Plato and Aristotle are, in contrast to Modern Europeans, consistent in crediting the Egyptians, respectively, with the kind of institutional stability and the division of labor, which each of them recommended as necessary for the wellbeing of the citizens of the well-ordered Hellenic *polis*. For instance, Plato's Athenian legislator praised the Egyptians for their wisdom to perceive the educational power of music, which they regulated for the benefit of their children and their state:

> Athenian: Then is it conceivable that anywhere where there are, or may hereafter be, sound laws in force touching this educative-playful function of the Muses, men of poetic gifts should be free to take whatever in the way of rhythm, melody, or diction tickles the composer's fancy in the act of composition and teach it through the choirs to the boys and lads of a law-respecting society leaving it to chance whether the result prove virtue or vice?
>
> Clinias: To be sure that does not sound rational, decidedly not.
>
> Athenian: And yet this is precisely what they are actually left free to do, I may say, in every community with the exception of Egypt.
>
> Clinias: And in Egypt itself, now—pray how has the law regulated the matter there?
>
> Athenian: The mere report will surprise you. That nation, it would seem, long enough ago recognized the truth we are now affirming, that poses and melodies must be good, if they are to be habitually practiced by the youthful generation of citizens. So they drew up the inventory of all the standard types, and consecrated specimens of them in their temples. Painters and practitioners of other arts of design were forbidden to innovate on these models or entertain any but the traditional standards, and the prohibition still persists, both for these arts and for music in all its branches. If you inspect their paintings and reliefs on the spot, you will find that the work of ten thousand years ago—I mean the expression not loosely but in all precision—is neither better nor worse than that of today; both exhibit an identical artistry.
>
> Clinias: A most amazing state of things!

Athenian: Or rather one immensely to the credit of their legislators and statesmen. No doubt one could find grounds for censure in other Egyptian institutions, but in this matter of music, at least, it is a fact, and a thought-provoking fact, that it has actually proved possible, in such a sphere, to canonize melodies which exhibit an intrinsic rightness by law. That must have been the doing of a god, or a godlike man—as in fact, the local tradition is that the melodies which have been preserved for so many ages were the work of Isis.[63]

One may read this passage as a paradigmatic case of Athenian subtle irony or of Platonic unmitigated conservatism. But, in my view, the philosopher should be praised both for his ability to see the importance of the Egyptian legislation on the matter of music and the respect he had for their legislators. From them perhaps he learned valuable lessons not only about the dangers of irrational experimentation in education, but also about the organization of the best possible state as a whole for the common political good.

With regard to the latter, Aristotle also is very explicit that the political philosophers at that time were looking to Egypt for enlightenment and discovering there some useful and important political lessons. Let us, therefore, listen carefully to his informed comments and take note of what the Hellenic philosopher has to say in this regard, because it will help us understand and appreciate better the vast gap which separates the classical Hellenic perspective from the biased Modern European perspective. Besides, Aristotle, unlike Plato, did not display a taste for irony in his serious writings, and can hardly be accused of political conservatism in comparison with his teacher. Consider this:

It appears that it is not new, nor has it recently become known to[64] political philosophers that the state ought to be divided into classes, and that the warriors should be separated from the husbandmen. The system has continued in Egypt and in Crete to this day, and was established, as tradition says, by a law of Sesostris in Egypt and of Minos in Crete ...[65] From this part of the world came the institution of common tables; the separation into castes from Egypt, for the reign of Sesostris is of far greater antiquity than that of Minos.[66] It is true indeed that these and many other things have been invented several times over in the course of ages, or rather times without number; for necessity may be supposed to have taught men the inventions which were absolutely required, and when these were provided, it was natural that other things which would adorn and enrich life should grow up by degrees. And we may infer that in political institutions the same rule holds. Egypt witnesses to the antiquity of all these things, for the Egyptians appear to be of all people the most ancient; and they have laws and a regular constitution existing from time immemorable. We should therefore make the best use of what has been already discovered, and try to supply defect.[67]

In this revealing passage Aristotle makes several important points, which are indicative of the Hellenic mind and method of approaching the problem of the origin/s of philosophy, science, and civilization. It contrasts sharply with the method of the European scholars, whose views will be discussed in the next section. First of all, Aristotle allows for the possibility that the same or similar political institutions may have been invented many times over, given the immensity of ages past. Secondly, he acknowledges the antiquity and civility of Egypt as a constitutionally organized state with a division of labor and a social order, which are factors of stability. They are, therefore, worthy of imitation by other civilized people, especially the Hellenes, whose love of excessive liberty was paid for by the tragedy of constant strife and civil war. Thirdly, he frankly admits that this method of inquiry permits one to appraise what has been "already discovered," which should be adopted without fear or shame, as well as what may be in need of improvement by further human activity.[68]

To corroborate what Aristotle and Plato have written about the Egyptians and their political institutions and practices as models for the Hellenes, I would also like to mention at this point another great name of Classical Hellas, Isocrates, not to be confused with Socrates. Although he is not mentioned in the histories of philosophy, this Athenian teacher of rhetoric considered himself a philosopher, who was interested in rational discourse and in addressing political problems in a practical manner by avoiding eristic triviality, sophistic trickery, and metaphysical oddity.

Isocrates was certainly one of very few sensible and sensitive men of letters, who saw in a pan-Hellenic union the solution to the problem of constant civil war.[69] If the Hellenes had to fight someone, Isocrates advised them to defend Hellenism against "the barbarians." By this he meant exclusively the Persians, who had been harassing the Hellenic city-states of Asia Minor. But if the Hellenes were to fight the great power of Persia successfully, in Isocrates' view, they should ally with the Egyptians, with whom they shared not only common political interests, but also important common cultural bonds.

We should keep in mind these complex political considerations, as we read Isocrates' praise of the legendary Busiris and, through him, the solid wisdom of the Egyptians. However, what he said is interesting and important for understanding the cultural link between the Hellenes and the Egyptians, because it accords well with the recorded views of the other two great Hellenic philosophers, Plato and Aristotle. So, let us listen to Isocrates' perceptive and sensitive speech on practical wisdom:

> So Busiris thus began, as wise men should, by occupying the fairest country and also by finding sustenance sufficient for his subjects. After-words, he divided them into classes: some he appointed to priestly services, others he turned to the arts and crafts, and others he forced to practice the arts of war. He judged that, while necessities and superfluous products must be provided by the land and the arts, the safest means of protecting these was practice in warfare and reverence for the gods. Including in all classes the right numbers for the best administration of the commonwealth, he gave orders that the same individuals should always engage in the same pursuits, because he knew that those who continually change their occupation never achieve proficiency in even a single one of their tasks, whereas those who apply themselves constantly to the

same activities perform each thing they do surpassingly well. Hence we shall find that in the arts the Egyptians surpass those who work at the same skilled occupations elsewhere more than artisans in general excel the laymen; also with respect to the system which enables them to preserve royalty and their political institutions in general, they have been so successful that philosophers who undertake to discuss such topics and have won the greatest reputation prefer above all others the Egyptian form of government, and that the Lacedaemonians, on the other hand, govern their own city in admirable fashion because they imitate certain of the Egyptian customs ... But the Lacedaemonians have made so much worse use of these institutions that all of them, being professional soldiers, claim the right to seize by force the property of everybody else, whereas the Egyptians live as people should who neither neglect their own possessions, nor plot how they may acquire the property of others. The difference in the aims of the two polities may be seen from the following: if we all imitate the sloth and greed of the Lacedaemonians, we should straightway perish through both the lack of the necessities of daily life and civil war; but if we should wish to adopt the laws of the Egyptians which prescribe that some must work and that the rest must protect the property of the workers, we should all possess our own goods and pass our days in happiness. [70]

So much about the Egyptian practical "wisdom" manifested in the organization of the state, which had attracted the attention even of Hellenic political philosophers, as Isocrates observed. It had also found rather immature imitators in the Spartans who, in his opinion, perverted the meaning of "the art of war" and, instead of using it defensively to protect their own country and liberty, they used it aggressively against other people and their property. The Egyptians also excelled in "piety" (*eusebeia*) and in "practical wisdom" (*phronesis*), which was closer to his heart and found many Hellenic imitators including the philosopher Pythagoras of Samos:

Furthermore, the cultivation of practical wisdom may also reasonably be attributed to Busiris. For example, he saw to it that from the revenue of the sacrifices the priests should acquire affluence, but self-control through the purifications prescribed by the laws, and leisure by exemption from the hazards of fighting and from all work. [71] And the priests, because they enjoyed such conditions of life, discovered for the body the aid which the medical art affords, not that which uses dangerous drugs, but drugs that are harmless as daily food, yet in their effects are so beneficial that all men agree that the Egyptians enjoy the best health and longevity; [72] and then for the soul they introduced philosophy's training, [73] a pursuit which has the power, not only to establish laws but also to investigate the nature of the universe. The older men Busiris appointed to have charge of the most important matters, but the younger he persuaded to forgo all pleasures and to devote themselves to the study of the stars, to arithmetic, and to geometry; the value of these sciences some praise for their utility in certain ways, while others attempt to demonstrate that they are conducive in the highest measure to the attainment of virtue ... [74] One might cite many admirable instances of the piety of the Egyptians, that piety which I am neither the first nor the only to have observed; on the contrary, many contemporaries and predecessors have remarked it, of whom Pythagoras of Samos is one. On a visit to Egypt he became a student of the religion of the people, and was first to bring to the Greeks all philosophy ...[75]

Evidently and reasonably, Isocrates concurs with Aristotle that leisure is the prerequisite for the development of science and philosophy, both of which he associates with Egypt originally. He agrees with the Platonic Socrates also regarding the importance of the division of labor politically, and the study of higher mathematics philosophically (that is, arithmetic, geometry, and astronomy). All this he refers to the wise Egyptians, with whom Pythagoras had allegedly studied. Finally he reiterates Homer's judgment regarding the cultivation of the medical art, in which the Ancient Egyptians had excelled, providing thus a model for the Ancient Hellenes to follow wisely in the centuries to come.

These are the facts, as reported by the Ancient Hellenes in their writings, regarding the way in which the Hellenic philosophers saw themselves and their relations to the civilized Egyptians. One would reasonably expect that the scholarship and "historiography" of Ancient Hellenic philosophy, as practiced by the scientific European historians would reflect these facts. But this is not the case, as we will see next, when the views of two influential European historians of Ancient Philosophy, Jaeger and Guthrie, will be examined.[76] The contrast between the views of the Hellenic philosophers and the Modern European historians of philosophy, as well as the manner in which they expressed their respective views, are indeed very striking.[77]

Modern Europeans vs. Ancient Hellenes

The two renowned scholars, Jaeger and Guthrie, are typical representatives of European scholarship. They have expressed opinions about the Ancient Hellenes and their relationship to the non-Hellenic peoples, which are rather astonishing. Their views on culture and civilization, and their dogmatic assertions about the origins of science and philosophy, are strangely contrary to the views of the (ostensibly admired) Ancient Hellenes. This fact may make one wonder about the possible causes and motives of such discrepancy between the Ancient Hellenes and the Modern Europeans. But it will be left to the readers to judge intelligently this culturally sensitive matter. Consider first the views expressed by Jaeger in the following passage, and compare them to those discussed in the previous section:

> The history of ancient Egypt, which is reckoned not in centuries but in millennia, is marked by a dreadful rigidity, which is almost fossilization. But among the Romans also, political and social stability was the highest good, and innovations were little desired or needed. Greece is in a special category. From the point of view of the present day, the Greeks constitute a fundamental advance on the great peoples of the Orient, a new stage in the development of society. They established an entirely new set of principles for communal life. However highly we may value the artistic, religious, and

political achievements of earlier nations, the history of what we truly call civilization[78]—the deliberate pursuit of an Ideal—does not begin until Greece ... [79] In this vague and analogical sense it is possible to talk of Chinese, Indian, Babylonian, Jewish or Egyptian culture, although none of these nations has a word or an idea which corresponds to real culture.[80]

Thus spoke Werner Jaeger, who dominated classical studies in the first half of the twentieth century, about culture and civilization. Most striking in the above statement is Jaeger's facility to pass from the reasonable judgment that Hellenic culture represents a new development on the historical scene, with which most people would agree, to the irrational assertion that African, Asian and Semitic peoples had no civilization and no "real culture."[81] Even the admired Ancient Hellenes are only temporarily spared. For, we are told subsequently, that they were to be surpassed by the so-called "Hellenocentric nations" of North Europe, especially the Germans.[82]

As the instruments of "the Spirit," the European Nations were chosen by the Christian God (of Semitic roots) to advance to new peaks of higher culture expressed by Lutheran Reformation first, and German Idealism and Romanticism later.[83] In spite of all the apparent praise and glorification of the Ancient Hellenes and the strenuous efforts to imitate the Hellenic artistic and intellectual achievements, the Northern Europeans cannot hide the feeling, felt deep in their hearts, that they do not feel at home in the lands of classical Hellas. Jaeger himself seems to have realized this fact:

> Of course each of the Hellenocentric nations feels that even Hellas and Rome are in some respects fundamentally alien to herself: the feeling is based partly on blood and sentiment, partly on organization and intellectual outlook, partly on historical distinctions. But there is a gigantic difference between that feeling and the sense of complete estrangement, which we have when we confront the Oriental nations, who are both racial and intellectually different from us; and it is undoubtedly a serious mistake in historical perspective to separate, as some modern writers do, the western nations from the Greeks and Romans by a barrier comparable to that which divides us from China, India and Egypt.[84]

This strange statement sounds as an apocalyptic confession because it reveals clearly the typically Teutonic attitude towards other nations and races. The German intellectuals of Jaeger's time might do well to debate whether to place themselves at equal or unequal distance of alienation from the Hellenes and the Romans, as from the Chinese, the Indians, and the Egyptians. Moreover Jaeger might be right in insisting upon the differentiation of unequal degrees of alienation from the various ancient nations. But this peculiar Northern European academic debate cannot alter the probability that the Ancient Hellenes and their philosophers would have felt at home in the pluralistic, tolerant, and civilized societies of China, Egypt, and India. They would have certainly preferred to live there rather than in the monolithic and intolerant societies of Medieval Northern Europe, under the double dominion of foxy Italian Popes and boorish German Emperors. The philosophic Hellenes would have probably felt even less at home in the religiously fanatical and "reformed" countries of the fragmented Europe, under the spiritual authority of philosophically unenlightened men.[85]

Be that as it may, we should perhaps not have allowed Jaeger to distract us from our goal here, by raising such thorny questions as what constitutes culture or civilization and which nation or race has contributed more or less to its advancement. Yet, it would have been inconsiderate to overlook his unreasonable assertions without any comments at least for two reasons. Firstly, because they come from a man who is usually reasonable in his judgments and very knowledgeable about Hellenic history, arts, religion, science, and philosophy. Secondly, because his views about civilization and culture provide a suitable context to evaluate his views regarding the origin of philosophy, which is our theme here. So, when it comes to science and philosophy, not surprisingly, Jaeger makes the following claims:

> Since Egypt and the Near Eastern countries were neighbors of Ionia, it is highly probable (and the probability is supported by sound tradition) that these older civilizations, through constant intellectual intercourse with the Ionians, influenced them not only to adopt their technical discoveries and skills in surveying, navigation, and astronomy, but also to penetrate the deeper problems to which the Egyptian and Oriental myths of creation and divinity gave answers far different from those of the Greeks ... But it was an innovation in the very principles of thought when the Ionians, assimilating and elaborating the empirical knowledge of the celestial and natural phenomena which they got from the Orient, used that knowledge independently to help them discover the origin and the nature of the universe; and when they subjected the myths dealing with the real and visible world, the myths of creation, to theoretical and causal inquiry. That is the true origin of scientific thought. That is the historical achievement of the Greeks ...[86]

Compared with the previous quoted passages these assertions appear to be more balanced. Jaeger appears to acknowledge here what he was denying earlier, that is, that other peoples, besides the Ancient Hellenes and Modern European Protestants, had developed civilizations, and that they influenced the Hellenes beyond doubt. However, Jaeger insists that there is a fundamental difference, a difference in kind, if you prefer, not just in degree, which sets the Hellenic scientific achievements apart from all the Oriental and non-Hellenic accomplishments.[87]

But if Jaeger is correct in his assessment of "the origin" of true science and philosophy, then the Ancient Hellenic philosophers must have been unaware of this alleged fact. For they believed, with Plato and Aristotle, that there has been not just one "origin" of scientific inquiry and philosophic speculation, but countless many, and that their own contribution was one of degree rather than one of kind.[88] For the Hellenes the emphasis was not on the primitive beginning but on the perfection of any art or science.[89] Thus they were proud only in the sense that, whatever they received from others, they did their best to improve upon it in their unique and Hellenic way.[90]

Turning now from Jaeger to Guthrie, we find here too the same reluctance to face the facts about the question of how the Hellenes saw their relation to other nations in terms of science and philosophy. If anything, his assertions are even more astonishing than Jaeger's. Consider, for example, the following passage and note his faulty reasoning. He suggests that the Egyptians could not possibly have influenced the Hellenes "philosophically" because they had no philosophy; and they did not have philosophy because they were naturally incapable of developing it, since they certainly lacked "the necessary spark," which the Hellenes possessed:

> In the application of various techniques to the amelioration of the human life the Egyptians of a thousand years before could probably have taught these Greeks some useful lessons. Yet the torch of philosophy was not lit in Egypt, for they lacked the necessary spark which the Greeks possessed so strongly and embodied in their word *philosophia*.[91]

Occasionally, even Guthrie, like Jaeger, is prepared to make some concessions with regard to the sciences. Take for example the following statement: "Thousands of clay tablets provided material for an appreciation of the science and philosophy of the ancient Near East and hence for a balanced estimate of what it could have taught the Greeks." Also, "the debt of Greek mathematics to Egypt and Babylon was one which the Greeks themselves acknowledged."[92] However, Guthrie does not hesitate, in the spirit of Jaeger, who had emphasized abstraction, generalization, formality, ideality, and universality, to make the inconsistent claim that follows:

> The uniqueness of their own achievement lies elsewhere. We get a glimpse of it if we consider that although philosophy and science are as yet inseparable, yet, whereas we speak of Egyptian and Babylonian science, it is more natural to refer to the philosophy of the Greeks. Why is this? The Egyptian and Mesopotamian peoples, so far as we can discover, felt no interest in knowledge for its own sake, but only in so far as it served a practical purpose. (p. 34)[93]

Now, if we were to ask how Guthrie, as a historian of Ancient Hellenic philosophy, would be able to reconcile his stated view with the contrary views held by both Aristotle and Plato, the answer would be that he would not even try. He simply thinks that they were wrong. Especially Aristotle is made the target here of Guthrie's attack for giving credit to the Egyptians for original contributions to science and philosophy, which they did not make. Consider his faulty argument in this regard:

Nevertheless Aristotle is too obviously advancing a favorite theory of his own, which he presses on many other occasions, and Herodotus' account of the practical limitations of Egyptian geometry remains the more probable. In holding that disinterested intellectual activity is a product of leisure, Aristotle is clearly right. His mistake lies in transferring to geometry in Egypt the character and the purpose that it had in fourth-century Athens, where it was part of a liberal education and also a subject of pure research. In Egypt it was the handmaid of land measuring or pyramid-building.[94]

The one who is in error here is certainly not Aristotle, but Professor Guthrie. He is wrong in all the three points, which he makes in this statement: that geometry was not part of the liberal education in Egypt; that the Egyptians had no advanced research in the subject of mathematics; and that the fourth-century Athens enjoyed both of these advantages. As a matter of fact, a man who knew mathematics and the state of education in the fourth-century Athens, and cared about these matters deeply, has confessed that he felt ashamed of all this. That man was Plato himself. As an educated Athenian, he felt shame when he compared the state of Hellenic pedagogy and mathematics of his time with that of Egypt of "many centuries ago." I will allow Plato to argue against the historian Guthrie here and invite you to be the arbitrators on this:

Ath. Well, then, I maintain that the freeborn men should learn of these various subjects as much as in Egypt is taught to vast number of children along with their letters. To begin with, lessons have been devised there [in Egypt] in ciphering for the very children, which they can learn with a good deal of fun and amusement ... They then go on to exercise in measurements of length, surface, and cubical content, by which they dispel the native and general, but ludicrous and shameful, ignorance of mankind about the whole matter.[95]

Cl. And in what way may this native ignorance consist?

Ath. My dear Clinias, when I was told, rather belatedly, about our condition in this matter, like you, I was astounded. Such ignorance seemed to me more worthy of a stupid beast like the hog than of a human being, and I blushed not for myself alone, but for the whole Hellenic world.

Cl. But what was the reason for your blushes? Let us have your account of it, Sir.

Ath. Why, so I will. Or rather I will make it plain by a question. Pray tell me one little thing. You know what is meant by *line*?... and *surface*?... and *volume*?...

Cl. Of course, I do.

Ath. And what of the relations of line and surface to volume, or of line and surface to one another? Is it not the fact that we Hellenes all imagine they are commensurable in some way or other?

Cl. Why certainly that is the fact.

Ath. Then if this is another impossibility, though we Hellenes as I said, all fancy it possible, are we not bound to blush for them all as we tell them, "Worthy Hellenes, here is one of the things of which we said the ignorance is a disgrace." (*Laws* 819b-820b)[96]

In light of this passage and previous texts from Plato, Aristotle, Isocrates, Jaeger, Guthrie, and others, the contrast between Ancient Hellenic philosophers and Modern European historians of philosophy should be strikingly evident. Unlike the Europeans, the Ancient Hellenes appear to be more objective and more sympathetic to the Egyptians, so that we may call them phil-egyptian and the Egyptians phil-hellenic. As genuine lovers of wisdom and truth, the Hellenic philosophers particularly were prepared to credit the wise and civilized Egyptians with achievements in music, medicine, mathematics, politics, religion, and practical wisdom, which were equal, if not superior, to those of their contemporary fellow Hellenes. In other words, in every field the Ancient Egyptians provided the models, which the Ancient Hellenes were eager to imitate and try to surpass.

In stark contrast to this sensible approach, European philologists and historians of Hellenic philosophy of the remarkable caliber of Jaeger and Guthrie, surprisingly, appear unwilling to follow the same prudent path, as the Ancient Hellenes, on this important matter.[97] In so doing, they give the impression of being friendly to neither Egypt nor Hellas, in a different sense regarding the latter, which is more subtle and serious. For if their appraisals of the origin of science, philosophy, civilization were correct, then it would follow that the admired Ancient Hellenes (their philosophers included) did not know what they were doing, when they praised the Egyptians for achievements in these areas highly, frequently, and in writing. One is left to wonder whether these European scholars realized their inconsistency and the magnitude of the insult, which they commit, not only against the admired Hellenic philosophers, but also against the intelligence of all sincere students of philosophy.

In this respect, then, and for these specific reasons, the Northern European approach is shown to have been unfair to the Egyptians and insulting to the Hellenes. In spite of all the praise of their "Hellenic genius," which the Ancients philosophers ostensibly receive from their modern admirers, the European tactic and logic here does not seem to serve the love of wisdom and truth, as understood by the beloved Ancient Hellenes. Therefore, it must be rejected as incorrect and unacceptable to those who, like the Hellenes and the Egyptian friends, believe that "sweet is truth."[98]

With these comments our discussion has reached its final goal. It remains now for us to draw the necessary conclusions from our analysis and discussion of the evidence presented. I would like to make some observations regarding the present state of affairs in the global order of things. I would also like to assess the potential role, which Hellenic philosophy may be called upon to play in the near future, in light of the unexpected reemergence of religious fanaticism of the two traditional enemies, that is, the fundamentalist faiths of militant Islam and messianic Christianity.

Conclusion

From our discussion at least three points should have become clear by now. First, we have seen through the provided historical evidence that the Ancient Hellenes had relatively easy access to the Mediterranean Egypt in the sixth and subsequent centuries, when the first Hellenic philosophers appeared in the horizon. Second, we have noticed that, as the newcomers on the historical scene, the Ancient Hellenes, especially the Hellenic philosophers, had much to learn from the civilized Egyptians. The Egyptian manifold wisdom, as expressed in their great achievements in the arts and sciences, in religion and medicine, in politics and law, the Hellenes quickly learned to admire and appreciate.[99] Third, we found that the Ancient Hellenes had good reason, drawn from their extensive experience, which justified their admiration of the Egyptian pedagogy, law, mathematics, medicine, and even their philosophic way of life in accordance with virtue and nature.

In different, but equally important, ways each of the Egyptian achievements appeared to have contributed to the ultimate cultural end of purifying the human soul and harmonizing it with the community and with the cosmos, so that it may become perfected to a maximum possible degree for mortal beings. It is perhaps no accident that this same noble goal is also found in the Hellenic tradition, as articulated in the Pythagorean and the Platonic schools of philosophy especially.[100]

Consequently, it would be prudent for the students of Hellenic philosophy to spend their time discovering any specific lessons or methods, which the Hellenes perhaps learned from the Egyptians and the ways in which they improved upon them, instead of trying to prove the impossible, like Jaeger and Guthrie. These two wanted to persuade us, for no evident reason, that the Ancient Hellenes alone and unassisted not only perfected, but also invented, every science and art, including philosophy, the great queen of arts and sciences.[101] In order to achieve such goal, the careful inquirer would do well to pay close attention to what the Hellenic philosophers actually said about their relations to their neighbors.

In this respect, it should be clear that our discussion has established at least this much: That Modern Europeans historians of Ancient Hellenic philosophy are essentially unlike the Ancient Hellenic philosophers and historians of philosophy. The latter were generous in giving measured credit, for achievements in the arts, sciences, religion, politics, and law, to those who, like the Ancient Egyptians, clearly deserved it. For instance, it would be wise to read Porphyry, who is a reliable Ancient historian of Hellenic Philosophy, carefully. Students should take note of his report about the doctrines, which Pythagoras brought to Hellas from abroad. They include: "That the soul is immortal; that it changes into other kinds of living beings; also that events recur in certain cycles, and that nothing is ever absolutely new; and finally that all living things should be regarded as akin."[102]

The doctrines of the immortality of the soul, the possibility of reincarnation, and the affinity of all life on earth, are very important philosophically and are echoed in some of the most advanced Platonic dialogues. But the most striking of

Porphyry's comments in this short passage, which seems pregnant with meaningful ancient wisdom, is that "nothing is ever absolutely new" in this world of ours with its cyclical history (in time and of time), as the Hellenic philosophers understood it. As Plato, Aristotle, and Isocrates have argued extensively, this good and sensible observation would apply to philosophy as well. For Hellenic minds, clearly philosophy could not have had one origin in time or space. Miletus and the sixth century BC are simply conventions.

Evidently, by the channel of Pythagorean tradition especially, some seeds and roots of Egyptian wisdom reached classical Hellas, where they grew into the magnificent tree of Platonism. When Platonism, centuries later (3th-6th AD), was reborn as Neoplatonism in Alexandria, it branched out into Christian (or religious) and Hellenic (or philosophical) versions.[103] As we will see in the next chapter, it was unfortunate, not only for the history of Europe, but for our civilization also, that the religious version prevailed. However, the fact remains that, in the prolonged struggle between the two versions of Platonism for the hearts and minds of the ancient peoples (Greeks, Romans, Europeans, Africans, and Asians), philosophy lost the battle to religion.[104]

Practicing monotheistic intolerance and theocratic despotism, particularly in Western and Northern Europe, the Popes managed to dominate European culture for the last two millennia.[105] In this qualified sense, it is correct to say that a general characterization of "European philosophy" would be, as A.N. Whitehead laconically put it, "a series of footnotes to Plato."[106] However, we should keep in mind that the Christianized Plato of Augustine to the extent that he was forced to serve the revealed dogmas of a theocratic religion, is different from the philosopher preserved in the Hellenic tradition, which was more philosophic, diverse, and tolerant.

In conclusion, it may be said that, for a perceptive student of the history of philosophy, the most profound crisis of our times cannot be the one associated with the collapse of the Soviet-style Socialism and the end of the Cold War, great as these events are in themselves. More serious is the other crisis, which pertains to the attempt to preserve the hegemony of European culture over the globe, and the dominance of the organized Church over Europe and the Western World using Platonic and Hellenic philosophy as "handmaids" of the Christian theocracy. This trend will inevitably antagonize and revitalize the fundamentalists of militant Islam. Thus, instead of moving forward to enlightenment, man will perhaps fall back again in the abyss of religious wars, fanaticism, and terrorism (as New York, Madrid, and London testify).

In view of this gloomy possibility, the time may be ripe for another rebirth of Platonism, hopefully more lasting and in its authentic Hellenic version this time.[107] Therefore, the friends of Pythagoras, Socrates, Plato, Aristotle, Plotinus, Porphyry, Proclus, Pletho, and all genuine Hellenic philosophers, should work together to prevent the lapsing of the World into "Dark Ages" again. On the contrary, they should resist religious fanaticism by the power of Hellenic *logos*. They should try to shape the new millennium in the renewed spirit of philosophic diversity, tolerance, and democratic freedom for the common good of humanity and its fragile sanity.[108]

Appendix

Hellenic Sources

The following texts may be considered as additional evidence in support of the presented thesis, which is not new, but the same Ancient Hellenic thesis (in so far as the author is concerned and can see):

From Herodotus (*ibid.*, Book II, 123):

"It is believed in Egypt that the rulers of the lower world are Demeter and Dionysus (Isis and Osiris). Moreover, the Egyptians were the first to teach that the human soul is immortal, and at the death of the body enters into some other living thing then coming to birth; and after passing through all creatures of land, sea, and air (which cycle it completes in three thousand years) it enters once more into a human body at birth. Some of the Greeks, early and late, have used this doctrine as if it were their own; I know their names, but do not here record them."

[Given what Herodotus says in IV, 95, we may be assured that Pythagoras would have been included in the list of those Greeks, who spoke of the immortality of the soul, its transmigration, and reincarnation, as if these doctrines were their own recent discoveries].

From Isocrates (*ibid.*, 28-29):

"On a visit to Egypt he [Pythagoras of Samos] became a student of the religion of the people, and was first to bring to the Greeks all philosophy, and more conspicuously than others he seriously interested himself in sacrifices and in ceremonial purity, since he believed that even if he should gain thereby no greater reward from the gods, among men, at any rate, his reputation would be greatly enhanced. And this, indeed happen to him. For so greatly did he surpass all others in reputation that all the younger desired to be his pupils, and their elders were more pleased to see their sons staying in his company than attending to their private affairs. And these reports we cannot disbelieve; for even now persons who profess to be followers of his teaching are more admired when silent than are those who have the greatest renown for eloquence."

From Plutarch (*Ibid.*, 9-10):

"At Sais the seated statue of Athena, whom they consider to be Isis also, bore the following inscription: 'I am all that has been and is and will be; and no mortal has ever lifted my mantle.' While the majority still believes that Amun (which we modify into Ammon) is the proper name of Zeus among the Egyptians, Manetho the Sebennyte thinks that it means 'what is concealed' and that concealment is signified by this word ... Hence they name the supreme god, whom they believe to be one with the universe, Amun, since they address him as one invisible and concealed, and exhort him to become manifest and clear to them. So great was the concern of the Egyptians for wisdom in religion. This is attested also by the wisest of the Greeks, Solon, Thales, Plato, Eudoxus, and Pythagoras, and, as some say, by Lycurgus as well; they came to Egypt and were in touch with the priests. Eudoxus indeed is said to have had instruction from Khonouphis the Memphite, Solon from Sonkhis the Saite, and Pythagoras from Oinouphis the Heliopolitan. Pythagoras, in particular, it appears, enjoying a state of mutual admiration with these people, imitated their symbolism and mysterious manner, interpreting his teachings with riddles; for many of the Pythagorean sayings are not at all lacking in the lore of the writing which is called hieroglyphic, such as 'Do not eat in a chariot; ... I myself believe that when these people call the monad Apollo, the dyad Artemis, the hebdomad Athena, and the first cube Poseidon, it is like what is established and assuredly enacted and written in the sacred rites."

From Iamblichus (*Vita Pythagorica*, 13-18):[109]

"Thales had helped him [Pythagoras] in many ways, especially in making good use of time. For this reason he had renounced wine, meat, and (even earlier) large meals, and had adjusted to light and digestible food. So he needed little sleep, and achieved alertness, clarity of soul, and perfect and unshakable health of body. Then he sailed to Sidon ... In Sidon he met the descendants of Mochos the natural philosopher and prophet, and the other Phoenician hierophants, and was initiated into the rites peculiar to Byblos, Tyre and the other districts of Syria. He did not, as one might unthinkingly suppose, undergo this experience from superstition, but far more from a passionate desire for knowledge, and as a precaution lest something worth learning should elude him by being kept secret in the mysteries or rituals of the gods. Besides, he had learnt that the Syrian rites were offshoots of those of Egypt, and hoped to share, in Egypt, in mysteries of a purer form, more beautiful and more divine. Awestruck, as his teacher Thales had promised, he crossed without delay to Egypt, conveyed by Egyptian seamen who had a timely landing on the shore below Mount Carmel in Phoenicia, where Pythagoras had been spending most of his time alone in the sanctuary ... He spent twenty years in the sacred places of Egypt, studying astronomy and geometry, and being initiated—but not just on impulse or as the occasion offered—into all the rites of the gods, until he was captured by the expedition of Kambyses and taken to Babylon. There he spent time with the Magi, to their mutual rejoicing, learning what was holy among them, acquiring perfected knowledge of the worship of the gods and reaching the heights of their mathematics and music and other disciplines. He spent twenty more years with them, and returned to Samos, aged by now about fifty-six."

From Proclus (*Commentary on Euclid*, 64. 16-70. 18):[110]

"Since it behooves us to examine the beginnings both of the arts and of the sciences with reference to the present cycle [of the universe], we say that according to most accounts geometry was first discovered among the Egyptians, taking the origin from the measurement of areas. For they found it necessary by reason of the rising of the Nile, which wiped out everybody's boundaries ... Thales was the first to go to Egypt and bring back to Greece this study; he himself discovered many propositions, and disclosed the underlying principles of many others to his successors, in some cases his method being more general, in other more empirical. After him Ameristus, the brother of poet Stesichorus, is mentioned as having touched the study of geometry, and Hippias of Elis spoke of him as acquired a reputation for geometry. After these Pythagoras transformed the study into the form of a liberal education, examining its principles from the beginning and tracking down the theorems immaterially and intellectually; he it was who discovered the theory of proportionals and the construction of the cosmic figures ... Plato, who came after them, made the other branches of mathematics as well as geometry take a great step forward by his zeal for them; and it is obvious how he filled his writings with mathematical arguments and everywhere stirred up admiration for mathematics in those who took up philosophy. At this time also lived Leodamas of Thasos, and Archytas of Taras and Theaetetus of Athens, by whom the theorems were increased and an advance was made towards a more scientific grouping ... Whatsoever offers a more profitable field of research and contributes to the whole of philosophy, we shall make the starting-point of further inquiry, therein imitating the Pythagoreans, among whom there was prevalent this motto, 'A figure and a platform, not a figure a sixpence,' by which they implied that the geometry deserving study is that which, at each theorem, sets up a platform for further ascent and lifts the soul on high, instead of allowing it to descend among the sensible objects of mortal men and in this lower aim neglect conversion to things above."

From Diodorus Siculus (Book I. 69. 1-6):[111]

"Now that we have discussed sufficiently the deeds of the kings of Egypt from the very earliest times down to the death of Amasis, we shall record the other events in their proper chronological setting; but at this point we shall give a summary account of the customs of Egypt, both those which are especially strange and those which can be of most value to our readers. For many of the customs that obtained in ancient times among the Egyptians have not only been accepted by the present inhabitants but have aroused no little admiration among the Greeks; and for that reason those men who have won the greatest repute in intellectual things have been eager to visit Egypt in order to acquaint themselves with its laws and institutions, which they considered to be worthy of note. For despite the fact that for the reasons mentioned above strangers found it difficult in early times to enter the country, it was nevertheless eagerly visited by Orpheus and the poet Homer in the earliest times and in later times by others, such as Pythagoras of Samos and Solon the lawgiver. Now it is maintained by the Egyptians that it was they who first discovered writing and the observation of the stars, who also discovered the first principles of geometry and most of the arts, and established the best laws. And the best proof of all this, they say, lies in the fact that Egypt for more than four thousand seven hundred years was ruled by kings of whom the majority were native Egyptians, and the land was the most prosperous of the whole inhabited world; for these things could not have been true of any people which did not enjoy most excellent customs and laws and the institutions which promote culture of every kind."[112]

Notes

1. Hellenic philosophy, like Hellenic culture and religion from which it developed, had many roots and connections. Some of these seem to reach out to the banks of the Nile. Others went as far as the banks of Euphrates and Indus; while some were certainly indigenous Hellenic or even pre-Hellenic.

2. By Africa, in this context, is meant Ancient Egypt, especially the part, which bordered with the Eastern Mediterranean. The same geographical restrictions apply to Asia and Europe. This triangle, formed by the meeting of the three continents, has been at the center of Hellenic civilization since the second millennium BC, and even more so since the second half of the first millennium BC. Our discussion will be focused on this culturally fertile triangle.

3. It is conceivable that a similar cultural fusion might have taken place a millennium earlier, during the flourishing of the Minoan and Mycenaean civilizations, in the second half of the second millennium BC (Late Bronze Age). The evidence from inscriptions for such a hypothesis is scanty, even after the decipherment of Linear B. One may sympathize with John Chadwick, when he states: "Our debt to the Greeks is sufficient reason for wanting to know more of the beginnings of their civilization, long before the historical period." *The Decipherment of Linear B* (Cambridge, 1967, 2nd edn), p. 139.

4. It is no accident that well-known representatives of these spiritual movements, such as Athanasius and Arius, Clement and Origen, Josephus and Philo, Basilides and Valentinus, Ammonius and Plotinus, were all connected with Alexandria in one way or another. They appeared there after the city lost its political independence in the battle of Actium in 31 BC. See on this, C. Bigg, *The Christian Platonists of Alexandria* (Oxford, 1886); and A.H. Armstrong, ed., *The Cambridge History of Later Greek and Early Medieval Philosophy* (Cambridge, 1967). The revival of Platonism in Alexandria and Northern Africa, and its contribution to the formulation of the Orthodox dogma of Apostolic Christianity is

fascinating and deserves a separate treatment. Suffice here to say that, for the next four centuries, Christian Alexandria (together with Antioch, Corinth, and Carthage), fought and conquered pagan Rome with the newly forged spiritual weapons of Christian theology, until Constantinople, as the New Rome, took its place in 330 AD. Then, proud Alexandria fought the New Rome alone over the question of "Christian Orthodoxy," for three more centuries. When it lost the decisive spiritual battle of Monophysitic Christology, Alexandria opened its gates and welcomed the fanatical followers of Mohammed's successors in 642. Since that time, it did its best to help the neophytes forge the spiritual weapons of militant Islam, destined to dominate the Middle East and the North Africa, to threaten Europe at Poitiers and Vienna, and finally to conquer Constantinople, the Citadel of Christendom, in 1453.

Parenthetically, it would appear that the long struggle between Christianity and Islam is still continuing, as is evident from the tragedies unfolding in Bosnia, the Balkans, Middle East, and Central Asia at the dawn of the third millennium. With the collapse of communism and the revival of nationalism and religious fanaticism, one can expect (perhaps with good reason, but also with great apprehension), that the strife between these two monotheistic and (by their nature) intolerant religions will intensify and spread to other areas of the globe. In the last two millennia, mankind has suffered greatly because of the folly of allowing the religious claims to a monopoly of God and to the title of "the chosen people" to take hold of its heart, in spite of the warnings of Platonic philosophers, like Porphyry and Pletho. This folly is still active.

5. To fail to discern the Pythagorean connection of Socrates and the Socratic movement, as represented by Plato and the early Academy, inevitably leads to a misunderstanding of Plato's mature philosophy and Socrates' deepest concerns. Yet this error is common among modern and contemporary scholars who, unlike the Neoplatonists, cannot see behind the mask of Socratic irony. The most recent manifestation of this anti-Platonic interpretation of Socratic philosophy is G. Vlastos' book, *Socrates: Ironist and Moral Philosopher* (Ithaca, 1991). See my review of it, in *Journal of Neoplatonic Studies*, I (1992): 133-141. The Platonic tradition from antiquity to Renaissance had a different view on this matter, which has been poetically expressed by Henry More (*Psychozoia*, I, 4):

"[Plato's school] ... well agrees with learned Pythagore,
Egyptian Trismegiste, and th' antique roll,
Of Chaldee wisdome, all which time hath tore,
But Plato and deep Plotin do restore ..."

Ficino (*De christiana religione*, XXII. 25), includes in "*prisca gentium theologia*" the names of Zoroaster, Hermes (Mercurius), Orpheus, Aglaophemus, Pythagoras and states: "*tota in Platonis nostri voluminibus continetur*." See also, C.A. Patrides, *The Cambridge Platonists* (Cambridge, 1969). For Aristotle, the link which connected the Pythagorean, Socratic, and Platonic philosophies was the search for definitions and the entities captured in them, that is, the Ideas or Forms: "But the Pythagoreans have said in the same way that there are two principles, but added this much, which is peculiar to them ... that infinity itself and unity itself were the substance of the things of which they are predicated. This is why number was the substance of all things ... Regarding the question of essence they began to make statements and definitions, but treated the matter too simply ... Socrates, however ... fixed his thought for the first time on definitions; Plato accepted his teaching, but held that the problem applied not to sensible things but to entities of another kind—for this reason, that the common definition could not be a definition of any sensible thing, as they were always changing. Things of this other sort, then, he called Ideas, and sensible things, he said, were all named after these, and in virtue of a relation to these; for the many existed by participation in the Ideas that have the same name as they. Only the name "participation" was new; for the Pythagoreans say that things exist by "imitation" of numbers, and Plato says they exist by participation, changing the name." (*Metaphysics*, 987a 12-987b 13) (W.D. Ross's translation).

Plotinus, in his turn, criticized Aristotle for not following the Pythagorean-Platonic tradition. On this see, "The Plotinian Reduction of Aristotle's Categories," in *Aristotle's Ontology*, A. Preus and J. Anton, eds (Albany, NY, 1992): 47-69. Also, H.J. Kramer *Plato and the Foundations of Metaphysics*, ed. and tr., J.R. Catan (Albany, NY: SUNY, 1990), pp. 115-130; E. Raven, *Pythagoreans and Eleatics* (Cambridge, 1948), pp. 1-19; and W. Burkert, *Lore and Science in Ancient Pythagoreanism* (Cambridge, Mass., 1972), pp. 83-125.

6.   Although the doctrines of transmigration [μετεμψύχωσις] and rebirth [παλιγγενεσία] of the soul are connected with Pythagoras' school, it is debated among scholars whether they were received from the Egyptians (through Melampus), the Thracians (through Orpheus), or the Indians (through the Gymnosophists). However, the Platonic Socrates insists on the ethical importance of "the care of the soul" which will allow one to live the life of excellence here on earth and, by purification [*catharsis*], to attain ultimate liberation and translation to the Gods. See A.B. Keith, "Pythagoras and the Doctrine of Transmigration," *The Journal of Royal Asiatic Society* (1909): 569-606; F.M. Cornford, *Principium Sapientiae: A Study of the Origins of Greek Philosophical Thought* (New York, 1965); W.K.C. Guthrie, *Orpheus and Greek Religion* (New York, 1966); by the same author, *The Earlier Presocratics and the Pythagoreans*, which is vol. 1 of the *A History of Greek Philosophy* (6 vols, Cambridge, 1978), pp. 146-340; G.S. Kirk and J.E. Raven, *The Presocratic Philosophers* (Cambridge, 1975), especially pp. 217-231; A.E. Taylor, *Plato: The Man and His Work* (London, 1926), especially, pp. 163ff.; W. Burkert, *ibid.*; C.A. Huffman, *Philolaus of Croton: Pythagorean and Presocratic* (Cambridge, 1993). Compare these views to the information provided by the three ancient *Vitae* of Pythagoras by Porphyry, Iamblichus, and Diogenes Laertius. For extensive bibliography on Pythagoras, L.E. Navia, *Pythagoras: An Annotated Bibliography* (New York, 1990).

7.   It is a great loss that Aristotle's book *On the Pythagoreans* has perished. Democritus' book on Pythagoras, if we accept Diogenes Laertius' claim that he wrote one, had the same fate. However, a careful reading of *Metaphysics* (987a-b, 989b-990a, 1074b 1-14, and 1078b 18-37); *De Anima* (404a 17-404b 29, 406b 26-407a 12, 411b 5-31); and *Politics* (1329b 1-36), would indicate that, in Aristotle's view, Plato's theory of Forms, as well as the theory of number, the theory of soul, and the corresponding theory of the city-state, including their respective divisions, were under the direct influence of Pythgoreanism. Evidently the same influence, which shaped Platonism, shaped also Neoplatonism. See D.J. O'Meara, *Pythagoras Revived* (Oxford, 1989); and my review of it in *Skepsis* 2 (1991): 162-165.

8.   The influence of the revived Platonism in Alexandria, Athens, Antioch, and Rome, on the formation of the Christian dogma calls for further systematic research. So does the struggle of Hellenism against Theocracy, which also made use of Platonic philosophy to defend polytheism and pluralism in the name of tolerance, diversity, and humanity. I have touched upon this subject in "Porphyry's Criticism of Christianity and the Problem of Augustine's Platonism," *Dionysius*, 13 (1989): 51-71; and in "Plotinus' Anti-Gnostic Polemic and Porphyry's *Against the Christians*," in *Neoplatonism and Gnosticism*, R. Wallis and J. Bregman, eds (New York, 1992), pp. 111-128.

9. In fact, "From Thales to Aristotle" is the conventional heading under which the story of Hellenic Philosophy has been told in Europe and the West in general. For example, a popular textbook, which is used for courses in Ancient Philosophy at American colleges and universities, is characteristically entitled, *Greek Philosophy: Thales to Aristotle*, R.E. Allen, ed. (London, 1985, 2nd edn). Also W.K.C. Guthrie' monumental *A History of Greek Philosophy* (6 vols, Cambridge, 1962-1981). Significantly, the first volume of it begins also with Thales and the sixth ends again with Aristotle.

10. This modern tendency overlooks the fact that Plato and Aristotle refer to the great poets of the Hellenic past with respect even when they disagree with them and criticize them. They treat the wise *gnomai* (precepts, maxims) of Homer, Hesiod, Solon, Pindar, and the seven Sages, in the same critical manner, as they would treat the *doxai* (opinions) of the pre-Socratic philosophers. As a matter of fact, both Plato and Aristotle quote and discuss the opinions of Homer and Hesiod more frequently than those of some philosophers, such as Xenophanes and Anaximenes. For later Platonists, like Porphyry, who anticipated Vico on this point, "the wisdom" of the poets, especially the one preserved in the Homeric epics, deserved to have extensive commentaries similar to those dedicated to the Platonic dialogues, the Aristotelian treatises, and the Plotinian *Enneads.* See J. Bidez, *Vie de Porphyre* (Hildesheim, 1964); my *Aristotle's Categories and Porphyry* (Leiden, 1988, 2nd edn, 1996); R. Lamberton, *Homer the Theologian: Neoplatonist Allegorical Readings and the Growth of the Epic Tradition* (Berkeley, 1989, 2nd edn, 1996), especially Chapters II and III. Also, J.M. Dillon, "Image, Symbol, and Analogy: Three Basic Concepts of Neoplatonic Allegorical Exegesis," in *The Significance of Neoplatonism*, R.B. Harris, ed. (Albany, NY, 1976): 247-262; and my review of this book in *Philosophy and Phenomenological Research* 38, no. 4 (1978): 593-594.

11. The root of this misconception is to be found perhaps in the reductionist tendency of translating the Greek word λόγος simply as reason, in the sense of deductive or inductive reasoning, which does not do justice to its multiple and diverse meanings. For it can also mean measure, proportion, analogy, speech, discourse, discursive reasoning, and noetic or intuitive apprehension of first principles, not to mention the Christian *Logos*, that it, the Incarnated Son of God in the person of Jesus Christ.

12. "In the days of Greek freedom to be a Greek had meant to be a citizen of a Greek canton; after Alexander it meant to have Greek culture," as W.R. Inge put it in "Religion," included in *The Legacy of Greece*, R. Livingstone, ed. (Oxford, 1969): 25-57. J.-P. Vernant's book, *The Origins of Greek Thought* (Ithaca, NY, 1982) is one of the latest and most forceful in stressing the importance of the connection between the emergence of the democratic city-state and the coming into being of the Hellenic philosophy in Ionia. See also the Proceedings of the International Symposium on *The Ionian Philosophy*, K. Boudouris, ed. (Athens, 1991); and A.J. Toynbee, *Hellenism: The History of a Civilization* (Oxford, 1959), pp. 8-17.

13. In this regard, European scholars appear to have followed the tradition going back to Augustine. As we will see in the second essay, for him Ancient Hellenes came as close to "the truth" as was possible for the unaided human reason (*De civitate Dei*, VII.5). The revelation of the "whole truth," of course, had to wait until the advent of Christ for the pious pastor of the Church and, for the modernists, until the coming of modern science and technology. For more on this important point, see the last essay.

For a good account of the deleterious influence of "race" on the distorted ways in which Northern European historians often perceive and interpret historical events and cultural phenomena of the Mediterranean world, see S. Vryonis, "Recent Scholarship on Continuity and Discontinuity of Culture: Classical Greeks, Byzantines, and Modern Greeks," in *The "Past" in Medieval and Modern Greek Culture*, ed., by same (Malibu, CA: 1978): 237-256.

14. A paradigmatic case is W.K.C. Guthrie's six volume *History of Greek Philosophy*, which is highly praised and used extensively. More about Guthrie and Jaeger below.

15. The limits of the present study and the limitations of my expertise would not allow me to go beyond the "literary evidence" as preserved in the Hellenic, Hellenistic, and Hellenized writers, poets, historians, and philosophers, from *circa* the eighth century BC to the fifteenth century AD. Unlike Bernal, I will resist the temptation to speculate boldly on archeological, geological, anthropological, mythological, glossological, Egyptological, and other potential evidence, which should be left to the specialists. See also note 77 below.

16. What impressed the Ancient Hellenic philosophers most about the Egyptians and their civilization was their antiquity. For example, Aristotle (*Politics* 1329b, 32) refers to them as "the most ancient people."

17. See, for instance, Thucydides *History*, I, 6.; Isocrates, *Panegyricus*, 45c; and Plato, *Phaedrus*, 258e-259d.

18. Theophrastus, according to Porphyry (*De Abstinentia*, II.3), characterized the Egyptians as "the most learned of all nations."

19. As Solon learned from the Egyptians: "There have been, and will be again, many destructions of mankind arising out of many causes; the greatest have been brought about by the agencies of fire and water, and other lesser ones by innumerable other causes ... And whatever happened either in your country or in ours, or in any other region of which we are informed—if there were any actions noble or great or in any way remarkable, they have all been written down by us of old and are preserved in our temples. Whereas just when you and other nations are beginning to be provided with letters and the other requisites of civilized life, after the usual interval, the stream of heaven, like a pestilence, comes pouring down and leaves only those of you who are destitute of letters and education, and so you have to begin all over again, like children, and know nothing of what happened in ancient times, either among us or among yourselves" (*Timaeus*, 22c-23b).

20. For ancient sources of this tradition, see note 49 below.

21. *Timaeus*, 22b.

22. The suggestion that someone, with good credentials and an unbiased mind, should undertake to clarify the relation of Ancient Hellenic philosophy and its possible Egyptian connections came from P. Morewedge, to whom I am grateful for this suggestion and encouragement. A shorter version of the essay was published as a monograph under the title, *When Greece Met Africa: The Genesis of Hellenic Philosophy* (Binghamton, NY, 1994), for class testing. Special thanks are due to J. Murungi and L. Bargeliotes for their constructive criticism after the testing.

23. Burckert, *ibid.*, pp. 15-28.

24. This is Socrates' persistent message, present in every Platonic Dialogue from first to last. Consider, for example:

"I shall go on saying, in my usual way, My very good friend, you are an Athenian and belong to a city which is the greatest and most famous in the world for its wisdom and strength. Are you not ashamed that you give your attention to acquiring as much money as possible, and similarly with reputation and honor, and give no attention or thought to truth and understanding and the caring of your soul?" (*Apology*, 29d-e).

"And so, Glaucon, the tale was saved, as the saying is, and was not lost. And it will save us if we believe it, and we shall safely cross the River of Lethe, and keep our soul unspotted from the world. But if we are guided by me we shall believe that the soul is immortal and capable of enduring all extremes of good and evil, and so we shall hold ever to the upward way and pursue righteousness with wisdom always and ever, that we may be dear to ourselves and to the gods both during our sojourn here and when receive our reward, as the victors in the games go about to gather in theirs. And thus both here and in that journey of a thousand years, whereof I have told you, we shall fare well" (*Republic*, 621c).

"And we should consider that God gave the sovereign part of the human soul to be the divinity of each one, being that part which, as we say, dwells as the top of the body, and inasmuch as we are a plant not of an earthly but of a heavenly growth, raises up from earth to our kindred who are in heaven. And in this we say truly, for the divine power suspends the head and root of us from that place where the generation of the soul first began, and thus makes the whole body upright" (*Timaeus*, 90a-b).

The translations of these and other Platonic passages are from *The Collected Dialogues of Plato*, E. Hamilton and H. Cairns, eds (Princeton, NJ, 1971).

25. All the signs seem to point to what Plato has called "a battle of gods and giants going on between them over their quarrel about reality" (*Sophist*, 246a); that is, the Pythagorean "friends of Ideas" and the Milesian naturalist philosophers. The "battle" is still continuing with the positivists now in the role of the "giants." See R. Rorty, "Pragmatism and Philosophy," in *After Philosophy*, K. Baynes et al., eds (Cambridge, Mass., 1987), pp. 20-66. Unfortunately for our curiosity (which demands to find out what exactly Pythagoras learned in his trips abroad, especially in Egypt, and how that learning might have influenced the Platonic traditions), the legendary Pythagorean silence regarding these matters is destined to frustrate our efforts. Since my task here is limited, I will try to draw attention only to some significant signs found in the texts of Hellenic historians, poets, and philosophers, especially Plato and Aristotle, from which I will quote extensively. This is an initial attempt to see clearly the contrast in perspective between Ancient Hellenic philosophers and Modern European scholars in its true dimensions. As an ancient philosopher put it: "Nothing greater can be attained by men, and nothing nobler can be granted by the gods, than truth." Plutarch, *De Iside et Osiride* (I.i. D, 4-5), J.G. Griffith, ed. (Wales, 1970).

26. Among the reasons which may account for this difference between the Ancient Hellenes and Modern Europeans, one may include, as I said, the fact that the Hellenes had a cyclical conception of history, as they had of nature and the cosmos in general. This perhaps prevented them from giving into the folly of believing that philosophy and civilization began with their genius alone or that they were destined "to end" with their own death. This folly, that is, the obsession of an absolute beginning, a linear progress, and an abrupt end, is characteristic of Christian theology and German "philosophy" which, in Nietzsche's sharp judgment, are virtually indistinguishable. He stated: "Among Germans one will understand immediately when I say that philosophy has been corrupted by theologian blood. The Protestant pastor is the grandfather of German philosophy, Protestantism itself is its original sin ... One has only to say the words 'College of Tubingen' to grasp what German philosophy is at bottom—a cunning theology," *Twilight of the Idols/The Anti-Christ*, R.J. Hollingdale, tr. (New York, 1968), p. 121.

On the other hand, according to R. Bernstein, the list of modern philosophers who have aspired "to end" philosophy includes Hegel, Kierkegaard, Marx, Heidegger, Wittgenstein,

Foucault, Derrida, and Rorty (and Hegel again, as revived). See *Philosophical Profiles* (Philadelphia, 1986), p. 85; and Chapter Five, "Why Hegel Now?" in which he reviews Ch. Taylor's *Hegel* (Cambridge, 1975); F. Fukuyama, *The End of History and the Last Man* (New York, 1992); and my "Philosophy, Human Wonder, and Hellenic Logos," *Skepsis* 2 (1991): 29-41.

27. I said, "the least biased," because it is possible that both approaches to the problem, the Ancient/Hellenic and the Modern/European, are not entirely free from prejudice. Given the political situations, which respectively prevailed in the fifth-fourth centuries BC, when Greeks and Egyptians as allies fought the Persian Empire, and in the nineteenth-twentieth centuries AD, when European imperialist powers scrambled for colonial control of Asia and Africa, it is understandable that the Egyptians would be perceived differently. Yet, there is a greater difference between the two perceptions than one would have reasonably expected. By portraying the Egyptians, not as the tutors of the admired Hellenes, but as another case of African barbarity, the Northern Europeans, perhaps unwittingly, appear to have accomplished the following three and ethically questionable tasks.

First, they have provided some justification for imperialistic aggression against Africa and for colonial occupation of Egypt.

Second, they have made the Ancient Hellenes look like fools, who were willing to give undue credit to non-Hellenes for the "Hellenic inventions" of philosophy, science, and civilization.

Third, and most ominous for the future of mankind, they have succeeded in appropriating the achievements of Hellenes (including the Hellenic philosophers who are, ironically, considered "Westerners," as we will see in the last essay) exclusively.

Thus, the Hellenes are separated from their Egyptian friends and, by implication, from the rest of the world. Paradoxically, even Modern Greeks, proud as they are of their Hellenic roots, have been taken in by this "scheme." Hence the eagerness to become "Europeans!" Homer, their poet, would have said: "Shame on you, Argives!"

28. According to Herodotus (VI. 283-5), the Ancient Hellenes considered Egypt as the "gift of the Nile," which is also called *Aigyptos* by Homer. The country stretches along the delta and the valley of the great river, surrounded by Asia from the East and by Libya from the South and the West. In fact, *Libya* was the name by which the Ancient Hellenes referred to Africa as a whole.

29. In the Homeric epics, the name "Hellenes" had not acquired as yet the broad meaning of applying to all those who fought the Trojans. They are generally identified as Argeans, Acheans, Danaans and Iaones. Hellenes were strictly the people of Phthiotis, the famed Myrmidons, who followed their hero Achilles in battle.

30. Odyssey, I, 20-25. The translation is E.V. Rieu's, in the Penguin Classics.

31. *Ibid.*, XIV, 256-344.

32. The version of the story which claims that Helen never went to Troy, but spent all those years in Egypt, while the Acheans and the Trojans were fighting for her (or "her image"), under the walls of Troy, has been always appealing to poets from Euripides to N. Kazantzakis. For example, in the Odyssey: *A Modern Sequel*, K. Friar, tr. (New York, 1958) the comrades of Odysseus, as they approached Egypt, could not help but sing of Helen, who was left in Crete as the poem's plot required:

and far, far off

on Egypt's sun-scorched sands, the piper's brain blazed up

till his mind whirled with vertigo and his heart pulsed:

"Oho! A north wind blows, and Helen sweeps my mind!"
What's happening, comrades, now, to her world-famous body?
(Book IX, 983-987).

33. Odyssey, IV, 217-230.

34. Herodotus (II, 112-120) extensively reports about Helen's adventure in Egypt as he heard it from the Egyptian priests and found the story convincing for this reasons: "So much was told me by the Egyptian priests. For myself, I believe their story about Helen. For I reason thus—that had Helen been in Ilion, then with or without the will of Alexandus she would have been given back to the Greeks. For surely neither was Priam so mad nor those nearest to him, as to consent to risk their own persons and their children and their city, that Alexandrus might have Helen to wife."

But Plato (*Phaedrus*, 274c-275c), speaks of a much more powerful drug (φάρμακον) than Helen's Egyptian gifts, that is, the invention of writing by Theuth, which would be of great help to memory and a "source of wisdom" for the Egyptians. The fame of the Egyptian doctors and their medicine was known to Aristotle also, as is evident from *Politics*, 1286a, 12.

35. *Helen*, 1-67, R. Lattimore, *Euripides II*, tr. (Chicago, 1969). Pindar also was familiar with some strange Egyptian customs, like the one he alluded to (in Fr. 201), and reported by Herodotus (in II. 46), regarding the copulation of women with he-goats.

36. For obvious political reasons, the Hellenes referred to the Persians as "barbarians." Herodotus asserts that "The Egyptians call anyone who does not speak their language 'barbarian'." So, among other things, the Ancient Hellenes, like the Hebrews, might have learned even this division of mankind from the Egyptians. However, given the egotistical bias of human beings, I suspect that the "us versus them" distinction is both the oldest and most universal expression of ethnocentrism. Plato disapproved of this division, although some times he used it. Consider, for instance: "Thank you, but what kind of mistake do you say that we made in our division just now? The kind of mistake a man would make who, seeking to divide the class of human beings into two, divide them into Greeks and barbarians. This is a division most people in this part of the world make. They separate the Greeks from all other nations making them a class apart; thus they group all other nations together as a class, ignoring the fact that it is an indeterminate class made up of peoples who have no intercourse with each other and speak different languages. Lumping all this non-Greek residue together, they think it must constitute one class because they have a common name 'barbarian' to attach to it" (*Statesman*, 262c-d).

37. Not surprisingly, the "Father of History" opens his great work, which is centered on the long struggle between the Greeks and the Barbarians (that is, the Persians), with some references to prehistoric or mythic times. At those distant times, the Hellenes abducted Europa and Medea to get even with the Barbarians who had carried off Io and Helen. The originators of the mischief were the Phoenicians, for they: "Among other places to which they carried Egyptian and Assyrian merchandise, they came to Argos, which was about that time preeminent in every way among the people of what is now called Hellas. The Phoenicians then came, as I say, to Argos, and set out their cargo. On the fifth or sixth day of their coming, their wares being now well-nigh all sold, there came to the sea shore among many other women the king's daughter, whose name (according to Persians and Greeks alike) was Io, the Daughter of Inachus. They stood about the stern of the ship; and while they bargained for such wares as they fancied, the Phoenicians heartened each other to the deed, and rushed to take them. Most of the women escaped: Io with others was carried off; the men cast her into the ship and made sail away for Egypt" (I. 1, in the Loeb translation).

Hence the connection between Io and Epaphus (or Apis) with Egypt (as Pindar remarked, Nem. X). Relevant, in this connection, are also Danaos, Aigyptos, and the story of Danaids, which Aeschylus treated skillfully in the *Suppliants*. Diodorus (I. 24), interestingly identifies the Argive Lady Io with the Egyptian Goddess Isis.

38. "Philosophy begins in Miletus, an Ionian city of the Mediterranean shore ... Every history of philosophy begins with Thales, and records with proper solemnity his opinion that the source of all things is water." R.E. Allen, *ibid.*, p. 1. This is typical of how histories of philosophy in general, not just histories of Ancient philosophy, begin. This tendency is perhaps due to a misunderstanding of a passage in Aristotle's Metaphysics, (983b 20), where the Stagirite refers to Thales as "the founder" of a "certain kind" of philosophy (ο της τοιαύτης αρχηγός φιλοσοφίας). In the Aristotelian text and its context, the emphasis is on the word τοιαύτης (of such a kind). He intends to identify Thales as the first philosopher, who postulated water, that is, a material natural element, as the first principle or αρχή of all things and, thus, he became the leader of those who followed him in the same direction. However, even in this narrowly conceived sense of natural and materialistic philosophy, Aristotle is careful to give due credit to those "ancient theologians," who had considered, "Ocean and Tethys the parents of creation, and described the oath of the gods as being by water, to which they give the name of Styx; for what is oldest is most honorable, and the most honorable thing is that by which one swears" (983b 30-32).

39. *Hist.* III, 191-192; also J.B. Bury et al., eds, *A History of Greece: To the Death of Alexander the Great* (New York, 1978, 4th edn), 84-85; and J. Boardman, *The Greeks Overseas* (Baltimore, MD, 1964), especially Chapter Four, "The Greeks in Egypt," pp. 127-162.

40. Herodotus, II. 178.

41. Plato mentioned King Amasis in the following passage: "In the Egyptian Delta, at the head of which the river Nile divides, there is a certain district which is called the district of Sais, and the great city of the district is also called Sais, and is the city from which King Amasis came. The citizens have a deity for their foundress; she is called in the Egyptian tongue Neith, and is asserted by them to be the same whom the Hellenes call Athena" (*Timaeus*, 21e).

42. Without the intervention of Aphrodite, the marriage would have ended in disaster for the following reason: "But it so fell out that Ladice was the only woman with whom Amasis could not have intercourse; and this continuing, Amasis said to this Ladice, 'Woman, you have cast a spell on me, and most assuredly you shall come to the most terrible end of all women.' So, the king's anger not abating for all her denial, Ladice vowed in her heart to Aphrodite that she would send the goddess a statue to Cyrene if Amasis had intercourse with her that night; for that would remedy the evil; and thereafter all went well, and Amasis loved his wife much. Ladice paid her vow to the goddess; she had an image made and sent it to Cyrene where it stood safe till my time, facing outward from the city. Cambyses, when he had conquered Egypt and learnt who Ladice was, sent her to Cyrene unharmed" (*Hist.* II. 181).

Amasis, we may recall, was also in friendly correspondence with the tyrant of Samos Polycrates. Is it possible that he had recommended the young Pythagoras to the Egyptian priests for advanced studies? Of course it is, as it is also likely that the mature philosopher Pythagoras turned against the tyrant of Samos after his soul had been set free by philosophia, just as the Platonic Socrates would have it. See on this Phaedo, 82e-84c; also the appendix to this essay.

43. H. Webster, *Early European History* (Boston, 1920), pp. 37-41.

44. Toynbee, *Ibid*, p. 114, gives a reason for the Athenian failure: "It might indeed have been expected that, after the failure, in 480-479 BC, of the Persians' attempt to annex European Greece to their empire, there would have been an immediate resumption, with greater energy than ever, of the Hellenic penetration of Egypt and South-West Asia, which had begun in the seventh century BC at the heels of the retreating Assyrians and had been cut short, in the sixth century, by the Persian Empire's sudden rise. The Persian Empire had been given a reprieve by the breach between Sparta and Athens. In 457 BC, Sparta had stabbed Athens in the back when Athens was wrenching Egypt out of Persia's grasp. In 393 Athens had stabbed Sparta in the back when Sparta was driving the Persians out of Western Anatolia. For a united Hellenic World the conquest of the Persian Empire would present no military difficulties."

Evidently, the Athenians did not learn, from this experience, the lesson that military adventures far from home are full of risks, otherwise they would have been more cautious with the ill-fated expedition to Sicily fifty years later.

45. Augustine writes (*De civitate Dei*, VIII. 5) that the Egyptian high priest had revealed to Alexander the great secret that even the Gods were once upon a time men, not only lesser gods like Heracles and Asclepius, but also Jupiter, Juno, Saturn, and so on. So, by accepting the appellation "Son of God," Alexander did not commit as great a hubris as it may seem at first glance. Besides, he seems to have prepared the way for the new Liberator, Jesus Christ, who was accepted as "the Messiah," the anointed "Son of God" and the God-man by the Hellenistic world without difficulty. As Alexander had liberated the Egyptians, the Jews, and the Asiatic Greeks from the Persians, the new Liberator Christ was expected to liberate them all from the Romans. Strangely enough, their dream came true.

Through the power of the new faith in the Christian Logos, in combination with the Hellenic logos and its protean expression, the Byzantine Greeks managed to take over the declining Roman Empire in the East (the Western part was taken over by the barbarians and completely de-hellenized, until the Renaissance). They renewed it, and built around Constantinople a new Greco-Romano-Egyptian theocratic civilization, which lasted for more than a millennium (330-1453). The fall of Constantinolpe to the Turks and the exodus of educated Byzantine refugees to the West happily coincided with the cultural awaking which is known as Renaissance. So as the Latin West was coming out of the darkness of the Middle Ages, the Greek East was falling into the darkness of Turkocracy, from which it has not as yet completely recovered.

46. The close cooperation between Hellas and Egypt during the Persian Wars, and their common front against the Persians, involved also the Hellenic Macedonia, as the following passage from Herodotus (IX. 45) indicates. The heroic deed by Alexander's great grandfather at the eve of the great battle at Plataeas clearly reveals the feelings of the King of Macedonia as a genuine Hellene: "Men of Athens, I give you this my message in trust as a secret that you must reveal to none but Pausanias, lest you even be my undoing; in truth I would not tell it to you were it not by reason of my great care for all Hellas; for I myself am by ancient descent a Greek [Hellene], I would not willingly see Hellas change her freedom for slavery. I tell you, then, that Mardonius and his army cannot get from the sacrifices omens to his liking; else had you fought long ere this. But now it is his purpose to pay no heed to the sacrifices, and join battle at the first glimmer of dawn; for he is in dread, as I surmise, lest you should muster to a greater host. Therefore I bid you make ready; and if (as may be) Mardonius delay and not join battle, wait patiently where you are; for he has but a few days' provisions left. But if this war end as you would wish, then must you take thought

how to save me too from slavery, who of my zeal have done so desperate a deed as this for the cause of Hellas, in my desire to declare to you Mardonius intent, that so the foreigners [barbarians] may not fall upon you suddenly ere you yet expect them. I that speak am Alexander the Macedonian."

47. Two hundred years before Alexander, the Milesians had settled in the Sais, where they founded Naukratis. According to Strabo (VIII. 17. 1. 18): "In the time of Psammitichus (who lived in the time of Cyaxares the Mede) the Milesians, with thirty ships, put in the Bublitine mouth, and then, disembarking, fortified with a wall the above-mentioned settlement; but in time they sailed up into the Saitic Nome, defeated the city of Inaros in a naval fight, and founded Naucratis, not far above Schedia."

48. The first Christian school of higher learning, the Catechetical School of Alexandria, produced such men of letters and great theologians as Clement, Origen, Dionysius, and Athanasius. Through their use of the Greek language and philosophic terminology and arguments in their writings, and in their prolonged Christological debates, they shaped the Christian Orthodox dogma, which made the Christianity intellectually respectable during the critical third and fourth centuries AD. On this see B. Altaner, *Partology*, H.C. Graef, tr. (New York, 1961, 2nd edn), pp. 212-245.

This tendency to use philosophical language and logical syllogisms in religious debates gave rise to the heresies of Christian Gnosticism, so much so that Harnak's characterization of the two movements as "the chronic" and "the acute" Hellenization of the Church seems proper. On this see H. Jonas, *The Gnostic Religion*, 2nd revised edn (Boston, 1963), p. 36; and "Plotinus' Anti-Gnostic Polemic and Porphyry's Against the Christians," in Neoplatonism and Gnosticism, R. Wallis and J. Bregman, eds (Albany, NY, 1992), pp. 111-128.

49. On this see, Herodotus II, 177; Diogenes Laertius IX, 35; Isocrates, Busiris, 28-29; Aetius I, 3, 1; Plutarch, De Is. et Osir., 10 and 34; Plato, Timaeus, 22b; Porphyry, Vita Pythagorae, 19; and Proclus, In Euclidem, 64-65.

50. As an eyewitness, Herodotus is invaluable in this regard, even when he exaggerates and gives the impression of being a "phil-Egyptian" (I would hesitate to use the term φιλοβάρβαρος because, to my knowledge, Hellenic authors do not refer to Egyptians specifically as "barbarians," except when they are included among other non-Greeks). This is especially true in Herodotus who knew that it was the Egyptians who first distinguished themselves from the "barbarians" (by this they meant primarily the Persians, as we saw). Consider, for example a passage from Book II, 49-50: "Nor yet will I hold that the Egyptians took either this or any other custom from the Greeks ... Indeed, well-nigh all the names of the gods came to Hellas from Egypt. For I am assured by inquiry that they have come from foreign parts, and I believe that they came from Egypt. Except the names of Poseidon and the Dioscuri, as I have already said, and Here, and Hestia, and Themis, and the Graces and the Nereids, the names of all the gods have ever existed in Egypt."

51. In spite of this fact, the language barrier has been adduced by modern historians, like Zeller and Burnet, as the strongest proof that the Greeks could not have borrowed any of their theories from the Egyptians because they would not have understood them, even if we assume that there was philosophy and science in Egypt.

52. According to Philo of Byblus, Tautos was also identified with Theuth whom the Greeks identified with Hermes. He later became known as Hermes Trismegistus. See A.I. Baumgarten, *The Phoenician History of Philo of Byblus: A Commentary* (Leiden, 1981), p. 18, (25).

53. Phaedrus, 274c-d.

54. "Wonders are many and none is more wonderful than man." Thus sings the Chorus in Sophocles' *Antigone*, indicating the close connection, which existed between philosophy and poetry as they were understood by the Hellenes. The inspired poet, the prudent lawgiver, the natural philosopher, and the dialectical metaphysician each had a claim to "wisdom," which was almost equal to that of Prometheus, the great benefactor of mankind. About the Protean nature of wisdom or *sophia*, Aristotle was most eloquent in *On Philosophy*, which unfortunately is not extant. But see *Aristotelis Fragmenta Selecta*, D.W. Ross, ed., *Oxford Classical Text* (Oxford, 1955), Fr. 8.

55. These favorite conditions for the development of the spirit of philosophical curiosity and of scientific inquiry existed not only in Ancient Greece but also, much earlier, in China, India, Mesopotamia, and Egypt. All these peoples created great civilizations, and cultivated the arts and the sciences, the letters and their gods in such ways and to such a degree that the Hellenes, according to their own accounts, did learn from them, especially from the Egyptians. With them, because of their proximity, they had certainly constant cultural intercourse at least since the seventh century BC.

56. *Theaetetus*, 155c-156a.

57. *Phaedrus*, 274c-275a (Hackforth's translation).

58. *Philebus*, 18a-b. See also *Enneads*, V.8.6. 1-10. Here Plotinus sets the hieroglyphic or ideogrammatic (if they are different, as Armstrong supposes) symbols in contrast to the letters: "The wise men of Egypt, I think, also understood this, either by scientific or innate knowledge, and when they wished to signify something wisely, did not use the forms of letters which follow the order of words and propositions and imitate sounds and the enunciation of philosophical statements, but by drawing images and inscribing in their temples one particular image of each particular thing, they manifested the non-discursiveness of the intelligible world, that is, that every image is a kind of knowledge and wisdom and is a subject of statements, all together in one, and not discursive or deliberation" (Armstrong's translation); and E.R. Dodds, *The Greeks and the Irrational* (Berkeley, 1951), p. 286.

59. *Metaphysics*, 982b 11-19. Note the agility with which Aristotle passes from the love of logic (and philosophy) to the love of myth (and mythology). He was a student of Plato for twenty years, and the latter's love for "likely stories" is well known, *Statesman*, 268d-e:

"Stranger: Then we must begin all over again from another starting point and travel by another road.

Y. Socrates: What kind of road must this be?

Stranger: We have to bring in some pleasant stories to relieve the strain. There is a mass of ancient legend a large part of which we must now use for our purposes; after that we must go on as before, dividing always and choosing one part only, until we arrive at the summit of our climb and the object of our journey. Shall we begin?

Y. Socrates: Yes certainly.

Stranger: Come, then, listen closely to my story as a child would; after all, you are not so very many years too old for stories.

Y. Socrates: Do continue, please.

Stranger: These old stories have been told before and will be told again. Among them is the one about the portent that settled the famous quarrel between Atreus and Thyestes. I expect that you have heard the story and remember the details of it as they are described to us."

60. *Ibid.* (981b 15-24). In this connection, consider also Porphyry's informed comment: "It is an undisputed fact that such mathematical sciences as geometry, arithmetic, and astronomy came to the Hellenes late. Yet they were known [to others], although the Hellenes had no knowledge of them." *Commentaria in Aristotelem Graeca*, IV, 1, A. Busse, ed. (Berlin, 1887), pp. 119, 37-120, 3 (the translation is mine). Porphyry's comment relates to the debate whether simultaneity applies to all cases of relatives, such as sensible and sense perception, knowable and knowledge, and so on. See also my Aristotle's Categories and Porphyry, op. cit., pp. 79-84. That the mathematical sciences came to Greece from Egypt, see also K. Vourveris, *Plato and the Barbarians* (Athens, 1966), pp. 130-140 (in Greek); that they were connected to medicine, see *Ptolemy: Tetrabiblos*, F.E. Robbins, ed. and tr. (Cambridge, Mass., 1956), I.3.16.

61. In these passages Aristotle attempts to bridge the gap between μύθος (mythical account) and λόγος (logical account), σοφία (wisdom) and θεωρία (contemplation). This last word is one of the Hellenic words, which have no monolectic English equivalent. It certainly does not mean only "theory" in the sense of a working hypothesis, which is in need of verification (for Logical Positivists) or falsification (for the followers of Popper). See D. Emmett, "Theoria and the Way of Life," *Journal of Theological Studies*, n.s. 17 (1966): 38-52; and G. Clark, *Iamblichus: On the Pythagorean Life* (Liverpool, 1989), pp. xiii-xiv.

62. *Phaedrus*, 257d; *Philebus*, 18b-c. Compare them with Herodotus, Histories II. 4, 50, 58, 82, 123, 177, 180; and Isocrates, Busiris 17, 28.

63. *Timaeus*, 656c-657b (B. Jowett's translation). In this passage, and others similar to this, Plato speaks as an eye-witness of the Egyptian works of art and, therefore, against those who doubt either his visit to Egypt or his knowledge and acquaintance with things Egyptian. Passages, like the above, may have prompted Popper to characterize Plato as an enemy of "the open society," as he envisioned it after World War II. See his *The Open Society and Its Enemies*, vol. 1, *The Spell of Plato* (Princeton, NJ, 1971, first published in 1962). However, at the end of that century Western societies certainly knew better than Professor Popper did, by having experienced the bitter fruits of too much openness, permissiveness, and excess of liberty.

64. Jowett's translation, from which I quote here, reads: "It is now new or recent discovery ...", which makes no sense in view of what follows. The discovery is anything but new. The Greek text reads: ἔοικε δε ου νυν ουδέ νεωστί τουτ' εἶναι γνώριμον, which I have translated as follows: "It appears that it is not new, nor has it recently become known to ..."

65. Notice Aristotle's respectful reference to "tradition" here and connect it to Plato's similar mention of tradition in the previous quotation. The contemporary practitioners of "logical analysis" and "deconstruction" could learn something from the Ancients' respect for tradition and their critical appraisal of it.

66. Herodotus also (II. 102-111), has much to say about this remarkable King of Egypt. Sesostris, it would appear, followed Diotima's recommendation (*Symposium*, 209d-3) of how to achieve immortality as a ruler. To him has been attributed the remark: "Only the king whose name is remembered on account of his work does not die," *The Columbia History of the World*, J. Garraty and P. Gay, eds (New York, 1984), p. 77. For Sesostris' memorial "stelae," see *Manetho Fr.* 35, ed., W.G. Waddell (Cambridge, Mass., 1956).

67. *Politics*, 1329b 1-35.

68. This method is typical of Aristotle. Its application extends over the entire Aristotelian corpus. Every major treatise opens dialectically in the sense that the opinions of

"the wise" or of "the majority" on a given subject are collected and scrutinized. If they are found to be sound, by the application of the criterion of human λόγος (with its multiple meanings), the opinions, customs, institutions, or whatever else is the matter under investigation are adopted as true, otherwise they are set aside. For more on the dialectic method and its importance for Aristotle's philosophy, see the third essay of this collection, "Aristotle and Western Rationality."

69. "His [Philip's] Athenian admirer, the more academic publicist and man of letters Isocrates, saw in the union of all the states of Hellas, under the leadership of a single power in the hands of a single great man, an opportunity for at last carrying through the Panhellenic counterattack on the Persian Empire which had been the unachieved aim of Cimon son of Miltiades ... The military triumph of Hellenic arms under Macedonian leadership had surpassed the dreams of Isocrates." A. Toynbee, *Hellenism: The History of a Civilization* (London, 1959) pp. 114-116. Isocrates was also an enlightened man, who understood that the essential characteristic of Hellenism was paideia (education). In his famous *Panathenaicus*, 50, Isocrates declared that the name "Hellenes" should apply not so much to those who were born in Hellas or happen to be of Hellenic blood, but to all men who shared in the Hellenic παιδεία (education and culture). He thus prepared the way for the coming of the cosmopolitan era of the Hellenistic world.

70. *Busiris* 13-20, Larue Van Hook, tr. (Cambridge, Mass., 1986). Regarding the stories about Busiris' and the Egyptians' reputation as being inhospitable to strangers, Eratosthenes' view, as reported by Strabo (VIII. 17. 1. 19), seems most reasonable. He explains them by "the lack of harbors at the Delta" and the presence of pirates.

71. Marx also, who actually quoted from *Busiris* (Ch. 8), remarks about the connection between Egypt and Hellenic political theory regarding the division of labor: "This aspect, from the stand-point of use-value alone, is taken as well by Plato, who treats division of labor as the foundation on which the division of society into classes is based, as by Xenophon, who with characteristic bourgeois instinct, approaches more nearly to division of labor within the workshop. Plato's Republic, in so far as division of labor is treated in it, as the formative system of the State, is merely the Athenian idealization of the Egyptian system of castes, Egypt having served as the model of an industrial country to many of his contemporaries also, amongst other to Isocrates, and it continued to have this importance to the Greeks of the Roman Empire." *Capital*, S. Moore and E. Aveling, tr. (3 vols, Moscow, 1978), vol. 1, pp. 345-346.

72. This is my simplified rendering of Isocrates' superlatives, which Van Hook translates, rather poetically, as "the healthiest and most long of life among men."

73. Again, "philosophy's training" is an awkward expression as a translation of the phrase "philosophias askesis." It would be better to render it simply as "practice of philosophy."

74. This may be another reference to Plato's *Republic* (Book Seven), where the connection between mathematics and virtue is emphasized. See also G.M.A. Grube, *Plato's Thought* (Indianapolis, 1980), pp. 248-251.

75. *Busiris*, 21-23. Even if we consider it an Isocratean rhetorical hyperbole that Pythagoras brought "all philosophy" to the Hellenes, the fact remains that he brought something important from his trips abroad. Perhaps that was the kind of intellectual pursuit, which attends to the mathematical sciences and allows philosophy to care for the needs of the soul, just as the art of medicine takes care of the bodily needs. Through Plato and the Platonic tradition, this type of philosophy more than any other contributed to shaping the

Hellenic view of man, as an ignorant captive whose true liberator was Lady Philosophy. The Platonic Socrates has stated it clearly: "Every seeker after wisdom knows that up to the time when philosophy takes it over, his soul is a helpless prisoner, chained hand and foot in the body, compelled to view reality not directly but only through its prison bars, and wallowing in utter ignorance. And philosophy can see that the imprisonment is ingeniously effected by the prisoner's own active desire, which makes him first accessory to his own confinement. Well, philosophy takes over the soul in this condition and by gentle persuasion tries to set it free" (*Phaedo*, 82e-83a). About the importance of the Platonic tradition, see *The Significance of Neoplatonism*, R. Baine Harris, ed. (Albany, NY, 1976), especially J.N. Findlay's essay, "The Neoplatonism of Plato," pp. 23-41.

76. Our discussion, in Section 5, does not pretend to be exhaustive in any sense. Jaeger and Guthrie are only two of the dozens of scholars who have dealt with the historiography of Hellenic philosophy. But they are considered as the most authoritative representatives of the Zeitgeist, so to speak. At any rate, the picture would be substantially the same even if we were to substitute, for example, the names of E. Zeller, *Die Philosophie der Griechen*, W. Nestle, ed. (Leipzig, 1923, 7th edn) and J. Burnet, *Early Greek Philosophy* (London, 1930, 4th edn), for Jaeger and Guthrie respectively.

There are many others who have followed in their steps. For example, Bernard Williams, "Philosophy," in *The Legacy of Greece*, M.I. Finley, ed. (Oxford, 1984), p. 202. He claims dogmatically that: "In philosophy, the Greeks initiated almost all its major fields—metaphysics, logic, the philosophy of language, the theory of knowledge; ethics, political philosophy, and (though to a much more restricted degree) the philosophy of art. Not only did they start these areas of inquiry, but also they progressively distinguished what would still be recognized as many of the most basic questions in those areas. In addition, among those who brought about these developments there were two, Plato and Aristotle, who have always, where philosophy has been known and studied in the Western world, been counted as supreme in philosophical genius ..." No doubt, Dr. Williams means to praise Plato and Aristotle, but what would they have thought of his eulogy?

77. In this respect, M. Bernal's hypothesis, in *Black Athena*, vol. 1 (New Brunswick, NJ, 1991), especially Chapters IV-X, regarding the strong racial motives of modern Northern European historiography, would seem plausible even to those critics, who are otherwise skeptical or critical of Bernal's project as a whole. Since not all of the four projected volumes have been published, we should be cautious not to commit the error of judging the whole by the part, as so many have done in reviewing the book.

Now, in so far as Bernal wishes to replace what he calls "the Aryan Model" with the "Ancient Model," which he seeks to revive and to revise, he would be moving in the right direction, especially if he does not go too far with the proposed "revision." But when he shows that he cannot resist the temptation of engaging in wild etymologies as proof of Levantine influence on the Hellenic language; or when he speculates on extensive Semitic colonization of prehistoric Hellas, he would seem to stand on slippery ground. But if, as he claims, "The political purpose of Black Athena is, of course, to lessen European cultural arrogance" (p. 73), then we can only wish his book the best of luck.

For a multiple response to Bernal's book, see *Black Athena Revisited*, M.R. Lefkowitz and G.M. Rogers, eds (Chapel Hill, NC, 1996); also, M.R. Lefkowitz, "Not Out of Africa," *New Republic* (1992): 29-36, and her book under the same title, *Not Out of Africa* (New York, 1996); and A. Preus, "Greek Philosophy: Egyptian Origins," in *Research Papers on the Humanities and Social Sciences* (Binghamton, 1992), which is equally critical of G.M.

James' book, *Stolen Legacy: Greek Philosophy is Stolen Egyptian Philosophy* (Trenton, NJ, 1992).

It is my understanding that the false dilemma, Eurocentrism or Afrocentrism, can be overcome by considering a third option, that of Hellenocentrism, as this essay has attempted to outline. The fierce debates between Afrocentrists and Eurocentrists at the present tend to ignore this option, because the former have uncritically accepted the latter's claim that Ancient Hellas and its great achievements, including Hellenic philosophy, belong exclusively to them, as an integral part of European civilization, which is only partially correct. See the last essay for more information on this issue.

78. By Jaeger's restrictive definition of "real culture" and civilization as "the deliberate pursuit of an Ideal," one may wonder whether any era or race (except for the Germans of the Romantic late nineteenth and early twentieth century), would qualify to be called civilized. Of course, German writers of that era, inspired as they were by the spirit of Romanticism, could dream that they were really pursuing the "Ideal of Ancient Hellas." But the Hellenes did not have such a foggy chimera to chase. For they lived their lives in the open air, under the clear blue Attic sky, and in the bright Mediterranean sun allowing its light to illuminate their arts, acts, and thoughts.

79. Even Hegel, whom Jaeger followed in his speculations on the origins of various institutions, is more cautious in his assertions. He writes, "Among the Greeks we feel ourselves immediately at home for we are in the region of Spirit; and though the origin of the nation, as also its philosophical peculiarities, may be traced further—even to India—the proper emergence, the Palingenesis of Spirit must be looked for in Greece first ... If the nation has a basis—such as the Greek world has in the Oriental—a foreign culture enters as an element into its primary condition, and it has a double culture one original, the other of foreign suggestion." *The Philosophy of History*, J. Sibree, tr. (New York, 1956), pp. 223-224.

However, inasmuch as Egypt and its civilization are concerned, Hegel's philosophy of history reads like a paraphrase of Herodotus: "This intelligent historiographer himself visited the country of which he wished to give an account, and at its chief towns made acquaintance with Egyptian priests" (p. 199). But occasionally Hegel spoils Herodotus' witty account with his own surprise: "It deserves mention here, that the Elians, in Herodotus' narrative, call the Egyptians the wisest of mankind. It also surprises us to find among them, in the vicinity of African stupidity, reflective intelligence, a thoroughly rational organization characterizing all institutions, and most astonishing works of art" (p. 204). Again: "This contrast of a vulgar soul and a keen intellect is characteristic in an Egyptian king" (p. 203). The reference is to the philhellene king Amasis, who was admired by both Herodotus and Plato.

80. *Paideia: The Ideals of Greek Culture*, G. Highet, tr. (New York, 1945, 2nd edn), pp. xiv-xvii. Similar prejudices seem to pervade also the commentary of two other authorities on Ancient Greek philosophy, G.S. Kirk and J.E. Raven, who, contrary to the evidence of ancient reliable sources, state: "It was the custom to credit the sixth-century sages with visits to Egypt, the traditional fountain-head of Greek science. Thales as the earliest known Greek geometer had a special reason for being associated with the home of land measurement. The implication that he spent a considerable time there is unique and not persuasive ... We have already seen that he had associations with Babylonia and with Egypt. The idea that the earth actually floats upon water was more clearly and more widely held in the latter of these countries; and the conjecture may be hazarded that Thales was indebted to Egypt for this

element of his world-picture." *The Presocratic Philosophers* (Cambridge, 1957), p. 77 and p. 91.

To clearly see the contrasting difference between the Ancient Hellenes and the Northern Europeans, we may compare these assertions with the statements of Aetius (1, 3, 1) and Plutarch (*De Is. et Os.* 34) respectively. According to Aetius, "Thales came to Miletus an old man having spent a long time studying philosophy in Egypt;" while Plutarch informs us that "Like Thales, Homer too had learned from the Egyptians to posit water as the principle and the genesis of all things." Lest one consider this a fantastic claim, we should recall that Plutarch, like Plato and Aristotle, refers to the famous lines of *Iliad* XIV 201 and 246, where the poet, like a Presocratic philosopher, states categorically:

"Both Ocean, the father of Gods, and Tethys their mother;" or

"...[O]f Ocean who is the source of all beings" (my translation).

The difference between Homer and Thales, or any other Presocratic philosopher, is that while they were serious regarding their dogmatic assertions about the ultimate nature of the universe, the poet playfully presents the same ontological view in a very funny scene. Hera, decked up like a peacock, is scheming to put Zeus to sleep (and Sleep was not far from his brother Death!) after arousing him erotically and passionately making love to him, so that she could pursue her plan of reversing the outcome of the battle to the advantage of her favorite Argives. The point is that, if the strange hypothesis that "water" [hydor] is the ultimate source of everything turned out to be true, Homer's poetry would have the advantage, over the dryness of philosophic prose, of having clothed the naked scientific "truth" in beautiful Hellenic hexameters!

81. But what is culture? "Culture is that complex whole which includes knowledge, belief, art, law, morals, custom, and any other capabilities and habits acquired by man as member of society." This definition is included in the list of one hundred sixty four definitions of culture to be found in, *Culture: A Critical Review of Concepts and Definitions* (New York, 1981), A.L. Krocber and C. Kluckhorn. See also S. Vryonis, *ibid.*, pp. 250-251, on the number and meaning of the diverse definitions of culture.

82. Jaeger, *Paideia*, p. xv. He developed this peculiar sense of "Hellenocentrism" fully in an introductory essay to the collection *Altertum und Gegenwart* (Leipzig, 1920, 2nd edn), reprinted in *Humanistische Reden und Vortaege* (Berlin, 1937). Part of my purpose in this essay was to show that Jaeger's claims regarding "Hellenocentrism" are not warranted historically or philosophically.

83. The most eloquent articulation of this fantastic scheme is to be found, of course, in Hegel, whose hypnotizing influence on the German mind a century after his death could not be shaken off even by a Classical Scholar of Jaeger's caliber. Consider, for example: "The solution and liberation of that Oriental Spirit, which in Egypt had advanced so far as to propose the problem, is certainly this: that the Inner Being [the Essence] of Nature is Thought, which has its existence only in the human consciousness ... In Persia begins the principle of Free Spirit as contrasted with imprisonment in Nature; mere natural existence, therefore, loses its bloom and fades away. The principle of separation from Nature is found in the Persian Empire, which, therefore, occupies a higher grade than those worlds immersed in the Natural. The necessity of advance has been thereby proclaimed. Spirit has disclosed its existence, and must complete its development ... For the Greeks surrender the sceptre of dominion and civilization [which they received from the Persians] to the Romans, and the Romans are subdued by the Germans" (*ibid.*, pp. 220-221). The Hegelian

connection between "dominion and civilization" perhaps explains Jaeger's hesitance to recognize the civilizations of non-Europeans.

84. *Ibid.*, xv. The Germanic tribes have (whereas others lack), what Hegel has called "the Heart," enabling them to become the bearers of the Higher Spirit as embodied in Lutheran Christianity: "The German Nation was characterized by the sense of Natural Totality—an idiosyncrasy which we may call Heart. Heart is that undeveloped, indeterminate totality of Spirit, in reference to the Will, in which satisfaction of the soul is attained in a correspondingly general and indeterminate way ... This is the abstract principle innate in the German peoples, and that subjective side which they present to the objective in Christianity. "Heart" has no particular object; in Christianity we have the Absolute Object ... [They] are recognized as the bearers of the higher principle of Spirit ... The Germans were predestined to be the bearers of the Christian principle, and to carry out the Idea as the absolutely Rational aim" (*ibid.*, pp. 350-354). What would a Hellenic philosopher say to this sort of thing? Amen or Alas?

85. Such as Luther and Calvin, for example. As H. Pirenne, *A History of Europe* (New York, 1965), p. 557, put it: "His [Luther's] doctrine of justification by faith was related to the doctrine of the mystics, and although, like the humanists, though for very different motives, he condemned celibacy and the ascetic life, he was in absolute opposition to them in his complete sacrifice of free-will and reason to faith." Hegel also declared: "Justly therefore did the Lutheran Reformation make this dogma [of Transubstantiation] an especial object of attack. Luther proclaimed the great doctrine that the Host had spiritual value and Christ was received only on the condition of faith in him" (*ibid.*, p. 377).

As for Calvin's fanaticism as it contrasts with Luther's mysticism, Pirrene again observes: "He had no need to seek for God. He was positive that he had God's Word in the Bible, and that it was to be found only in the Bible. He was to devote his life to arriving at an understanding of the Bible, and imposing upon other men the teachings, which he discovered in it. His heart and his emotions played no part in his religion. In him there was no trace of the Lutheran mysticism. Reflection, reasoning, logic—these were his means of conviction" (p. 577).

What a degradation of logic and philosophy as the Hellenes had conceived and practiced them, one might be tempted to say. But one should not forget that, with a few luminous exceptions of heretics or apostates, the role which was assigned to "philosophy" by the organized and dominating Church in Christian Europe has been for the most part of last two millennia precisely that of *ancilla ecclesiae*. In modern times, "philosophy" simply changed masters and became *ancilla scientiae* or *ancilla ideologiae*. See also the last essay on this.

86. *Ibid.*, p.156. Regarding medicine, Jaeger ponders: "Why Egyptian medicine did not become a science in our sense of the word? ... The Egyptians could not conceive of nature as a universal whole, as the Ionians could and did," *ibid.*, vol. III, p. 5. Not only the Homeric Helen, Herodotus, Isocrates, Plato, and Aristotle, whom we have already quoted on this subject, but also contemporary historians of science and religion would find it difficult to agree with Jaeger on the point regarding medicine. David Lindberg, for example, in *The Beginnings of Western Science* (Chicago, 1992), p. 20, writes: "This brief sketch of Egyptian and Mesopotamian contributions to mathematics, astronomy, and the healing arts offers us a glimpse of the beginnings of Western scientific tradition, as well as a context within which to view the Greek achievement. There is no doubt that the Greeks were aware of the work of their Egyptian and Mesopotamian predecessors, and profited from it. In the chapters that follow, we will see how these products of Egyptian and Mesopotamian thought

entered and helped shape Greek natural philosophy." In addition to this, Siegfried Morenz explains: "What is so clearly true of art hold good also for science. Religion was the basis of Egyptian science ... Certainly science, where unlike art the idea of absolute progress is in order, suffered from the fact that religion was so closely bound up with ancient notions about the cosmos, and adhered to them so tenaciously. But this does not refute the fact that science, medicine included, had its origin in religion. Institutionally the medical profession was associated with the priesthood. Greek authors testify to this connection, and this is amply confirmed by ancient Egyptian sources. Indeed, ritual requirements may be responsible for the creation of a branch of science." *Egyptian Religion*, Ann E. Keep, tr. (Ithaca, NY, 1992), pp. 7-8.

87. Jaeger does not seem to be aware that what he collectively calls "Orientals," especially the Indians, had developed very diverse conceptual schemes some of which would have been envied by the Presocratic philosophers. Democritus, for instance, would have felt at home with the thoroughly monistic, materialistic, and therefore heterodox system of Carvaka; Pythagoras would have sympathized with the Samkhya orthodox system of dualism; and Socrates would have approved wholeheartedly the ultimate purpose of philosophy as articulated by one of the most eloquent contemporary Indian thinkers, Sarvepalli Radhakrishnan. He said: "In its pursuit of the truth, Indian philosophy has always been strongly dominated by concern with the inner life and self of man, rather than the external world of physical nature. Physical science, though developed extensively in the Golden Age of Indian culture, was never considered the road to ultimate truth; truth is to be sought and found within." *Indian Philosophy* (Princeton, 1973), p. xxiv. Compare this with Socrates' words of prayer, with which this essay ends.

88. Consider the following exchange between two friends:

"Athenian: Enough, then of this matter. But what may we take to have been the beginning of a state? I wonder whether the best and easiest way to treat the problem may be this?

Clinias: What?

Athenian: To start from the same point with which we regularly have to begin when we would study the double progressive development of a city in virtue and vice.

Clinias: And that point is?

Athenian: Why, the interminable length of time, I conceive, and the changes which it brings with it.

Clinias: Pray explain yourself.

Athenian: Well, cities have existed and men have lived in civil societies for a long time. Do you think you could possibly tell how long?

Clinias: Not readily, to say the least of it.

Athenian: But you admit at least that it must have been so for an immense and incredible time?

Clinias: Oh yes, there is no doubt about that.

Athenian: And you will surely grant that thousands and thousands of cities have come into being during this time, and no less a number have ceased to exist? Moreover, every form of constitution has repeatedly appeared in one or other of them ...

Clinias: Indubitably."

Laws, 676b-c (A.E. Taylor's translation).

89. As we saw, Aristotle put it succinctly: "It is true indeed that those and many other things have been invented many times over in the course of ages, or rather times without

number" (*Politics*, 1329b). In this light, it would seem that what differentiates the Hellenic philosophy from both the pre-Hellenic and the post-Hellenic philosophical speculations was its autonomy and its freedom. The Hellenic philosophers, as we read through their extant texts, give the impression of men who were eponymous and free to search for the truth regarding the nature of man and the nature of the cosmos without the fetters of any authority, whether autocratic or theocratic, whether political or priestly. However, whereas the Egyptian priests had to serve the interests of their state, the European "philosophers" served the interest of the medieval Church and its theology, or those of modern technology and political ideology in more recent times.

The point is that, to put it blandly, philosophy has not as yet recovered the autonomy, which it enjoyed during the Hellenic period. It is for us to try to help philosophy recover what it has lost in the last two millennia, its Hellenic dignity and freedom, so that it can once again serve as a guide to the good life to be lived in harmony with nature, with other human beings, and with Socratic "beauty within."

90. "Whatever the Hellenes would receive from the non-Hellenic peoples, at the end, they would improve on it" (*Epinomis*, 987d, translation mine).

91. Guthrie, *ibid.*, vol. 1, p. 31. To see more clearly the absurdity of Guthrie's claim let us compare it with Zeller's more balanced judgment. Although Zeller, like Guthrie, denies any borrowing, on the part of the Ancient Hellenes, from Egypt or India, he accepts the fact that the Egyptians and the Hindus had developed philosophical doctrines, which were very similar to those of the admired Hellenic philosophers: "It must have been very astonishing to the followers of Alexander to find among the Brahmans not only their Dionysus and Heracles, but also their Hellenic philosophy; to hear of water being the origin of the world, as with Thales; of Deity permeating all things, as with Heracleitus; of a transmigration of souls, as with Pythagoras and Plato; of five elements, as with Aristotle; of the prohibition of flesh diet, as with Empedocles and the Orphics; and no doubt Herodotus and his successors must have been often inclined to derive Greek doctrines and usages from Egypt. But for us, all this is not sufficient proof that Heracleitus, Plato, Thales and Aristotle borrowed their theorems from the Hindus or Egyptians." *A History of Greek Philosophy*, tr. S.E. Alleyne (London, 1881), pp. 42-43. See also *Strabo* (*xv.* 1, 58), for the valuable reports of Megasthenes, Aristoboulus, Onesicritus and Nearchus in their eastward adventures.

92. *Op. cit.*, pp. 32-33.

93. Compare this to Proclus' sensible view that: "The sciences did not arise for the first time among the men of whom we know, but at countless other cycles in the past they have appeared and vanished and will do so in the future." *A Commentary on the First Book of Euclid's Elements*, G.R. Morrow, ed. (Princeton, NJ, 1970), p. 51; and the *Appendix*. Herodotus also, II. 2, would certainly disagree with Guthrie's assessment because, as an eyewitness, he knew that the Egyptians had more accurate astronomical calculations than the Hellenes, even in the fifth century BC, the golden age of Hellas. At any rate, lofty as it may be, the Aristotelian expression "knowledge for its own sake," was applied by the philosopher only to what he called First Philosophy. So one should not use it as an essential characteristic of all sciences and all branches of philosophy, especially Hellenic philosophy. For, to use the apt simile of Martin West: "Early Greek Philosophy was not a single vessel which a succession of pilots briefly commanded and tried to steer towards an agreed destination, one taking one way, the next altering course in the light of his own perceptions. It was more like a flotilla of small craft whose navigators did not all start from the same

point or at the same time, nor all aim at for the same goal." *The Oxford History of the Classical World*, J. Boardman et al., eds (Oxford, 1987), p. 113.

94. Guthrie, *ibid.*, p. 35. Guthrie ignores the fact that Aristotle had devoted the entire First Book of his earlier work *On Philosophy* to reviewing the philosophical principles of the non-Hellenic nations in the same critical manner, in which he discussed the Platonic and the Pythagorean doctrines in the Second Book.

95. This is perhaps an idealized picture of Egyptian pedagogy. For a more realistic description of the situation, see R.A. Caminos, *Late Egyptian Miscellanies, Brown Egyptological Studies*, vol. 1 (London, 1954).

96. Plato's view is clear and needs no further commentary. We can trust that Plato was better informed than Guthrie because, according to Strabo (VIII. 17. 1. 29): "At Heliopolis the houses of the priests and schools of Plato and Eudoxus were pointed out to us; for Eudoxus went up that place with Plato, and they both passed three years with the priests, as is stated by some writers; for since these priests excelled in their knowledge of the heavenly bodies, albeit secretive and slow to impart it, Plato and Eudoxus prevailed upon them in time and by courting their favor to let them learn some of the principles of their doctrines." A little earlier (VIII. 17. 1. 3), Strabo had stated that the Egyptians were praised, among other thing, for having divided the people into three classes, the producers, the soldiers, and the priests, and in less than two lines he has refuted Guthrie and all those who have found neither science nor philosophy in Egypt: "The priests were used to study both philosophy and astronomy, and to meet and converse with the kings" (translation mine).

Even Professor Jaeger, in spite of what he said about culture and science in *Paideia*, did not hesitate to make the following statement about Eudoxus in his *Aristotle*: "After their intercourse with Eudoxus, Plato and his followers took a very great interest in the attempt of the Cyzicenian School to explain the irregular movements of the planets by simple mathematical suppositions. This was not the only way in which Eudoxus stimulated them. He tremendously enlarged their notions of geography and human culture by bringing exact reports of Asia and Egypt, and by describing from extended personal experience the status of astronomy in those parts. His contribution to ethical questions was also important." *Aristotle: Fundamentals of the History of his Development*, R. Robinson, tr. (Oxford, 1934), p. 17.

97. As we have seen, in their opposition to any suggestion that other nations, beside the Hellenes, might have had something to do with philosophy and science, Jaeger and Guthrie are in the company of E. Zeller and J. Burnet. Since we have already quoted Zeller, we should perhaps balance the account by quoting Burnet too: "The truth is that we are far more likely to underestimate the originality of the Greeks than to exaggerate it, and we do not always remember the very short time they took to lay down the lines of scientific inquiry which science has followed ever since ... The only eastern people that can bear comparison with the Greeks in Science and philosophy are the Indians ... [The] analogy of Egypt and Babylon certainly suggests that this reached India from the Hellenic kingdom of the North West." *Greek Philosophy* (New York, 1968), p. 7. He expresses similar views in *Early Greek Philosophy* (London: Adam and Charles Black, 1948), especially the Introduction, where he discusses the "Alleged Oriental origin of philosophy" and dogmatically asserts that: "Much that has been regarded as Oriental may just be native. As for later influences, we must insist that no writer of the period during which Greek philosophy flourished knows anything of its having come from the East" (p. 15). Compare this very strange claim with the Hellenic sources, which are cited in Section 4, and the *Appendix*.

B. Russell, although usually a good logician, is inconsistent on this point, since he asserts that: "Philosophy begins when someone asks a general question, and so does science. The first people to evince this kind of activity were the Greeks. Philosophy and science, as we know them, are Greek inventions ... Philosophy and science begin with Thales of Miletus in the early sixth century BC." *Wisdom of the West* (New York, 1989), p. 10. Ancient Hellenes, especially Hellenic philosophers, would not be persuaded by Russell's dogmatic assertion that no man, Greek or Barbarian had even asked a general question before "the early sixth century," and least of all Thales of Miletus. For he knew better on this because he had learned in Egypt from the priests.

Even Hegel, whom Russell considers as a great obfuscator, seems more reasonable and better informed than the other European historians of philosophy on this essential point: "They [the Greeks] certainly received the substantial beginnings of their religion, culture, their common bonds of friendship, more or less from Asia, Syria and Egypt ... From Egypt Pythagoras thus without doubt brought the idea of his Order, which was a regular community brought together for purposes of scientific and moral culture, which endured during the whole of life. Egypt at that time was regarded as a highly cultivated country, and it was so when compared with Greece." *Lectures on the History of Philosophy*, E.S. Haldane, tr. (London, 1963), p. 150.

98. Plutarch, *De Is. et Os.* 68. He writes: "Therefore in these matters above all we should take as a guide into the mysteries the understanding which philosophy gives ... On the nineteenth, for instance, of the first month they [Egyptians] keep a festival to Hermes and eat honey and figs, saying the while 'sweet is truth.'"

99. It would appear, then, that the good will and kind feelings were mutual between the Ancient Hellenes and the Egyptians, as is evident from the following Platonic passage, *Timaeus*, 21e-22a: "They [the citizens of Sais] are great lovers of the Athenians and say that they are in some way related to them. To this city came Solon and was received there with great honor."

100. The same holds for the Indian philosophical tradition, especially as it was expressed in the Upanishads. At least this was the consensus among the participants in the IX International Conference on *Neoplatonism and Indian Thought*, held in New Delhi, India, December 29, 1992-January 2, 1993. The Upanishads are both the concluding portions of the Vedas and the basis for the systematic Vedanta philosophy in which, as Max Muller put it: "Human speculation seems to have reached its very acme." S. Radhakrishnan and Ch. Moore, eds, *Indian Philosophy* (Princeton, NJ, 1973), p. 37.

101. This is a task worthy of further serious research. For it is important for us and necessary to have a better understanding of what specifically the Hellenes learned from their Egyptian friends and from other non-Hellenic peoples, and how they transformed it.

102. *Vita Pythagorae*, 19, and *De antro Nympharum*, 75-76. It cannot be coincidental that Porphyry confirms what Herodotus, Isocrates, and Plutarch had written on this issue, not to mention Plato and Aristotle. There must be a kernel of truth in the tradition, which invariably connects Plato with the Pythagoreans and Pythagoras with the "learned Egyptians." See also the *Appendix*.

103. As Aristotle saw it (*On Philosophy*, Fr. 8), *sophia* covers any ingenious invention or conception in the five basic areas of human activity which aims at satisfying man's multiple needs, bodily, aesthetic, political, theoretical, and religious or metaphysical. So it is a great loss when philosophy is restricted to the "analysis" of language and logic, as it has been in recent times.

104. On this prolonged conflict, see "Porphyry's Criticism of Christianity and the Problem of Augustine's Platonism," *Dionysius* 13 (1989): 51-70.

105. In the process the Church itself was "barbarized," in the apt characterization of H. Pirenne, *A History of European: From the Invasions to XVI Century* (New York, 1965), p. 55. He writes: "The apathy of the Church, however, is very simply explained. Something had happened to it, which had happened, though in a greater degree, to the whole society after the invasions: it had become barbarized ... after this the life of the mind became dormant." Thus, Europe entered the Dark Ages from the snares of which perhaps it has not, as yet, liberated itself completely. Even so, and perhaps ironically, the "barbarized" Western Church succeeded in bringing some rays of light of Mediterranean civilization to the North of the Alps and East of the Rhine. This must tell us something of the state of "barbarism" in which it found the Teutonic tribes there, Nietzsche's protestations to the contrary not withstanding: "Christianity, growing from Jewish roots and comprehensible only as a product of this soil, represents the reaction against morality of breeding, of race, of privilege—it is the anti-Aryan religion *par excellence*: Christianity the revaluation of all Aryan values, the victory of Chandala values, the evangel preached to the poor and lowly, the collective rebellion of everything downtrodden, wretched, ill-constituted, underprivileged against the 'race'—undying Chandala revenge as the religion of love," *ibid.*, p. 58.

106. *Process and Reality*, D.R. Griffin and D.W. Sherburne, eds (New York, 1978), p. 39. In this essay I have implicitly claimed that the Pythagorean/Platonic tradition represents the nobler aspects of the Hellenic spirit. I have also implied that it is more relevant to the present and more promising for the future than the Milesian tradition. So I would like to allow Whitehead to provide us with his reasons in support of such claim. Consider: "Newton could have accepted a molecular theory as easily as Plato, but there is this difference between them: Newton would have been surprised at the modern quantum theory and at the dissolution of quanta into vibrations; Plato would have expected it. While we note the many things said by Plato in the *Timaeus* ... we must also give him [Plato] credit for that aspect of his teaching in which he was two thousand years ahead of his time. Plato accounted for the sharp-cut differences between kinds of natural things, by assuming an approximation of the molecules of the fundamental kinds respectively to the mathematical forms of the regular solids ... Again Newton's *Scholium* gives no hint of the ninety-two possibilities for atoms, or of the limited number of ways in which atoms can be combined so as to form molecules. Physicists are now explaining these chemical facts by means of conceptions, which Plato would have welcomed ... There is another point in which the organic philosophy only repeats Plato. In the *Timaeus* the origin of the present cosmic epoch is traced back to an aboriginal disorder, chaotic according to our ideals. This is the evolutionary doctrine of the philosophy of organism. Plato's notion has puzzled critics who are obsessed with the Semitic theory of a wholly transcendent God creating out of nothing an accidental universe. Newton held the Semitic theory. The *Scholium* made no provision for the evolution of matter ... Until the last few years the sole alternatives were: either the material universe, with its present type of order, is eternal; or else it came into being, and will pass out of being, according to the fiat of Jehovah. Thus, on all sides, Plato's allegory of the evolution of a new type of order based on new types of dominant societies became a daydream, puzzling the commentators" (pp. 94-95).

107. In this way the dream of George Gemistos or Pletho, the Renaissance Neoplatonist who tried unsuccessfully to politically (and religiously) revive Hellenism and the Hellenic

version of Platonism, may come true. For Toynbee there is a real possibility for such a revival: "The Plethonian renaissance of pre-Christian and pre-Muslim nature-worship may turn out to be as shocking for twentieth-century Western rationalists as it was for the fifteenth-century Ecumenical Patriarch Yennadhios. Yet nature-worship has never been extirpated in India or in Eastern Asia, and these two regions, together, are the habitat of much more than half the human race. A god's power is demonstrated by his ability to take vengeance on human beings who dispute it. This is how Dionysos made Pentheus aware of who and what he was. In our day Mother Earth has begun to demonstrate to modern Man that he cannot violate her realm, the biosphere, with impunity ... Between gods, as between human sovereign states, force is the *ultima ratio*. In the present conflict between the chthonic gods and the thunderer from Sinai, do ex-Christian rationalists feel confident that Yahweh will prevail? If we are in doubt, it will be rash to dismiss, as 'the rotten nonsense of the Hellenes', a religion that was already immemorially old before Judaism and Christianity and Islam were heard of." *The Greeks and their Heritages* (Oxford, 1981), p. 314.

108. If only the voice of reason could be heard by the fanatics (Muslims and Christians), who have been abusing each other in the name of the one true God! For God and "the other gods" may not be as incompatible as it appears in the eyes of those, who have been brought up in the climate of the Western monomania of monotheism, whether Christian or Islamic, which perhaps prepared the way for Marxist atheism. For, "This sort of monotheistic complacency is becoming more and more difficult to maintain as we become more and more vividly aware of other religious traditions than the Judeo-Christian-Islamic, notably that of India ... [I shall consider] one or two points about the most powerful polytheism within our own tradition, the Hellenic, which has influenced that tradition in many important ways. The Greeks in the end found it possible to combine this with monotheism, to believe in God without ceasing to believe in the gods ... [W]e shall do well to keep their theology and their gods in our thoughts and in our prayers, in the way which seems appropriate to each of us. It is not by one path only that so great mystery can be approached." A.H. Armstrong, "Some Advantages of Polytheism," *Dionysius* 5 (1981): 181-188.

In this connection, I would also like to note, with sadness, the tragic irony, which the situation in India presents to the world, after the Ayodya incident in December 6, 1992. This great land of many gods and goddesses, of civility and tolerance, showed disturbing signs of adopting the kind of religious fanaticism and violent militancy which, till now, was the trademark of the crusades and the holy wars of the two monotheistic religions, Christianity and Islam, whose aggression during the centuries of occupation of India has caused its people great suffering. But if the Indians, in response, adopt the same religious fanaticism as their opponents, even in self-defense, they will lose a precious and attractive aspect of their honorable tradition of religious tolerance and cultural diversity. Hence the tragic dilemma they face, and our sincere sympathy for them. May the examples of Socrates, Ghandi, and other sages, who would prefer to "suffer rather than do wrong," enlighten the Indians to find a way out of the present predicament!

109. *On the Pythagorean Life*, Gillian Clark, tr. (Liverpool, 1989), pp. 6-8.

110. *Greek Mathematical Works: Thales to Euclid*, I. Thomas, tr. (Cambridge, 1980), pp. 144-175.

111. *Diodorus of Sicily*, vol. 1, Books I and II, C.H. Oldfather, tr. (Cambridge, 1933).

112. In these lines, Diodorus gives the appropriate response to Jaeger, to Guthrie, and those who have questioned the close cultural relation of Ancient Hellenes and the Egyptians. The great admiration, which the former felt for the achievements of the latter in government,

law, arts and sciences, and for their search for first principles and practical wisdom, is clearly stated by Diodorus and the other Hellenic authors cited already. No further comments are needed.

Chapter 2

Plato and European Philosophy

Introduction

One of the valuable products of the Hellenic mind, which has been offered freely to the world at large, is Hellenic philosophy, especially Platonic philosophy. With its roots in the Pythagorean tradition, its Socratic flavor, and its powerful influence, Platonic philosophy occupies a central place in the history of Hellenic philosophy and, by extension, the history of "European philosophy," which has been characterized as "footnotes to Plato."[1]

My purpose in this study will be to take a synoptic look at the adventures of Plato and Platonism in Europe,[2] in light of the above quoted aphorism, in order to determine its truth-value. I will attempt to specify the limited sense, in which it is correct so that it may be accepted as a true statement, that is, philosophically or historically true, and with or without significant qualifications.

In outline my thesis will be developed in the following sequence: First, I will argue that it was the Christian version of Platonism, as opposed to the Hellenic version, which influenced "European philosophy" to the extend that we can speak of "philosophy" in Christian Europe without a serious equivocation.[3] I shall maintain that there were fundamental differences between these two versions of Platonism, the Hellenic and the Christian. The differences should not be overlooked by anyone who wishes to understand the European mind and ethos; the kind of "philosophy" which was produced during the Middle Ages and beyond; and the "bad habits" acquired during philosophy's servitude to dogmatic theology and theocracy. These forces dominated Europe so thoroughly and for so long that it lost contact with its pre-Christian cultural roots in terms of freedom and dignity. From this major handicap European culture, in spite of significant progress, has not recovered completely as yet.[4]

I will argue further that the acquired "bad habits" of European "philosophy," especially its docile servitude to alien authorities, appear to have been transferred from medieval theology to modern technology, since the seventeenth century, and to Marxist political ideology since the nineteenth century. These "Masters" have been served well by faithful European "philosophers." But, by reason of this triple servitude and lack of freedom, "philosophy" in Europe, I will argue, has become something very different from what it was in Hellenic times. This "philosophy" would appear to Hellenic eyes and minds as a simple pseudonym or "homonym," having only the name in common with the Hellenic philosophy. In this respect the novelty, which characterizes the thinking of A.N. Whitehead, would seem to fall, despite his hope, outside the "European tradition." But this is perhaps an advantage over the traditional "European "philosophy" and a hopeful sign of better things to come.[5]

I will conclude the discussion of this chapter with the bleak observation that the recent demise of Soviet-style socialism in Eastern Europe may have become a milestone, but is just the beginning of troubles ahead. For there is a growing suspicion that science and technology will not solve all our problems soon enough, as many had hoped in the past. This fact, in conjunction with the recent revival of fundamentalism and religious fanaticism, to which foolish claims of monopoly of God inevitably lead, are perhaps factors serving as significant signs of culturally troubled times ahead.

At the same time these factors seem to have prepared the way for the revival of the free, tolerant, diverse, and playful spirit of philosophy as the Hellenic philosophers understood and practiced it. So it is reasonable to expect that a possible restoration of philosophy to its Hellenic freedom and dignity will help us, as we enter the post-modern era, to learn the civil lesson of how to live together with respect for cultural differences, and to work together for common global goals.[6]

Plato and Platonism

For the perceptive student of Hellenic philosophy, Plato, his teacher Socrates, and his pupil Aristotle constitute a triad of genuine philosophic wisdom, which is unique in the annals of Mediterranean culture. Ancient Hellenic philosophy began with the bold speculations of philosophers about the nature of nature (*physis*), the origin of *kosmos*, the role of *logos* or *nous* (reason, intelligence, mind) in structuring the cosmic order, and the meaning of being (*einai*) in general. Conventionally, it all started in sunny Ionia, in Asia Minor, in the beginning of the sixth century and reached a climax two centuries later in Athens, where Plato's thought came to a felicitous fruition.[7]

Like a skillful craftsman, Plato knew how to use the Socratic method of dialectic in his writings, in order to blend the various threads of the Ionian, the Pythagorean, and the Parmenidean philosophical traditions harmoniously. Thus, he created wonderful Platonic *Dialogues*, which were then, and became more so as time went on, a rich mine of spiritual gems. These included suggestive speculations about the Gods and the mortals; about the cosmos and the ideal city-state (*polis*); and, above all, about the human soul (*psyche*) and its proper Socratic *paideia* and erotic care. All these virtues made the appeal of the Platonic philosophy permanently felt in the historical world, whether Greco-Roman, Judeo-Christian, Judeo-Islamic, or ecumenical as it is now.[8]

In addition to this achievement, Plato initiated an innovative educational program, a philosophically oriented *paideia*, which was based on literacy and the written word. The innovation successfully challenged the traditional pattern of poetically sanctioned and orally transmitted Hellenic culture. That oral culture had trained many generations of Hellenes to imitate the exemplars of heroic virtue as immortalized by Homer in the great epics of *Iliad* and *Odyssey*.[9] According to the new ideal of excellence, the body and its athletic training were to be given their due share of attention, always in preparation for the citizens to perform their main task, that is, to defend their freedom.

Such precious political freedom would allow them to act and to philosophize as free men. But the emphasis was now Platonically shifted from body to soul; from external goods to internal virtues, both ethical and intellectual; from mere economic interests to common political pursuits, and from petty city-state antagonisms and demagogic party strife, to broad pan-Hellenic and ecumenical aspirations.[10] In the "School of Hellas," as the city of Athens came to be known after Plato, like a beacon of bright light, the Platonic Academy attracted many searching minds and sensitive souls. They came from everywhere looking for epistemic knowledge and for the art of living well, according to the lived wisdom of Socrates and his philosophic friends.[11]

From every part of the Hellenic or Hellenized Mediterranean world students came to the Platonic Academy to study with Plato and his successors the mathematical and natural sciences. They also came to discuss with the philosophers the possibility of an ideal political constitution, which would liberate the restless Hellenes from the tragedy of constant civil strife and fratricidal wars. Later, when the Hellenes lost their political independence to the Romans, it was the revived Platonism in Alexandria, which taught them the lesson of the true consolation of philosophy, that the freedom of the human spirit, unlike the freedom of the human body, cannot be bounded.[12]

The successfully revived Platonism (known as Neoplatonism) was brought from Alexandria to Rome by Plotinus and his bright pupils who, like the Eleatics and the Pythagoreans a thousand years earlier, dreamed of establishing a city, a *Platonopolis*, in Campania, in the heart of *Magna Graecia*.[13] From imperial Rome Platonism spread to every corner of the Mediterranean world contributing to its hellenization and civilization.[14]

Two Versions of Platonism

It was at the critical time of the third and fourth centuries AD, when the Roman Empire was collapsing under external barbarian attacks and internal political and religious strife, that the revived Platonism, especially in the Hellenized Eastern parts of the Empire, split into two opposite camps. They opposed each other bitterly and fought to the end a sort of intellectual "civil war."

The first group felt more hellenized. It was aristocratic, culturally conservative, and in favor of the time-sanctioned religious tradition of polytheism, cultural diversity, and tolerance towards new ideas, trends, cults, gods, and goddesses. They asserted that salvation was a personal achievement demanding hard work to purify the soul and cultivate the mind to contemplate the order of cosmos and to ascend steadily towards the supreme and ineffable Platonic Good.[15]

The second group was less Hellenized and included apostates from polytheistic Hellenism and messianic Judaism. They had accepted the new Christian faith and behaved rather strangely. They were more egalitarian and revolutionary, demanding radical change in every aspect of civil tradition, especially the honored tradition of religious tolerance and the worship of many gods. For instance, the Christians claimed that they had found the one and only "true way" to the one and only true God, who was worshiped, paradoxically, in the name of a trinity: Father, Son, and Holy Spirit.[16]

This triadic God, as the Christians believed, had created the world miraculously out of nothing (*ex nihilo*) and intended to destroy it but, like an irrational Despot, had changed His mind at the last minute. He had decided to give sinful men a last chance to save themselves by accepting a man, Jesus son of Virgin Mary, as God's only begotten Son! The Son of God, miraculously again, had become a man in order to mediate between the fallen man on earth and a furious God/Father in heaven, who strangely still cared for this pitiful creature, despite its multiple sins and follies.[17]

The semi-Hellenized Christian party also believed that the pre-Christian world had been prepared by God (*preparatio evangelica*) to receive the sacrificial Lamb of God and the Gospel of salvation, by two great gifts: the Hebraic Law and the Hellenic philosophy.[18] For educated Christians, men like Clement, Origen, and Augustine, Hellenic philosophy, especially Platonic philosophy, came very close to the "revealed truth" of the Christian faith, in fact as close as it was humanly possible. Even so, for them Hellenic philosophic wisdom was definitely deficient in comparison with the "revealed" divine Wisdom, as embodied in the Mosaic Law (divine *Nomos*) of the Old Testament, and the Incarnated Son of God (divine *Logos*) of the New Testament.[19]

This being the case, it is not surprising that the second group, which was more fanatical and numerous in the Eastern Mediterranean part of the Roman Empire, emerged victorious from the ensuing long struggle for the hearts and minds of the Greco-Romans. In the hands of such inspired men as Origen, Clement of Alexandria, and the Cappadocean Fathers (St. Basil and the two Gregories) in the Hellenistic East; and Lactantius, Ambrose, and Augustine in the Latin West, the Christian message was dressed up in linguistic fineries. It was armed with the complete spiritual panoply of the Christian version of Platonism, and it was turned against pagan Rome, its political hegemony and, especially, its polytheism. Under the attacks of such a formidable foe, weakened and tolerant Rome could not last for long. Ironically, the Imperial City was finally "conquered spiritually" by the

Christianized remnants of four great old cities, Alexandria, Antioch, Corinth, and Carthage. They were ready to take their revenge, having been conquered by Rome and humiliated militarily centuries earlier.[20]

Thus the Hellenistic East, in spiritual cooperation with the Hellenized part of Northern Africa, seem to have taken revenge on Rome and the semi-barbarous West, which had dared to subjugate them, the more learned and cultured, by the brute force of Roman and Latin legions.[21] An African Bishop, rhetorician and apostate from Hellenic Platonism, Augustine of Hippo, wrote the epitaph of the fallen Old Rome, and envisioned the rising of the glorious Christian Church, as the new *City of God*.[22]

In the ruins of the Roman Empire, far away from idolatrous Rome, in the dark blue waters of the Bosporus a New Rome was to rise. It was destined to become the seat of the Byzantine or Eastern Christian Roman Empire, which embraced the Hellenized and Christianized Mediterranean world. It was comprised of Greco-Romans, Jews, Armenians, Syrians, Africans and many more. Named Constantinople after its founder, Constantine the Great, the New Rome became and remained for more than a thousand years (330-1453) the powerful center of Byzantine civilization, which was a rather strange, but potent blend of Hellenic, Roman and Christian cultural elements.[23]

During the long life of the Byzantine Empire, the power of the established Church, based on the authority of the Scriptures and protected by the Imperial Power in the East and by the almost equally monarchic Papal Power in the West, was never seriously challenged by Hellenic philosophy. This, in the form of an anemic Christian Platonism, had become by then only a humble "handmaid" of dogmatic theology and oppressive theocracy.[24] Consequently, it is not surprising that in the hearts and minds of many Europeans even today, Christian Faith and Platonic Philosophy are so closely connected that it would be impossible to separate them, without diminishing the cultural value of them both.

Thus, the truth of Whitehead's statement, regarding the alleged close relation of Platonism and "European Philosophy," seems obvious to Northern Europeans, in view of certain basic historical facts. These include the fact that European culture, especially in the North, is essentially a Christian and Protestant culture. There is not much, if anything, in the pre-Christian semi-barbarous past of Northern Europe, which the Europeans can honestly admire or wish to revive.[25] Besides, European Christian theologians and so-called "philosophers," Catholic and Protestant, from the time of Augustine to Hegel and beyond, felt an intellectual affinity with Platonic philosophy, especially in its Neoplatonic elaboration. Systematically, therefore, they have tried to adopt and adapt it to the requirements of revelations of respective religious dogmas.[26]

Yet, as a matter of historical fact, the free and inquisitive spirit of Hellenism, as expressed in philosophy and democracy particularly, and the scriptural spirit of early Christianity, as it developed from its Judaic roots, were culturally incompatible. So they opposed each other bitterly for several centuries before they were "harmonized" and learned to peacefully co-exist in what was seen as "The Glory of Byzantium."[27] For the first five centuries, however, Hellenic Platonism vigorously opposed the dogmatic, fanatic, and intolerant Church and became the champion of Hellenism.

In the minds of Hellenic philosophers and Platonists, Hellenism was identified with certain fundamental freedoms. Such freedoms would include the following: the freedom to worship one or many gods; the freedom to speculate about the origin of the ordered cosmos and the cause of its order; the freedom to investigate the nature of man and the nature of things by rational means; the freedom to cultivate a life of virtue and excellence, both ethical and intellectual excellences; and, perhaps more significantly, the freedom to tolerate a variety of theories, ideas and innovations without discriminating against them on the basis of some "sacred revelations."[28]

Even in the fifteenth century, with the revival of Platonism under the inspired teaching of Pletho, as we will see below, the conflict between the two versions of Platonism, the Hellenic and the Christian, resurfaced. In addition to this, the broader conflict between tolerant, polytheistic and humanistic Hellenism and intolerant, monotheistic and theocratic Christianity became apparent in the declining Byzantine Empire and in renascent Italy, especially after the founding of the Florentine Platonic Academy and the spread of Hellenic Platonism in Christian Europe.[29]

From this prolonged conflict between the two versions of Platonism, the Christian and the Hellenic, I will indicatively discuss only some aspects of a significant historical episode, the case of Augustine vs Porphyry, that is, the Christian Theologian vs the Hellenic Philosopher. Both of them claimed to be Platonists and used Platonic philosophy to defend their respective cause, Christianity and Hellenism.

It would be instructive to see what really divided the two Platonists, who distinguished themselves as thinkers and writers. Apparently, their differences have shaped the European consciousness of Judeo-Christian heritage and, at the same time, have fostered a tension within it, which remains unresolved and acutely felt even today by some sensitive souls and questioning European or Neo-Hellenic minds.

From this consideration we will be in a better position to view Whitehead's generous evaluation of Plato's influence on "European philosophy." For the specific case of Augustine vs Porphyry is a characteristic case of the Christian theologian's acquired "bad habit" of using and even abusing conveniently the Hellenic philosophy, especially Platonic philosophy. The goal of such abuse is to provide philosophical coverage for the Church dogma, and intellectual respectability and political support for ecclesiastic, theocratic hierarchies. Since this tactic became in time the pattern of "philosophizing" in Christian Europe for more than a millennium, it deserves, in my view, more serious consideration.[30]

Augustine vs Porphyry the Platonist

In the *De civitate Dei* (hereafter abbreviated as *DcD*),[31] Augustine distinguished three types of theology: the mythical or fabulous, the physical or natural, and the political or civil, to use both the Latin and the Greek terminology of which he was very fond.[32] Of these three types Augustine considered natural theology as the most important because it deals with the opinions of the Greek philosophers about the cosmos, the soul, and God and their respective relationships. The Greek philosophers are divided by him into two groups, the true lovers of wisdom and lovers of God, duly acknowledged as the source of all wisdom; and those who use the glorious name of philosophy for theories and activities which have no relation to truth or God's goodness. The Platonists are identified with the former group and the materialists with the latter. By Platonists, Augustine does not mean the followers of Plato in general, but rather Plotinus and Porphyry in particular, who lived and philosophized in Rome earlier on.[33]

Augustine believed that, of all Hellenic philosophical schools, Platonism came as close to the revealed truth of the Christian faith as it did, because its founder Plato had connections with the sources of "ancient wisdom" in the Near East. For he states: "When Plato went to Egypt he had heard the prophet Jeremiah;"[34] and "whilst traveling in the same country, [he] had read the prophetic scriptures;" and, more likely, "as he was most earnest in the pursuit of knowledge, he also studied those writings through an interpreter, as he did those of the Egyptians."[35]

Even so, in Augustine's view, Platonism stood in need of correction on some important points such as the structure of the Holy Trinity, the creation and the final destruction of the cosmos in time and, more importantly, the nature and destiny of the human soul. Such correction would be done, of course, in the light of the higher authority and divine wisdom of the Holy Scriptures, which early Christianity had adopted faithfully as the revealed will of the one and only true God of the Trinity.

In this section I will briefly consider only a few of the errors of the non-Christian Platonists. Special emphasis will be placed on those "errors" regarding the destiny of the soul and its relation to the body after death as articulated by Augustine in *DcD*, and his attempt to correct them with the help of Scriptural authority. Our discussion will reveal that Augustine's goal was not to correctly understand the Hellenic Platonists and their philosophical differences, for which he could not care less as a practical Bishop and servant of the Catholic Church. Rather, he was prepared to intensify the philosophers' differences in order to prepare the way for the final theological solution of all the problems relating to the soul and its salvation.

For the faithful Christian, there was only one way to salvation, Christ crucified and resurrected, as a pre-figuration of what was to follow for his faithful followers. He appears to suggest (rather shamelessly for a man who considered himself a Platonist at one time),[36] that philosophical speculation, inquiry, and argument about this important matter must yield to the authoritative wisdom of the Church and its established dogma. This dogma was to be interpreted authoritatively by the Bishop of Rome or Pope, destined to become "infallible."

In this respect, Augustine can be seen as the first in a long series of "Western philosophers" and "Christian theologians," Catholic and Protestant,[37] who sought to subordinate inquisitive Hellenic philosophy successfully to "revealed" and dogmatic Christian theology, which it served faithfully for millennia as the *ancilla theologiae*.[38]

However, Augustine, unlike many other Christian theologians, had to confront the non-Christian and Hellenic Platonists, like Porphyry, who had elegantly defended philosophy's autonomy and dignity, as well as its sufficiency to guide the rational soul to its ultimate destination, the union with its supreme source, the Platonic Good.[39]

With these preliminary observations, we may now consider some of the specifics of this interesting case of Augustine against Porphyry and other Platonist philosophers of that time, as it is presented in his *magnum opus*, the *De civitate Dei* (*DcD*).

The careful reader of *DcD* will notice that the treatise is thematically divided into two parts. In Books XI-XXII, Augustine traces the development and destiny of both the earthly and the divine cities, from the beginning to the end of time. At that time, the sinful inhabitants of the one will be punished eternally in hell, while the sanctified bodies of the citizens of the other will enjoy the blissfulness of eternal life in heaven. Books I-X, on the other hand, are devoted to the task of answering the impious pagans who accused the Christians of being responsible for the calamities, which befell Rome as a result of the barbarian invasions. It also attacks the polytheistic Hellenic religion in its three aspects, as specified above, especially its natural theology, as presented and defended by the non-Christian Platonic philosophers of his time. Consider the following programmatic statement:

> And this, if I am not mistaken, will be the most difficult part of my task, and will be worthy of the loftiest argument; for we must then enter the lists with the philosophers, not the mere common herd of philosophers, but the most renowned, who in many points agree with ourselves, as regarding the immortality of the soul, and that the true God created the world, and by His providence rules all He has created. But as they differ from us on other points, we must not shrink from the task of exposing their errors. (*DcD*, I, 36)

It is indicative of the importance of this metaphysical issue that both parts of his work culminate with discussions of the various philosophical views about the soul and its relation to God, as well as their differences from the revealed Christian truth. The philosophers whom Augustine has in mind here are identified by him as "The Platonic Philosophers, who derive their name from their master Plato" (*ibid.*, VII, 1).

These are the philosophers, whose works had liberated Augustine from the snares of Manicheism in his youth, and whose divergent views on the soul and its destiny after death he was determined to artfully explore in order to achieve his stated theological and apologetic goals.[40] He had great respect for them as well as for Plato who, he emphasizes, "among the disciples of Socrates shone with a glory which far excelled that of the others, and who not unjustly eclipsed them all" (*ibid.*, VIII, 4).

But even Plato must yield to the superior "wisdom" of the prophetic utterances of the Holy Scriptures, whose authority the convert Christian does not dare to question.[41] Plato's merit, as Augustine sees it, derives from the fact that he perfected philosophy by combining into one its two, and hitherto separate, aspects, the Pythagorean contemplative and the Socratic practical.

As for "those who are praised as having most closely followed Plato," they are highly esteemed because of their exalted view of God. This is such that: "In Him are to be found the cause of existence, the ultimate reason for the understanding, and the end in reference to which the whole life is to be regulated. Of which three things, the first is understood to pertain to the natural, the second to the rational, and the third to the moral part of philosophy" (*ibid.*, 4).

According to Augustine, the Platonists have excelled in each of the three branches of philosophy, natural or physical, rational or logical, and moral or ethical. Especially praiseworthy is the fact that: "Plato determined the final good to be to live according to virtue, and affirmed that he only can attain to virtue who knows and imitates God—which knowledge and imitation are the only cause of blessedness" (*ibid.*, 5).[42]

In spite of all this praise, however, Augustine believed that the Platonists, beginning with Plato himself, erred in many ways. Included in the Platonic doctrines, which he found most defective and in need of correction, are the following:

1. that the Cosmos, although it had a beginning, will not have an end;
2. that sacred rites and sacrifices ought to be performed in honor of many gods, though they [the Hellenic Platonists] insist that the philosopher is a lover of God only;
3. that there are three kinds of rational souls belonging to terrestrial men, to aerial spirits (or demons), and to celestial gods respectively;
4. that gods have direct intercourse with demons, though the demons mediate between gods and men;
5. that they have adopted many methods and principles of purification, such as the theurgic arts, which are "impure;"
6. that the rational human soul is co-eternal with God and of the same essence as He;
7. that the human rational soul undergoes a number of rebirths and can achieve no permanent release from the body;
8. that they do not acknowledge Christ as "the Mediator" and as the "one and universal way" to salvation; and

9. that the Platonists, unlike the Scriptures, disagree with each other on several important points.[43]

In view of this list of philosophical errors committed by Platonists, the perceptive reader of the *DcD* cannot fail to notice that Augustine praises Porphyry highly for his significant improvement upon both Plato and Plotinus with regard to the destiny of the soul. This improvement was welcome to Augustine not only because it seemed to bring Platonism closer to the Christian doctrine, but also because it was an indication that even the admired Plato, was not immune to error and in need of emendation and correction. For him, "If it is considered unseemly to emend anything which Plato touched, why did Porphyry himself make the emendations, and these not a few?"[44]

Presumably what Plato held, in some of his philosophical myths[45] and Porphyry tactfully rejected, was the possibility of human souls entering the bodies of beasts in one of their many rebirths, which they must undergo as penal catharsis for wrongs done in this life. Augustine's interpretation of the assumed Platonic divergence on this is as follows:

> For it is certain that Plato wrote that the souls of men return after death to the bodies of beasts. Plotinus also, Porphyry's teacher, held this opinion; yet Porphyry justly rejected it. He was of opinion that human souls return into human bodies, but not into the bodies they had left, but other new bodies. He shrank of the other opinion, lest a woman who had returned into a mule might possibly carry her own son on her back. He did not shrink, however, from a theory, which admitted the possibility of a mother coming back into a girl and marrying her own son. (*DcD*, X, 30)

It is regrettable that Augustine does not back up his assertions with quotations from or references to specific works of these philosophers, especially Porphyry, whom he likes to set in contrast to both his teacher Plotinus and the respected founder of Platonism, Plato himself.[46] Considering Porphyry's position in *De Abstinentia*[47] regarding "rationality" in animals and our responsibility to treat them with sensitivity, it is hard to believe that he would have expressed so strong reservations about the souls of some brutish people being born again as brutes. Unless, of course, the Platonic philosopher was arguing on behalf of the defenseless animals involved here. But that is not the reason, which Augustine hints at, when he mentions the image of the mother reborn as a mule and used as such by her own son for a ride.

Morally it is also difficult to see whether Porphyry really improved the situation by giving the son the opportunity of marrying his own mother, who may be reborn as an attractive girl, instead of riding on her when reborn as a mule. Yet, Augustine sees it as an improvement and a correction of Plato, which, he thinks, opens the way for him to proceed with further and more radical corrections of the Platonists. This might have been his motive for setting Porphyry against these men, his teacher Plotinus and Plato.

By claiming that Porphyry had taken issue with the towering figures of Platonism, Plato and Plotinus, Augustine is not really praising the bold student, who dared to correct his teachers. Such praise would have been questionable in the eyes of the Hellenic and the hellenizing Neoplatonists, who did not want to appear original as much as they desired to preserve the purity of Plato's thought by clarifying the meaning of his words. Apparently, Augustine wanted to suggest to his readers that these Platonists disagree among themselves about the soul's destiny after death, so that the illumination of the Christian Scripture and the safety of "faith" were needed to settle the matter once and for all. Consider, for instance the following:

> How much more honorable a creed is that which was taught by the holy and truthful angels, uttered by the prophets who were moved by God's Spirit, preached by Him who was foretold as the coming Savior by His forerunning heralds, and by the apostles whom He sent forth, and who filled the whole world with the gospel—how much more honorable, I say, is the belief that souls return once for all to their own bodies, than they return again and again to divers bodies? Nevertheless Porphyry, I have said, did considerably improve upon this opinion, in so far, at least, as he maintained that human souls could transmigrate only into human bodies, and made no scruple about demolishing the bestial prisons into which Plato had wished to cast them ... Here is a Platonist emending Plato, here is a man who saw what Plato did not see, and who did not shrink from correcting so illustrious a master, but preferred truth to Plato. (*Ibid.*)

By preferring "truth to Plato," Porphyry would follow Aristotle. But in addition to this improvement, Porphyry made another and greater correction of the Platonic doctrine regarding reincarnation and the recycling of the soul:

> He [Porphyry] says, too, that God put the soul into the world that it might recognize the evils of matter and return to the Father, and be for ever emancipated from the polluting contact of matter ... Yet he corrects the opinion of other Platonists, and that on a point of no small importance, inasmuch as he avows that the soul, which is purged from all evil and received to the Father's presence, shall never again suffer the ills of this life ... Porphyry saw this, and therefore said that the purified soul returns to the Father, that it may never more be entangled in the polluting contact with evil. (*Ibid.*)

Of this move Augustine approved, of course, and rejoiced to find in Porphyry a Platonist adopting a view different from Plato's view and better, since he saw "what Plato failed to see." This would certainly be high praise for Porphyry if it were documented by Augustine and proven to be the case. At any rate, the shrewd African bishop, as we said, was not so much interested in sorting out the differences of the philosophers, as he was in showing the way of salvation to seeking souls and in fortifying the faithful in the truth of their faith. So, he was ready to use Porphyry's alleged departure from the Platonic tradition on this point, in order to present the doctrine of the Church as being even better than Porphyry's emended Platonism. For it was seen as a combination of what is best in Platonism, as understood and interpreted by Augustine.

Indeed, if Porphyry is correct that the cleansed soul will remain united with the Supreme Source or Father forever, this is good news. For it means that something, which had a beginning in time, that is the state of the perfected soul's bliss, will have no end in time. And if so, the Christian view that the human soul, though created in time, is destined to live forever should not have offended the non-Christian Platonists who, in Augustine's view, insisted that whatever has a beginning in time must, by logical necessity, have an end in time too.[48] Evidently, Augustine is searching for a way of combining what he thinks is best in Porphyry and Plato so that he may reach the correct Catholic dogma of resurrection not of the soul only, but of the body too, which would thus be spiritualized and saved for eternity:

> Statements were made by Plato and Porphyry singly, which if they could have seen their way to hold in common, they might possibly have become Christians. Plato said that souls could not exist eternally without bodies; for it was on this account, he said, that the souls even of wise men must some time or other return to their bodies. Porphyry, again, said that the purified soul, when it has returned to the Father, shall never return to the ills of this world ... And therefore, if Plato and Porphyry, or rather, if their disciples now living, agree with us that holy souls shall return to the body, as Plato says, and that, nevertheless, they shall not return to misery, as Porphyry maintains—if they accept the consequence of these two propositions which is taught by the Christian faith, that they shall receive bodies in which they may live eternally without suffering any misery—let them also adopt from Varro the opinion that they shall return to the same bodies as they were formerly in, and thus the whole question of the eternal resurrection of the body shall be resolved out of their own mouths. (*DcD*, XXII, 27-28)[49]

Augustine should have known that neither Porphyry nor any other genuine Platonist philosopher (to leave aside the astrologers quoted by Varro) would agree with him that, from the acceptance of the premise of the blissful state of the soul, would follow the consequence of "the eternal resurrection of the body." On the contrary, these philosophers were convinced that, as Socrates had stated in the *Phaedo* and Porphyry repeated: "In order for the soul to be happy, it must avoid any close contact with the body."[50] This aphorism is not characteristically Porphyrian, as Augustine claims, but a Platonic commonplace.[51]

However, Augustine was well aware that pagan adversaries, especially Porphyry, had questioned and even mocked the Christian claim about "resurrected bodies," through the example of the drowned fisherman. Echoing Porphyry's question about the fish and the fishermen endlessly consuming each other, and about his assertion that even God cannot do the logically impossible of restoring the original body, Augustine resorted to the omnipotence of God once again. He believed in God's ability to make miracles and trusted the supreme authority of the Bible, arguing as follows:

> That flesh, therefore, shall be restored to the man in whom it first became flesh. For it must be looked upon as borrowed by the other person, and, like the pecuniary loan, must be returned to the lender. His own flesh, however, which he lost by famine, shall be restored to him by Him who can recover even what has evaporated. And though it had been absolutely annihilated, so that no part of its substance remained in any secret spot of nature, the Almighty could restore it by such means as He saw fit. For the sentence, uttered by the Truth, "Not a hair of your head shall perish," forbids us to suppose that, though no hair of a man's head can perish, yet the large portions of his flesh eaten and consumed by the famishing can perish ... But even in his body he will be spiritual when the same flesh shall have had that resurrection of which these words speak, "It is sown an animal body, it shall rise a spiritual body." (*DcD*, XXII, 20-21)

This brings the discussion to the central question about the means by which this miracle would be accomplished, that is "the way" or *via universalis*. This Porphyry had rejected as impossible and foolish on philosophical and historical grounds, while Augustine accepted it as necessary on the authority of the Scriptures:

> This is the religion, which possesses the universal way for delivering the soul; for, except by this way, none can be delivered. This is a kind of royal way, which alone leads to a kingdom which does not totter like all temporal dignities, but stands firm on eternal foundations. And when Porphyry says, towards the end of the first book *De Regressu Animae*, that no system of doctrine which furnishes the universal way for delivering the soul has as yet been received, either from the truest philosophy, or from the ideas of the Indians, or from the reasoning of the Chaldaeans, or from any source whatever, and that no historical reading had made him acquainted with that way, he manifestly acknowledges that there is such a way, but that as yet he was not acquainted with it ... For Porphyry lived in an age when this universal way of the soul's deliverance—in other words the Christian religion—was exposed to the persecutions of the idolaters and demon-worshipers, and earthly rulers. (*DcD*, X, 32)

Once again, by "universal" Porphyry and Augustine meant two different things. For the Hellenic philosopher, it does not make sense to speak of the Christian "way of salvation" as universal, since millions and millions of people have lived and died, or will live and die, without having even heard of the *evangelion* (gospel). But, for Augustine the Bishop and the Church Father, the way is called "universal" because, to paraphrase him, either it is "the universal way of salvation for those who believe" which, of course, excludes the non-believers, who are the great majority; or because it purifies "the entire man," soul and body.[52] All this is accomplished "through Christ," by whose incarnation "purification comes to the faithful." His preference for Scriptural authority, dogmatic assertion and stubborn opposition to Porphyry's subtle distinctions are apparent in these and similar points, which make the gap between reasoned Hellenic philosophy and Christian revealed faith unbridgeable.

Evidently echoing Porphyry's many jibes regarding the doctrine of incarnation, he deplores the Platonist's blindness. He explains Porphyry's failure to recognize the principal importance of Christ's mediation as being caused by his lack of humility:

> But Porphyry, being under the dominion of these envious powers, whose influence he was at once ashamed of and afraid to throw off, refused to recognize that Christ is the Principle by whose incarnation we are purified. Indeed he despised Him because of the flesh itself which He assumed, that He might offer a sacrifice for our purification—a great mystery, unintelligible to Porphyry's pride, which that true and benignant Redeemer brought low by His humility, manifesting Himself to mortals by the mortality which He assumed. (*DcD*, X, 24)

Passages like the above clearly indicate the gap which separates the faithful heart of the believer, which is filled with the light of revelation and feels sorry for those who are still blind, from the critical mind of the philosopher, which rejects any sort of consolation that does not pass the test of reason. Augustine would have been delighted if a learned Platonist, like Porphyry, had accepted the baptism "in the name of the Father and of the Son and of the Holy Spirit." But he was convinced that the philosopher's pride prevented him from seeing the light of faith by joining the Church. He also knew that even in the fifth century many men were following Porphyry in defying the Church and the Christian emperors, who found it necessary to condemn Porphyry's books for a second time in 448. It is in this light that we should read exclamations like the one that follows, in order to grasp the full impact of its urgency:

> Oh, had you but recognized the grace of God in Jesus Christ our Lord, and that very incarnation of His, wherein He assumed a human soul and body, you might have seen it to be the brightest example of grace! But what am I doing? I know it is useless to speak to a dead man ... But perhaps not in vain for those who esteem you highly, and love you on account of their love of wisdom or curiosity about those arts, which you ought not to have learned; and these persons I address in your name. (*DcD*, *X*, 29)

Thus, Augustine would appear to have learned at the end of his life that Hellenic Platonists, like Porphyry, and Platonism itself were radically incompatible with the faith demanding belief in the revealed grace of God, as manifested in His incarnated Son, Jesus, the living *Logos* of God's *sophia*. By setting Porphyry against Plato and by rhetorically exposing their apparent differences, Augustine apparently thought that he would be able to minimize the philosopher's appeal to educated non-Christians and Christians alike. Thus he had hoped that the Christian readers of his book would be fortified in their faith, whereas the pagan readers would change their minds, convert to Catholicism, and be saved. Otherwise they would have to live with some feeling of regret for their inability to see the saving light of the one and only "true faith."

This being the case, it would seem that Augustine's response to Platonism in general, and his criticism of Plato and Porphyry in particular, is neither clear-cut nor one-sided. When he compares Porphyry to other Platonists, like Plotinus, Augustine praises the philosopher highly for his improvement of philosophical doctrines, as they had been developed traditionally up to his time, which had great influence on the lives of the non-Christians. But when he considers Porphyry as the best advocate of Hellenic polytheism and religious tolerance, Augustine is critical of the philosopher, who is portrayed as having betrayed lofty Platonic philosophy to accommodate pagan "demonology."

Finally, when he looks at Porphyry as the determined adversary of Christianity, Augustine sees in him the most impious and blasphemous philosopher whose intellectual pride prevented him from finding true wisdom in the Incarnated *Logos* of God. In addition to this, his philosophical writings misled many souls away from the one and only true path of salvation, Christ's incarnation, crucifixion and resurrection. At the end, not surprisingly, Augustine, the ardent defender of the Catholic Church and the Christian faith, would sacrifice philosophy at the altar of dogmatic theology.

From the scattered remarks in *DcD*, it is evident that Augustine would be happy if Porphyry, like Victorinus, had accepted the Christian faith or, at least, if he had been as discreet as Plotinus about Christianity. But the most admired Platonist, who had allegedly corrected Plato himself, had done neither of these things, and Augustine had to face this unpleasant fact. It is also clear that, when Augustine mentions Porphyry and Plato or refers to their differences, he is doing so not for the sake of theoretical concerns, but for practical purposes. For his target appears to have been not the dead philosophers, but the group of Porphyry's followers whom he wanted to convert to the cause of the Church by all means. As a believer, Augustine thought that he had found *the way* to salvation and he could not see why others were so blind as to have missed it. Thus, he took it upon himself to show them how a combination of selective doctrines from Plato and Porphyry would yield essentially the same truth, which he had found in the Bible, when he learned to read it with pious humility and ardent faith.

However, this was not the way a philosopher, like Porphyry, or his philosophical friends and followers, had elected to look at the matter. The contact with Plotinus and the study of Platonism had helped Porphyry and many other minds to rise above the common superstitions of their time in search for the philosophical way which does not exclude other ways for other souls, but tolerates them by giving each "its due."[53] This openness and philosophical tolerance was perceived by Augustine as compromising the one and only true way of salvation and, therefore, as objectionable and censurable. However, the same philosophic spirit of diversity and religious tolerance has inspired thoughtful people through the centuries with its truth and nobility, even in the West.[54]

Evidently, Augustine and Porphyry were destined to oppose each other and to place their great abilities as writers in the service of the cause of Christian faith and Hellenism respectively. It is perhaps ironic that, in spite of Porphyry's critique of the Church and Augustine's reservations regarding the compatibility of Christian faith and Hellenic philosophy, the Byzantine theologians succeeded in molding the two traditions together in what came to be known as their Greco-Roman and Christian heritage. During the Italian Renaissance, as we will see in the next section, the tradition was passed on to Europe, where it became and remained a distinct philosophic trend, in spite of the traditional tension between its Christian and Hellenic aspects.

It would be difficult indeed to conceive of European culture without the Platonic philosophy in its Christian version. In this regard, "European philosophy," and even Christian theology, would appear to have been nothing but a "series of footnotes to Plato," as Whitehead said. Coming from one of the great representatives of "European philosophy" in our times, this statement is a great tribute to Plato and to the everlasting appeal of Platonism. But, in light of our discussion, it is not true without qualifications. For it was the Christian version of Platonism that influenced Europe, and this version was very unlike the Hellenic version, because it was forced to serve alien masters and strange authorities in its many adventures in Christian Europe.[55]

Platonism in the Italian Renaissance

With the decline of the Byzantine Empire in the East and the fall of Constantinople first to Western Crusaders (1204) and then to the infidel Turks (1453), the Byzantine Greeks began to feel more like Hellenes and less like Romans.[56] After all, their language, their traditions, their much Hellenized Christian education, and even simple comparison with the semi-barbarous Crusaders, whether Franks, Goths, Saxons or other Northerners, made the difference perfectly clear to their eyes.[57] It was during the time of the awaking of the national consciousness of the Byzantine Greeks that the study of Ancient Hellenic philosophy was unexpectedly revived and the search for their ancestral roots began slowly. In this intellectually pregnant atmosphere, the Hellenic version of Platonism was revived and found a worthy spokesman in Pletho.[58]

Pletho had the courage and intellectual honesty to advocate, as a necessary means to the survival and renewal of the decaying Empire, radical reform in every field: the army, politics, religion, education, and philosophy. His message was heard and signs of revival of the Ancient Hellenic traditions started to appear in the horizon in the heart of Hellas, the Peloponnese. Pletho's message and the subsequent movement of revival came too late and had no time to grow sufficient strength to stop the advancement of Turkish barbarism into Europe. But before the final collapse of the Byzantine Empire, Pletho had the chance to travel to Italy briefly. There he introduced some Florentine humanists to the Hellenic version of Platonism, as opposed to its Christian version, which had prevailed in the West since Augustine's time and, like the Aristotelian Scholasticism of the Middle Ages, had degenerated entirely.[59]

In this light, it is no accident that the rebirth of letters in renascent Italy coincided with the flooding of its markets with precious Greek manuscripts, after the capture of Constantinople and other centers of culture of the Hellenized Christian East by the Western Christian Crusaders. Nor should it be seen as an accident that the flourishing of philosophy, art and mathematics in Florence in the fifteenth century, coincided with the spreading of Pletho's teaching of Hellenic Platonism after the founding of the Florentine Platonic Academy.[60] It is the case that, despite Pletho's effort to prevent it, the Platonism of the Academy was Christianized, under Ficino's leadership and with the influence of Bessarion, a student of Pletho. He converted to Catholicism, became a Cardinal and was twice seriously considered a candidate for the throne of St. Peter.[61]

It would seem, therefore, that the literary activities of the late Renaissance Platonists, like those of Augustine in the Patristic Era, were meant to render Platonism safe for Catholic Christianity. However, by then, the spirit of freedom-loving Hellenic Platonism was out of the secure bottle of ecclesiastic dogmatism and it was difficult to put it back again as safely as before. Thus, in spite of the efforts of Inquisitors and the flames that burned the flesh of Jordano Bruno and other like-minded innovators and modern martyrs of philosophy, the spirit of free inquiry, which the Hellenic version of Platonism had generated in renascent Europe, could not be completely stifled.[62]

Besides Erasmus, and the sixteenth-century Humanists, we may mention in this connection, some groups and intellectual circles, which in one way or another made some use of Platonism.[63] First to be mentioned are the Cambridge Platonists in the seventeenth century, who used a refined version of Platonic idealism to combat, among other things, fanatical Puritanism and the crude materialism of Thomas Hobbes. Then followed the Berlin academics, under the leadership of Schleirmacher and his friends in the nineteenth century, using the Platonic texts in order to test the validity of the historical, the critical and the hermeneutic methods, which they had devised in their studies of the Scriptures.[64] The third group was made up by the literary critics of Schlegel's circle, who saw the Platonic texts aesthetically, and used the theoretical tools of Platonism to provide philosophical backing to Romanticism as a legitimate theory of literature.[65]

They were followed by the German Idealists, especially Schelling and Hegel, who attempted to build philosophical systems with heavy borrowing from Neoplatonists, especially Plotinus and Proclus.[66] In the twentieth century, we have Bergson's theory of *elan vital* and Russell's early version of Realism, both of which seem to have also been influenced respectively, by the dynamic and the static aspects of Hellenic Platonism. Last, but not least, Whitehead's process philosophy, or the philosophy of organism, is acknowledged by the author himself as a fair child of Platonism:

> The safest general characterization of the European philosophical tradition is that it consists of a series of footnotes to Plato ... In one sense by stating my belief that the train of thought in these lectures is Platonic, I am doing no more than to express the hope that it falls within the European tradition ... If we had to render Plato's general point of view with the least change ... we should have to set about the construction of a philosophy of organism.[67]

Adventures of Platonic Philosophy

I would like to open a parenthesis at this point to say something about this strange statement which comes from one of the innovative philosophical minds produced by Europe in the twentieth century.[68] For in light of the adventures of Platonism, as were schematically presented here, and in view of the fact that European culture, especially in North Europe, is fundamentally a Christian culture, "European philosophy" can correctly be characterized as a series of footnotes to the Bible rather than to Plato.[69]

Moreover, unlike Platonic/Hellenic philosophy in general, "European philosophy" has been written traditionally by trained theologians. They do occasionally make use of philosophical texts and logical tools in order to elucidate the truth of revelation by their Scriptural hermeneutics;[70] or to provide philosophical backing for doctrines which, by their own nature, demand not the light of reason, but the comfort of faith.[71]

In other words, rather than accepting Whitehead's aphorism uncritically, it would be safer to apply to "European philosophy" what Nietzsche perceived and expressly stated about German philosophy. The latter, in his view, had been in the hands of German theologians, Catholic and Lutheran, for so long and had been corrupted by Biblical hermeneutics to such a degree, that it did not deserve the name of philosophy. This glorious name, as understood by Hellenic philosophers who invented the dangerous art of bold thinking, was intended for that kind of intellectual activity fitting only for the "Free Spirits."[72] For, like an exotic plant of the mountains, philosophy needs much sunshine and fresh air to breathe freely in order to bear its sweet fruit.[73]

Platonic philosophy in particular acknowledges only one ruler, who rules heaven and earth and the lives of the lovers of wisdom.[74] For, according to Platonic Socrates, "All the wise agree, thereby glorifying themselves in earnest, that in reason [*logos*] we have the king of heaven and earth."[75] Accordingly, philosophy would seem to become atrophic, when it is forced to serve other masters and other authorities than reason and truth, which is to be sought and seen by the eye of the human mind (the intuitive intellect or the Hellenic *nous*). It would seem, from the history of Platonism that, what happened in Europe, for the most part of two millennia of Christian culture, was precisely this kind of philosophic atrophy. It is, therefore, prime time for change there.

This resulted mainly from the lack of freedom to philosophize and speculate on the nature of the divine, the order of the cosmos, the good of the state and, above all, the care and destiny of the human soul. About these daring themes the Ancient Hellenic philosophers matched their wits against each other and produced an incredible wealth of wise suggestions and practical solutions to these problems. But in the Christian era, the Catholic Church formulated and fixed specific doctrines or dogmas regarding all these matters. Faithful clergy and laymen, doctors and lawyers, theologians and "philosophers" had to follow the given direction unquestioningly, if they were not prepared to face the stake or an ecclesiastical *anathema*.

Much of the energy of brilliant men like Augustine, Erigena, Anselm, Abelard, Aquinas, Scotus, Ockham, Descartes, Pascal, Locke, Berkeley, Leibniz, Kant, Hegel, and countless others, was spent in an effort to keep their thinking within the boundaries of the Church dogma. Some of them had to pretend that their writing had nothing to do with the things of which the divine revelation had spoken, lest they scandalize the faithful flock and upset the powerful ecclesiastical authorities of their respective regional sects. Now, one may uncritically call the products of these European minds "philosophy," but it is really a clear case of Aristotelian "homonymy."

For to the extent that the thinking was conditioned or restricted by the fixed dogma of the Christian Church on crucial philosophical questions, such as the nature of nature, the nature of man, and the destiny of the human soul, these "philosophies" were essentially different from authentic Hellenic philosophy. Their producers differ much from Anaxagoras and Pythagoras, Plato and Aristotle, Plotinus and Porphyry, Proclus and Pletho who engaged, for more than a thousand years, in philosophic activity as free persons in the spirit of Hellenic *philosophia*.

It is only recently that a few bold European minds dared to shake free from the yoke that despotic Roman Catholicism and anarchic, but economically powerful, Protestant fundamentalism had imposed on European minds and cultures for about two millennia. But even the voices of modern anti-religious thinkers, such as Nietzsche, Kazantzakis, and Sartre, for example, sound like cries of frustrated and desperate theologians, who have lost faith in the God of their fathers, than anything like the serene and measured *logos* of the pre-Christian Hellenic philosophers.

The Hellenes disagreed philosophically, but their *logos* remained always clear and strong, whether they were Platonic or Peripatetic, Stoic or Epicurean, Eclectic or Skeptic. In this respect, Hellenic philosophers were unlike the European thinkers, who seem tortured either by an unbearable "existential angst" or by revolutionary fervor to "change the world." On the contrary, the ancient Hellenic philosophers give the impression that they knew the secret of how to live in harmony with the natural world and in peace within themselves, with their friends or even their adversaries.[76]

So, at the present, there should be concern among thinkers and scientists that even the short period of relative freedom for daring philosophical speculation, scientific inquiry, and free thinking, might be coming to an end with the unification of Christian Europe, opposed by a militant and radicalized Islam. We should pose and think as we witness the process of unification of Europe under way; the collapse of Socialism in Eastern Europe; the revitalization of the Catholic Church in Europe, and so on.

Particularly ominous is the Vatican's renewed aspirations of reviving the role of the Pope as "Caesar" in the medieval manner, by aggressively moving into the desperate Eastern European countries to re-baptize ex-Communists and other nominally Orthodox Christians.[77] Fanatical Islam is also stirring up once again, just like it did in the seventh and the fourteenth centuries, and is ready to apply all means, including terror, to spread God's message. Hence the real Dark Ages may not be in Europe's medieval past, but ahead of it, unless philosophy is revived and nurtured.[78]

With this cautious note, let us return to Whitehead's quoted aphorism and try to understand it correctly by placing it in the context of his philosophical system.[79] We should keep in mind a few facts about the author of *Process and Reality*, in which the statement is found, regarding the characterization of the European philosophical tradition as a "series of footnotes to Plato."

First, we note that Whitehead came to philosophy from science and rather late in his life, after a long and successful academic career as mathematician at Cambridge and other British Colleges. He was co-author, with B. Russell, of the monumental *Principia Mathematica* at the beginning of the twentieth century.[80] Afterwards their paths diverged, so that they developed different philosophical outlooks.

Unlike Russell, who was caught up in the webs of the Vienna Circle with its emphasis on logical analysis,[81] Whitehead tried to create a new metaphysics based on modern scientific discoveries in physics and biology, in order to provide an adequate philosophical account of the nature of reality.[82] As he saw it, the new Cosmology was closer to Plato's *Timaeus* than to Newton's *Scholium*:

> The appeal to Plato in this section has been an appeal to the facts against the modes of expression prevalent in the last few centuries. These recent modes of expression are partly the outcome of a mixture of theology and philosophy, and partly due to the Newtonian physics, no longer accepted as a fundamental statement. But language and thought have been framed according to that mould; and it is necessary to remind ourselves that this is not the way in which the world has been described by some of the greatest intellects. Both for Plato and for Aristotle the process of the actual world has been conceived as a real incoming of forms into real potentiality, issuing into real togetherness which is an actual thing.[83]

In this way, then, Whitehead wants to honor Plato, by placing him at the head of the philosophical tradition which, he thinks, has inspired every major scientific and philosophical development in Europe including his own philosophy of organism. But he intends to do more than this as the following passage clearly indicates:

> Thus in one sense by stating my belief that the train of thought in these lectures is Platonic, I am doing no more than expressing the hope that it falls within the European tradition. But I do mean more: I mean that if we had to render Plato's general point of view with the least changes made necessary by the intervening two thousand years of human experience in social organization, in aesthetic attainments, in science, and in religion, we should have to set about the construction of a philosophy of organism.[84]

From these quotations and similar others it is clear that Whitehead had great admiration for Plato and wished to associate his process philosophy with traditional Platonism.[85] But, since he was not a historian of philosophy or even a historian of ideas, he seems to have failed to notice the two versions of Platonism, the Christian and the Hellenic, which we discussed in section three. Ironically, although he had no taste for irony being puritanically serious about his work, Whitehead had hoped to be part of the "European tradition," which he characterized as "a series of footnotes to Plato." He did not realize perhaps that this tradition represented the Christian version of Platonism, while his cosmology and his free metaphysical speculations are closer to the Hellenic version of Platonism, as we have described these two versions in section two above. In this sense, his version of Platonism, as presented in *Process and Reality*, does not really fall within the European tradition of Christian Platonism.

For, in spite of his respect for what he describes as the humility of the gentle Galilean religion of love, the cosmos and the God we meet in the pages of Whitehead's book do not have the familiar characteristics found in the Biblical stories and portraits of the Christian God.[86] Rather, like the dancing Shiva, like Bergson's *elan vital* or like Kazantzakis' marching-on God-General, Whitehead's "ultimate principle of creativity" lures the "primordial nature of God" out of the realm of pure potentiality in a constant cosmic adventure into novel actuality.

Thus it would seem that creativity gives birth naturally to "the only begotten" actual world of sensibility, which is for ever in-the-making, permanently changing, like Heraclitus' river, and constantly advancing to "novelty." This provides God with a new mask or, as Whitehead calls it, "the consequent nature of God."[87] Consider, for example, the following revealing passages and see whether you recognize anything traditionally Christian about this new cosmological conception of God:

> The immediacy of the concrescent subject is constituted by its living aim at its own self-constitution. Thus the initial stage of the aim is rooted in the nature of God, and its completion depends on the self-causation of the subject-super-ject. This function of God

is analogous to the remorseless working of things in Greek and in Buddhist thought. The initial aim is the best for that *impasse*. But if the best is bad, then the ruthlessness of God can be personified as *Ate*, the goddess of mischief. The chaff is burnt. What is inexorable in God, is valuation as an aim towards "order"... If we prefer the phraseology, we can say that God and the actual world jointly constitute the character of the creativity for the initial phase of the novel concrescence. The subject, thus constituted, is the autonomous master of its-own concrescence into subject-super-ject. It passes from a subjective aim in concrescence into a super-ject, into objective immortality. (*P&R*, pp. 244-245)

Thus, when we make a distinction of reason, and consider God in the abstraction of a primordial actuality, we must ascribe to him neither fullness of feeling, nor consciousness. He is the unconditioned actuality of conceptual feeling at the base of things so that, by reason of this primordial actuality, there is an order in the relevance of eternal objects to the process of creation. His unity of conceptual operations is a free creative act, untrammeled by reference to any particular course of things. It is deflected neither by love, nor by hatred, for what in fact comes to pass. The *particularities* of the actual world presuppose it; while it merely presupposes the general metaphysical character of creative advance, of which it is the primordial exemplification. The primordial nature of God is the acquirement by creativity of a primordial character ... He is the lure for feeling, the eternal urge of desire. (*Ibid.*, p. 344)[88]

And again:

Thus, so far, the primordial side of the nature of God has alone been relevant. But God, as well as being primordial, is also consequent. He is the beginning and the end. He is not the beginning in the sense of in the past of all members. He is the presupposed actuality of conceptual operation, in unison of becoming with every other creative act. Thus, by reason of the relativity of all things, there is a reaction of the world on God. The completion of God's nature into fullness of physical feeling is derived from the objectification of the world in God. He shares with every new creation its actual world; and the con-crescent creature is objectified in God as a novel in God's objectification of the actual world ... God's conceptual nature is unchanged, by reason of its final completeness. But his derivative nature is consequent upon the creative advance of the world. (*Ibid.*, p. 345)

So much, then, about Whitehead's innovations regarding the conception of God and God's relation to the world's creative activity and to the destiny of the human soul. God is just one of "the actual entities," which populate the physical world. Let us close this discussion on Whitehead's aphorism by quoting his view on Catholic traditional Christianity, which is illuminating and directly related to our theme here:

When the Western world accepted Christianity, Caesar conquered; and the text of Western theology was edited by his lawyers. The code of Justinian and the theology of Justinian are two volumes expressing one movement of the human spirit. The brief Galilean vision of humility flickered throughout the ages, uncertainly ... But the deeper idolatry, of the fashioning of God in the image of the Egyptian, the Persian, and the Roman imperial rulers, was retained. The Church gave unto God the attributes, which belonged exclusively to Caesar ... The divine Caesars merely represent the most natural, obvious, idolatrous theistic symbolism, at all epochs and places. (*Ibid.*, pp. 342-343)

With this statement I fully agree. However, as we have seen, precisely because of Caesar's (and Pope's, one may add, for Western Europeans) domination of Christianity and of Christianity's domination of the European mind and ethos, the so-called "European philosophy" cannot be characterized simply as "a series of footnotes to Plato" without serious equivocation. For it is inadequate without qualification or explanation as to what historically happened to Platonism and to Hellenic philosophy in general in Christian Europe.

In other words, "The Passion of Hellenic Philosophy in Europe"[89] needs to be uncovered and stated clearly, while Whitehead's aphorism naively suggests that there is no such misfortune, no "passion of philosophy" in the Christian Europe, which needs to be told and to be brought to light. On this point we respectfully disagree.

Conclusion

In the light of the preceding discussion and analysis, we are in a position to clearly see now the reason why many Europeans would not hesitate to claim that Platonic philosophy belongs exclusively to them, as part of their "philosophical tradition." By analogous reasoning even Modern Greeks, for purely economic and political considerations, declare proudly that "Greece belongs to the West." By this statement they mean that Greece should be an economic partner in the emerging and prosperous European Union.[90] In my view, it is historically more accurate and intellectually more honest to reverse the statement and declare that Europe and the West belong to Greece, in the sense that some of their best traditions came from the Greco-Roman-Byzantine civilization with its Christianized Platonic philosophy. However, Hellenic and Platonic philosophy belong to mankind as a whole, which needs it today more than ever before; and to the world at large by reason of its ecumenical values, and its perennial and universal virtues. For, if it is true that Christianity appropriated Platonic philosophy, it is equally true that Islam did the same.[91]

But Christians and Muslims should not forget that Platonic/Hellenic philosophy, which they have used or abused in the service of their respective theologies and theocracies, antedates the monomania of the new religions with their exclusive claims to the monopoly of God and truth. Such claims inevitably lead to fanaticism, hatred, and intolerance. In contrast to these claims, Hellenic philosophy, by its entertainment of many methods of searching for the truth, has a natural affinity to certain pre-Christian and pre-Islamic civilizations, which flourished around the Mediterranean Sea in Ancient Hellas, Asia Minor, North Africa, and the Far East, especially in India and China.[92]

Hellenic philosophy, therefore, can serve as a window and a bridge for these peoples, but especially for the Europeans, to look at other exotic worlds and to reach out to them as friends and as students of their stored human wisdom of ages past. From the considerable humane wisdom of these different ancient civilizations and their present manifestations, Europeans and others can learn valuable lessons which may assist us all in building, for the generations to come, a better future, humane, socially secure, and conducive to a culturally diverse and richer life.[93]

For the benefit of students, who thirst for wisdom and may care to learn from Plato and the Platonic Socrates, I would like to close this study with a list of five valuable Socratic lessons. They derive from genuine Platonic and Hellenic philosophy and may be of some help to sensitive souls and inquisitive minds living in the troubled post-modern world and searching for some sensible order in the present ethical chaos.

First of all, we may learn from Platonic Socrates and genuine Hellenic philosophy the lesson of how to live in harmony with nature and "Mother Earth." She deserves our loving-care as she gets older and more polluted every day by us, her naughty children, perhaps her present shame, but potentially her greatest glory, as "Father Kronos" makes us wiser through suffering. Learn also how to look upon the Cosmos as our "Big Brother," with a body much bigger than ours, but made from the same elements like our bodies, and with a "Sister Soul" much wiser than our little souls. These human souls should be disciplined to occasionally stop the frenetic pace, turn inward and try to discover who they are, where they come from, where they go to, and what this life on earth is all about.

Second, we may learn from Platonic Socrates and genuine Hellenic philosophy the lesson of how to live in peace with ourselves and in peaceful co-operation or, as the case may be, in competition with our neighbors. But remembering to always have tolerance for their strange ways, respect for their weird ideas, and sincere human sympathy for their real suffering here and now, as if we were all brothers and sisters of the same Mother Earth, who may need our constant care and love for our sake.

Third, we may learn from Platonic Socrates and genuine Platonic philosophy that it is wise to fill our political offices with prudent persons, who have put their own house in order before they dare to ask for our vote and our trust. Leaders, political leaders specifically, should have the self-mastery to withstand the many temptations, which attend the holding of high office and power. They should have the trained will to dedicate themselves to the service of "the common good" and not of private profit. Above all, they should be wise enough to know that they do not know everything, so they should not promise all things to all people cleverly or foolishly. Nor should they do anything else but what would serve well or better the common good of their small or large *polis*, keeping in mind also the great *Cosmopolis*, which we share with other peoples, animals and living beings.

Fourth, we may learn from Platonic Socrates and genuine Platonic philosophy that as human beings we cannot live only on bread, meat, and wine; on the contrary, we also need food for the mind and the spirit. We must become philosophically aware that we will be able to find true human happiness, flourishing and wellbeing (*eudaimonia*), not by excessive accumulation of material goods, but by following the Delphic and Socratic precept, "know thyself " and "take care of the soul." This can be accomplished by the right kind of Socratic erotic *paideia* in athletics and *philosophia*.

Fifth, we may also learn from genuine Platonic and Hellenic philosophy the valuable lesson of how to pray as human beings, when there is such need for prayer. This should be done without allowing monistic obsessions, and talk about the one "true God" and the one and only "true way," to offend other peoples and their perhaps different approach to the Divine. We are too fallible to know "the only way." So, we may follow the wise example of the Platonic Socrates, who prayed to "God and the other gods" and asked only for one thing, the gift of becoming "beautiful within."[94]

Notes

1. A.N. Whitehead, *Process and Reality*, D.R. Griffin and D.W. Sherburne, eds (New York, 1978), p. 39. To see the context of this famous statement, consider: "The safest general characterization of the European philosophical tradition is that it consists of a series of footnotes to Plato. I do not mean the systematic scheme of thought which scholars have doubtfully extracted from his writings. I allude to the wealth of general ideas scattered through them. His personal endowments, his wide opportunities for experience at a great period of civilization, his inheritance of an intellectual tradition not yet stiffened by excessive systematization, have made his writings an inexhaustible mine of suggestion. Thus in one sense by stating my belief that the train of thought in these lectures is Platonic, I am doing no more than to express the hope that it falls within the European tradition. But I do mean more: I mean that if we had to render Plato's general point of view with the least change made necessary by the intervening two thousand years of human experience in social organization, in aesthetic attainments, in science, and in religion, we should have to set about the construction of a philosophy of organism." As we will see, Whitehead's hope that his "philosophy of organism" will fall "within the European tradition" is not fulfilled because, among other things, his cosmology and theology go beyond the religious restrictions of the traditional European "philosophy."

2. For more detailed historical discussion and analysis of the different aspects of the influence of Plato and Platonism on European thought, I refer the interested reader to the following works, since my intention in this study is not to provide another history of "this

phenomenon," but only a new interpretation of its philosophical aspect: A.H. Armstrong, ed., *The Cambridge History of Later Greek and Early Medieval Philosophy* (Cambridge, 1967); R. Klibansky, *The Continuity of the Platonic Tradition during the Middle Ages* (London, 1939); E. Gilson, *History of Christian Philosophy in the Middle Ages* (New York, 1955); E. von Ivanka, *Plato Christianus: Uebernahme und Umgestaltung des Platonismus durch die Vaeter* (Einsiedeln, 1964); W. Beierwaltes, ed., *Platonismus in der Philosophie des Mittelalters* (Darmstadt, 1969); B. Tatakis, *La Philosophie Byzantine* (Paris, 1949); F. Masai, *Plethon et le platonisme de Mistra* (Paris, 1956); S. Runciman, *The Last Byzantine Renaissance* (Cambridge, 1970); N.A. Robb, *Neoplatonism of the Italian Renaissance* (New York, 1968); P.O. Kristeller, *Renaissance Thought* (New York, 1961); and by same *Eight Philosophers of the Italian Renaissance* (Stanford, 1965); J. Hankins, *Plato in the Italian Renaissance* (Leiden, 1990); C.A. Patrides, ed., *The Cambridge Platonists* (London, 1969); J. Miles, *John Colet and the Platonic Tradition* (La Salle, Ill, 1961); E.N. Tigerstedt, *The Decline and Fall of the Neoplatonic Interpretation of Plato: An Outline and Some Observations* (Helsinki, 1974); R.T. Wallis, *Neoplatonism* (New York, 1972), especially Chapter Six, "The Influence of Neoplatonism;" and D. O'Meara, ed., *Neoplatonism and Christian Thought* (Albany, NY, 1982).

    3. I shall argue in more detail in the last assay of this collection that philosophy, as Plato, Aristotle, and the Hellenic philosophers understood and practiced it, did not and could not flourish in Christian Europe in the last two millennia. The dominion of the Catholic Church with its hierarchical structure and its theocratic proclivity would not have allowed it. The promise of the Renaissance for a revival of Hellenic philosophy was soon to be frustrated by the "fundamentalist fury" of Reformation and Counter-Reformation. So was the hope of the Enlightenment for a genuine revival of the free philosophic spirit. It soon gave way to the "Catholic spiritualism" in France and to "Lutheran evangelicalism" and "pietism" in Germany. The efficacy of Hegel's dialectics prepared German "philosophy" to play the familiar servile role of handmaid of Protestant theology: "Sustained by philosophy, religion [the Christian religion, the true religion, as he calls it] receives its justification from thinking consciousness ... Philosophy is to this extent theology." *Hegel's Lecture on the Philosophy of Religion*, P.C. Hodgson, ed. (Berkeley, 1988), pp. 488-489.

    It is my thesis that even with the coming of modern science in the sixteenth and seventeenth centuries, philosophy did not become free, as one might have reasonably expected and as it had been in the Hellenic era. It simply and sadly changed "masters" and began to serve science and technology, instead of revelation and theology, when it was not made to serve both simultaneously under the old sophistic trick of "double truth." J. Locke, for example, endeavored to prove "rationally" not only God's existence, but also the absurd Christian doctrine of creation *ex nihilo*. See, *An Essay Concerning Human Understanding*, 2 vols (London, 1972), vol. 2, pp. 265-267. He described himself with obvious pride as "an under-laborer of the incomparable Mr. Newton." In his turn, the great Physicist stated sincerely that: "The Church is constituted and her extent and bounds of communion are defined by the laws of God, and these laws are unchangeable. The laws of the king extended only to things that are left indifferent and undetermined by the laws of God ... For the law was good if a man could keep it, but we were to be saved not by the works of the law, but by faith in Jesus Christ." Quoted from *On Our Religion to God, to Christ, and the Church*, by E.A. Burtt, *The Metaphysical Foundations of Modern Science* (Garden City, NY, 1954), p. 286.

The propagation of Marxist "scientific socialism" in the nineteenth and its political application in the twentieth century by the Stalinist and Maoist versions of the "dictatorship of the proletariat," in Eastern Europe and in China respectively, could hardly provide a suitable environment for philosophy's emancipation. Thus its practitioners in these lands simply changed "masters" once again, when they did not serve more than one at the same time, that is, revolutionary ideology, scientific technology, and apocalyptic theology. For the affinities between revolutionary Marxism and traditional Christianity see, for instance, L. Stevenson, *Seven Theories of Human Nature* (Oxford, 1974), pp. 35-60.

4. Such great cultural misfortunes are difficult to overcome. As E.A. Burtt put it blandly: "[W]e must wait for the complete extinction of theological superstition before these things can be said without misunderstanding. Such is the misfortune of modern thought as compared with that of Greece" (*ibid.*, p. 324). Although he is writing at the second half of the twentieth century, the author advises us "to wait." But for how long, one may ask. The answer to this question, and even the asking of it, indicates the magnitude of this "misfortune" for Europe and the world at large.

5. My optimism for a global and better future, in contrast to the pessimism regarding the European philosophical past and present, is based on the reasons which are summarized in the *Introduction* and, especially, the *Conclusion* of this study.

6. In this respect, the need for the restoration of genuine Hellenic philosophy, for which I shall argue in this and the other essays of the collection, is of real global concern, and not some kind of antiquarian nostalgia. It is for the sake of a better future for humanity that "the humanism" of Hellenic philosophy must be revived and restored to its ancestral freedom and dignity.

7. The process was completed during the thousand yearlong life of the Platonic Academy. Three works may be of interest in this connection, G.M.A. Grube, *Plato's Thought* (Indianapolis, 1980), presents a thematic arrangement of Plato's views on various topics; H.J. Kraemer, *Plato and the Foundations of Metaphysics* (New York, 1990), in J.R. Catan's translation, gives an account of the "indirect tradition" regarding Plato's unwritten doctrines, the principles of his philosophy, and his teaching in the Academy; and Philip Merlan, *From Platonism to Neoplatonism* (The Hague, 1960), traces the development of Platonism in the Schools of Neoplatonism.

8. The probability of the ecumenical and global appeal of Platonic philosophy in the coming millennium would seem to be high, given its dialectic and non-dogmatic nature. Time will show. But the question, "Why did Plato write dialogues?" is still debated seriously by Platonists. See, for instance, Ch. Griswold, *Platonic Writings and Platonic Readings* (New York, 1988); and H.J. Kraemer (*ibid.*).

9. For the transition from orality to literacy and the relation between the Homeric culture and the Platonic program of reform, see E. Havelock, *Preface to Plato* (Cambridge, Mass, 1982), especially pp. 254-311.

10. See W. Jaeger, *Paideia: The Ideals of Greek Culture* (3 vols, New York, 1943), especially vol. 2, pp. 220-373; for a detailed discussion of each Platonic Dialogue, see W.K.C. Guthrie, *A History of Greek Philosophy* (6 vols, Cambridge, 1962-1981), vols. 4 and 5; and for a critique of some of their views regarding the origin of Hellenic philosophy, see the first essay, "The Origin of Hellenic Philosophy."

11. The expression "School of Hellas" comes from Isocrates who, like Plato, emphasized in his writings the need of pan-Hellenic cooperation. The need of our times is,

of course, that of pan-anthropic and ecumenical cooperation and understanding, in view of the recent revival of religious fanaticism and the resulting blind terrorism. For more on this point see the last essay of the present collection.

12. Consider Boethius' reply to the song of Lady Philosophy:

"The man who searches deeply for truth, and wishes to avoid being deceived by false leads, must turn the light of his inner vision upon himself. He must guide his soaring thoughts back again and teach his spirit that it possesses hidden among its own treasures whatever it seeks outside itself.

Then all that was hidden by the dark cloud of error will shine more clearly than Phoebus; for the body, with its burden of forgetfulness, cannot drive all light from the mind. The seed of truth grows deep within and is roused to life by the breath of learning. For how can you answer questions truly unless the spark of truth glows deep in your heart? If Plato's Muse speaks truly, whatever is learned is recollection of something forgotten.

I agree fully with Plato, I [Boethius] said. For this is the second time I have been reminded of these truths. I forgot them first under the oppressive influence of my body, then later when I was depressed by grief."

The Consolation of Philosophy, R. Green, tr. (Indianapolis: Bobbs-Merrill, 1975), pp. 69-70; and compare it to *Republic*, Book VII.

13. Under the then present favorite conditions and the imperial favor, which the Plotinian school enjoyed, this was probably not a utopian dream. Porphyry reports on the project and its fate thus: "The Emperor Gallienus and his wife Salonina greatly honored and venerated Plotinus. He tried to make full use of their friendship: there was said to have been in Campania a city of philosophers which had fallen into ruins; this he asked them to revive, and to present the surrounding territory to the city when they had founded it. Those who settled there were to live according to the laws of Plato, and it was to be called Platonopolis; and he undertook to move there with his companions. The philosopher would easily have gained his wish if some of the courtiers, moved by jealousy, spite, or some such motive, had not prevented it. *Vita Plotini*, 12. 1-13, *Enneads*, vol. 1, A.H. Armstrong, ed. (Cambridge, Mass, 1978).

14. But as it spread, Hellenic Platonism encountered its great rival, Hellenized Christianity. On the revived Platonism, its sources, and its variety, see R. Wallis, *Neoplatonism* (New York: Scribner's, 1972); for its relation to and conflict with Christianity, see D.O'Meara, ed., *Neoplatonism and Christian Thought* (New York, 1982); and my review of the book in *Journal of the History of Philosophy* 21, no. 4 (1983): 565-568.

15. See "Porphyry's Criticism of Christianity and the Problem of Augustine's Platonism," *Dionysius* 13 (1989): 51-70.

16. On this see, R. Wallis, ed., *Neoplatonism and Gnosticism* (Albany, NY Press, 1992); and my "Plotinus' Anti-Gnostic Polemic and Porphyry's *Against the Christians*" in the same volume.

17. *Ibid.* To Porphyry's mind such Christian claims were irrational and arrogant. But for St. Paul, his followers, and the faithful Christians for many generations to come, the end of the world and the "Second Coming" of the Lord were near, which must have been a terrifying expectation. On this matter, Whitehead comments thus: "In the early days of Christianity, there was a general belief among Christians that the world was coming to an end in the lifetime of people then living. We can make only indirect inferences as to how far this belief was authoritatively proclaimed; but it is certain that it was widely held, and that it

formed an impressive part of the popular religious doctrine. The belief proved itself to be mistaken, and Christian doctrine adjusted itself to the change." *Science and the Modern World* (New York: The Free Press, 1967), p. 182. From these observations, Whitehead concludes (rather hastily and to the amusement of his friend B. Russell), that the Christian religion, just like the modern science, has "constantly progressed."

As for folly and its relation to Christians and non-Christians, see the delightful treatise of Desiderius Erasmus, *The Praise of Folly*, C. H. Miller, tr. (New Haven: Yale University Press, 1979), from which I would like to offer the reader a relevant sample here: "As for the theologians, perhaps it would be better to pass them over in silence, *not stirring up the hornets' nest and not laying a finger on the stinkweed*, since this race of men is incredibly arrogant and touchy. For they might rise up *en masse* and march in ranks against me with six hundred conclusions and force me to recant. And if I should refuse, they would immediately shout 'heretic.' For this is the thunderbolt they always keep ready at a moment's notice to terrify anyone to whom they are not very favorably inclined." (p. 87) One might have hope that things would have changed since Erasmus' time, but the recent rise of fundamentalism (Islamic and Christian, especially) indicates that the contrary is the case.

18. Consider on this, for example, the revealing statement of Clement of Alexandria: "Accordingly, before the advent of the Lord, philosophy was necessary to the Greeks for righteousness. And now it becomes conducive to piety; being a kind of preparatory training for those who attain to faith through demonstration ... For God is the cause of all good things; but of some primarily, as of the Old and New Testament; and of others by consequence, as philosophy. Perchance, too, philosophy was given to the Greeks directly and primarily, till the Lord should call the Greeks. For this was a schoolmaster to bring 'the Hellenic mind,' as the Law, the Hebrews, 'to Christ.' Philosophy, therefore, was a preparation, paving the way for him who is perfected in Christ." *Stromata*, in *Greek and Roman Philosophy after Aristotle*, J.L. Saunders, ed. (New York: The Free Press, 1966), p. 306.

19. The transformation of Jesus, from son of Virgin Mary to the only Begotten Son of God, and the stories of His Incarnation and Resurrection, had scandalized Hellenic Platonists; for the faithful, they constituted the great mystery of salvation. On this and the conflict between Christian and Hellenic Platonism, see also my "Plotinus' Anti-Gnostic Polemic and Porphyry's *Against the Christians*," in *Neoplatonism and Gnosticism*.

20. This account of Rome's decline and fall is obviously synoptic, speculative, and oversimplified; but it would have looked so to the theoretic minds of Platonic philosophers. For more extended historical accounts of this event, see *The Cambridge Ancient History*, vols. XII-XIII (London, 1961); *The Columbia History of the World*, Part One, J.A. Garraty and P. Gay, eds, (New York, 1894); and E. Gibbon, *The Decline and Fall of Rome* (London and New York, 1911).

21. Rome's rise and fall is, of course, a complicated story as noted above, note no. 20. But it may be helpful to keep in mind that it is the classical case of a historical pattern, according to which the rule of the less cultured people over the more cultured peoples tends to become tenuous with time, and sooner or later the roles are reversed. Accordingly, Rome was destined to be conquered both spiritually and politically from within by its more civilized citizens, that is, the Hellenized inhabitants of the Hellenistic centers of Africa and Asia, such as Alexandria, Antioch, Rhodes, Corinth, and so forth. When the Hellenized peoples of these cities found in their new faith in Christ risen from the dead a unifying force

and a powerful weapon, which could be effectively used to regain their lost political power and freedom, Rome's rule in the East was finished. However, Rome itself learned from them the lesson so well that, when it fell into the hands of Germanic barbarians, Rome succeeded in ruling over them again through the power of the Cross, not only spiritually but also politically, during the Middle Ages in parts of Europe. The Teutonic tribes of the North had to wait until the time of Reformation to follow Luther's fury to victory and freedom in the name of "true faith" in the Lord. Stalin and Hitler underestimated the power of apostles like Peter, Paul, and Luther. They could have learned a lesson from them and, thus, perhaps foresee the impending failure of their anti-Christian campaigns of totalitarian endeavor in the still nominally "Christian Europe" of the twentieth century.

22. The *De civitate Dei* is divided into two parts, books I-X and XI-XXII, dealing respectively, as noted, with the earthly and the heavenly cities as conceived by Augustine. On this, as well as the thesis that in his *magnum opus* Augustine was responding to Porphyry's attack on the Church, see my "Porphyry's Criticism of Christianity and the Problem of Augustine's Platonism," *Dionysius* XIII (1989): 51-70, and the relevant bibliography provided there.

23. Evidently, the edifice of European civilization is based on three Byzantine foundations: Christian religion, Roman law, and some relics of Hellenic literature that miraculously survived in the Theocratic New Order. Whether the Northern Europeans are aware of this historical fact and willing to admit it is, of course, another matter.

24. The only serious challenge to the established Christian version of Judaic monotheism after the sixth century AD, that is, after the closure of the philosophical schools including the Platonic Academy by Justinian in 529, came from Islam. But Islam can be seen as a new version of Judaic monotheism, much more militant and fanatical than Christianity. In Marxism one can see the last extreme phase of the same dangerous process, where the Prophet has replaced even God Him-self. There is hope now that, with the collapse of Marxism in *praxis*, the other two versions of Judaism and intolerant monotheism may follow, but it will take time. Hence the chance for the revival of Hellenic philosophy.

25. The Nazi view to the contrary not withstanding. In this respect, the Northern Europeans differ significantly from the Mediterranean Europeans (Spanish, Provencal French, Italians and Greeks), who have retained some memory of their glorious pre-Christian and pre-Islamic past, the Greco-Roman world. Thus, unless the economic domination of the South by the North changes which is unlikely, there cannot be much hope for a revival of Hellenic philosophy even in the European Union. The only place for such revival would seem to be America. For in philosophy, as in other things, this Great Democracy of Thomas Jefferson and other Founding Fathers and admirers of Hellenic civilization, has been innocent of the sins, which the Europeans have committed against genuine Hellenic philosophy, freedom and democracy, not only in medieval but also in modern times. Besides, only through an ecumenical philosophy of the Hellenic, Platonic and pre-Christian type, America will be perhaps able to peacefully attain and sustain world hegemony in freedom and democracy. As long as it is perceived as a Christian superpower, it will be resented and resisted by the non-Christian countries around the world, especially Japan, China, and India, which make up about half of the world's population. It will be resisted also, and more ominously for Freedom and Democracy, by fundamentalist Islam, that is, Christianity's younger, more militant and sinister sister.

26. In this respect, any believer in divine revelations, whether Christian or Muslim, must think and "philosophize" within the strict limits set by dogmatic faith as defined and interpreted by religious hierarchical authorities, otherwise he becomes a heretic, "anathema" is pronounced upon him, and his books go into the *Index*. But, such sort of sick and sickening "philosophy" (to use Nietzsche's acute diagnosis), is a corruption of *philosophia* as the Ancient Hellenes knew it and personified it in Athena, the Virgin Warrior Goddess, defender of freedom and dispenser of wisdom. This is a great loss for the world. Will it be able to recover the gift ever again? That is a good question.

27. "The Glory of Byzantium" was the title of a successful exhibit of Byzantine icons and manuscripts, from the different parts of the Eastern Roman Empire, at the Metropolitan Museum of New York in spring of 1997.

28. That kind of freedom, as enjoyed by the Ancient Hellenic philosophers, was impossible for European "thinkers." They had to either directly provide support for the established Church dogma, Catholic or Protestant, or at least pretend that philosophy and science had different areas of concern and concepts of "truth," so that they could not possibly come into conflict with dogmatic faith. What a hypocrisy, what a lack of honesty and human dignity, you may think. Yet, the timid attitude is found in Aquinas and Averroes, in Duns Scotus and William of Ockham, in Descartes and Pascal, in Locke and Leibniz, in Hegel and right-wing Hegelians, in skeptical Hume and critical Kant, and many more icons of the slavish pantheon of European "philosophers."

The few notable exceptions to the rule, the rare heroic voices of protest, are just that, exceptions which verify the rule; protests which do not alter the deep-rooted tradition of servitude, so characteristic of the so-called "philosophy" in Europe. I believe that it is time for change and America may be the only promising land for the re-birth of genuine philosophy of the Hellenic and pre-Christian kind. We need it now, and will need it more in the near future, if the American society is to remain free, open, tolerant, diverse, democratic, humanistic, pluralistic and "hegemonic" in world affairs.

29. It is true that Ficino's and Bessarion's Christian version of Platonism prevailed in the Italian Renaissance by the end of the fifteenth century and spread Northward by the Humanist movement. However, there always remained an undercurrent of the other, the Hellenic version of Platonism, which was characterized by a freer and non-dogmatic spirit of philosophical speculation and tolerance. The fate of Jordano Bruno, who was burned at the stake, clearly indicates that this version of Platonism was perceived as "dangerous" to the well established and monarchically ruled Catholic Church. The burning of Servetus in Calvinist Geneva in 1555, indicates that the Christianity of the Reformed Church, whether Calvinist or Lutheran, was ready to continue its antithesis to philosophy and science, which Catholicism had blessed from the beginning. On this see also J. McManners, ed., *The Oxford Illustrated History of Christianity* (Oxford, 1990), pp. 233-266.

30. The Augustinian tactic of using Platonic philosophy as *ancilla theologiae* (handmaiden of theology) was not challenged until the thirteenth century, when Thomas Aquinas decided to put Aristotle to the same task and thus created the high tide of Scholasticism. This dominated Europe until the Renaissance, when a revival of Platonism occurred, under the main influence of Pletho.

31. Material in this section was first published in "Porphyry's Criticism of Christianity and the Problem of Augustine's Platonism," *Dionysius* 13 (1989): 51-70.

32. *De civitate Dei* (*DcD*), VI, 5. Throughout this work Augustine uses key Greek words without translation, and provides etymologies and comments on their meanings.

33. For Porphyry Augustine has both high praise and much criticism, for reasons which will become evident as we proceed.

34. *De doctrina Christiana*, II, 43.

35. *De civitate Dei*. VIII, 11. Here he seems more aware of the chronological discrepancies between Jeremiah's and Plato's dates, as well as the difficulties involved in the communication problem. The only valuable information in this connection is that Augustine was aware (as some modern scholars are not, or they refuse to admit it) of the long tradition which insisted on Plato's visit to Egypt. For more details, see the first essay of the collection and the *Appendix.*

36. "The sense of shame is found in all men," said the Chinese sage, Mencius. *The Wisdom of Confucius* (New York, 1966), p. 281. If Mencius were correct, then Augustine would seem to be the exception to the rule. For he abandoned Platonic philosophy "without a blushing" in order to serve the monarchically structured hierarchy of Catholic Church.

37. For Nietzsche, there is virtually no difference between Protestant Pastors and German "philosophers." In his view, "Philosophy has been corrupted by theological blood. The Protestant pastor is the grandfather of German philosophy, Protestantism itself is its *peccatum originale.*" *Twilight of the Idols*, R.J. Hollingdale, tr. (New York, 1985), p. 121. In my view, his apt characterization applies to "European philosophy" as a whole, from Augustine to Heidegger. Because of his sharp perception of matters of the spirit, and his acute diagnosis of the malady of the European mind, Nietzsche is recognized as one of the very few "Free Spirits," to be born in Christian Europe, over the Alps and beyond the Rhine.

38. In spite of the Renaissance, the Reformation, the Scientific Revolution, and other revolutions that followed, it seems that "European philosophy" from Descartes to Hegel and beyond has not liberated itself from the fetters of Christian theology, whether traditional or "moral theology," which was Kant's preference. Nietzsche saw this historical fact clearly and felt disgusted with "German philosophy." Even Whitehead felt restrained by Judeo-Christian Scriptural stipulations concerning the natural world, and he would prefer Plato's *Timaeus* as a safer guide to "Mathematical Cosmology." The last section of this essay has additional information on this important point.

39. Our troubled times of post-modern skepticism and deconstructionism can be seen as the final phase of philosophy's struggle to break away from the uncomfortable embrace of theology or, alternatively, as the prelude to a renewed alliance between the two. In the new millennium each may assume the familiar roles of slave and master respectively. The stakes are high and the responsibility of philosophers and enlightened political leaders is great. Will they assume it and act accordingly? Time will tell this tale too.

40. For more on this problem, see "Porphyry's Criticism of Christianity and the Problem of Augustine's Platonism," *Dionysius* 13 (1989): 51-70.

41. Consider the following confession which, coming from a grown up man, sounds childish, but it is indicative of what "true conversion" and otherworldliness does even to a mature person.

"By reading of these books of the Platonists I had been prompted to look for truth as something incorporeal, and I *caught sight of your invisible nature, as is known through your creatures*. Though I was thwarted in my wish to know more, I was conscious of what it was that my mind was too clouded to see ... For if I had not come across these books until after I had been formed in the mould of your Holy Scriptures and had learnt to love you through familiarity with them, the Platonist teaching might have swept me from my foothold on the solid ground of piety, and even if I had held firm to the spirit which the Scriptures had imbued me for my salvation, I might have thought it possible for a man who read nothing but the Platonist books to derive the same spirit from them alone. So I seized eagerly upon the venerable writings inspired by your Holy Spirit, especially those of the apostle Paul. At one time it had seemed to me that he sometimes contradicted himself and that the purport of his words did not agree with the evidence of the law and the prophets, but these difficulties now disappeared once and for all. I began to read and discovered that whatever truth I had found in the Platonists was set down here as well, and with it there was praise for your grace bestowed ... Nothing of this is contained in the Platonists' books. Their pages have not the mien of the true love of God. They make no mention of the tears of confession or of *the sacrifice that you will never disdain, a broken spirit, a heart that is humble and contrite, nor do they speak of the salvation of your people, the city adorned like a bride, the foretaste of your spirit, or the chalice of our redemption.* In them no one sings *No rest has my heart but in God's hands; to him I look for deliverance.*"

Emphasis is in the text. *St. Augustine's Confessions*, R.S. Pine-Coffin, tr. (New York, 1986), pp. 154-156.

42. The Platonists were also favored because their writings were better known: "For the Greeks, whose tongue holds the highest place among the languages of the Gentiles, are loud in their praises of these writings; and the Latins, taken with their excellence, or their renown, have studied them more heartily than other writings, and, by translating them into our tongue, have given them greater celebrity and notoriety" (*DcD*, VII, 10)

43. These points have been selected from *DcD*, VIII-X.

44. *DcD*, X, 3o.

45. *Republic*, 618a-620d.

46. The identification of the *De regressu animae* is still uncertain. See J. O'Meara, *Porphyry's Philosophy from Oracles in Augustine* (Paris: Etudes augustiniennes, 1959), p. 36; compare it with P. Hadot, "Citacion de Porphyre chez Augustine," *Revue des etudes augustiniennes* (1960): 205-244.

47. A. Nauck, ed., *Porphyrii philosophi Platonici: Opuscula selecta* (Hildesheim, 1963).

48. What Augustine seems to forget here is that, from a Platonic point of view, the ultimate return of a soul to its Fatherland, which we should not confuse with its temporary release, as Augustine seems to do here, simply ends a soul's temporary adventure into the material world. In this sense, and regardless of whether the release of a soul from the body is permanent or not, it would seem that all is well and as it should be, platonically speaking, if that which had a beginning in time came to an end in time.

49. Earlier, Augustine had quoted from Varro's *On the Origin of the Roman People* as follows: "Certain astrologers have written that men are destined to a new birth, which was called *palingenesia*. This will take place after four hundred and forty years have elapsed; and then the same soul and the same body which were formerly united in the person, shall again be reunited."

50. In Augustine's words: "*ut beata sit anima, corpus esse omne fugiendum.*"

51. In *Theaetetus*, 176a-b, they would read the exchange between Socrates and Theodorus:

"Socrates: Such are the two characters, Theodorus. The one is nursed in freedom and leisure, the philosopher, as you call him. He may be excused if he looks foolish or useless when faced with some menial task, if he cannot tie up bedclothes into a neat bundle or flavor a dish with spices and a speech with flattery. The other is smart in the dispatch of all such services, but has not learned to wear his cloak like a gentleman, or caught the accent of discourse that will rightly celebrate the true life of happiness for the gods and men.

Theodorus: If you could convince everyone, Socrates, as you convince me, there will be more peace and fewer evils in the world.

Socrates: Evils, Theodorus, can never be done away with, for the good must always have its contrary; nor have they any place in the divine world, but they must needs haunt this region of our mortal nature. That is why we should make all speed to take flight from this world to the other, and that means becoming like the divine so far as we can, and that again is to become righteous with the help of wisdom. But it is no such easy matter to convince men that the reasons for avoiding wickedness and seeking after goodness are not those which the world gives ... "

52. According to Augustine, we need not seek out one kind of purification for the part that Porphyry calls intellectual, and another for that part that he calls spiritual, and still another for the body. In his eyes, these divisions complicate the matter.

53. The philosophical way of life is not recommended for everybody, but only for those who may have higher intellectual and spiritual aspirations, as Porphyry has argued thoroughly throughout his long treatise, *De abstinentia*.

54. This is especially true in Eastern religions and cultures which tend to be more tolerant probably because they are diverse and polytheistic societies, in a sense that Western European societies have not been able to be historically. At recent times, they have made some progress towards that goal, but it has been painful to them, especially to those in Islamic societies, because of their historical conditioning. For the same reason it is precarious. For: "Despite the protestations of Islamic apologists for such radicalism, or more precisely religious militancy, I would like to suggest that there can be no convivial accommodation between the best in the traditional society and the best in what we somewhat euphemistically characterize as *modern society*. The former—whether Islamic, Christian, or Judaic—insists on strict adherence to the norms which are essentially a closed religio-political system, one in which any separation between the spiritual and profane is not tolerated. In such authoritarian system, civil liberties, participation, joint decision making, or willingness to accommodate secular necessity are greatly diminished." W.H. Lewis, *The Mediterranean Quarterly* 6, 3 (1995): 1-13.

55. The question "Is Whitehead's version of Platonism part of the traditional Christian Platonism or something different?" will be addressed below.

56. G. Ostrogorsky, *History of the Byzantine State* (New Brunswick, 1957), pp. 356-402.

57. Especially the area North of the Danube and East of the Rhine, which was not penetrated by the civilizing breeze of the Hellenized pre-Christian Mediterranean world, appeared barbarous to Hellenic eyes. Perhaps it is not an accident that the same area became, in time, the birthplace of furious Protestantism and brutal Nazism.

58. He is better known by his Hellenized name. See also, Leo Bargeliotes, "Pletho as Forerunner of the Neo-Hellenic and Modern European Consciousness," *Diotima* 1 (1973): 33-60.

59. It seems that the tradition is still alive. For instance, the majority of articles published by the two leading journals in the English-speaking world, *Ancient Philosophy* and *Phronesis*, seem to fall into this category. There are, of course, notable exceptions of excellent studies on Plato and Aristotle published in these journals, as well as in two recent collections of critical essays edited by G. Vlastos, *Plato* (2 vols, Garden City, NY, 1971); and J.P. Anton and A. Preus, *Essays in Ancient Greek Philosophy*, vol. *3*, *Plato* (New York, 1989). However, most of them are narrowly analytical and "philological" rather than philosophical, in the Hellenic sense of *philosophia*.

60. J. Hankins, *Plato in the Italian Renaissance* (Leiden, 1991), pp. 193-217 and 267-299.

61. *Ibid.*, pp. 217-236.

62. With the coming of the Reformation in the sixteenth century the Catholic Church, with its tendency towards scholastic legalism and despotic Papism, lost control over parts of Northern Europe, where for a short time Platonism found more hospitality.

63. My intention is not to provide a history of the influence of Platonism here, which would take us far off the limits of this study, but only a few traces which will lead us to Whitehead and his famous aphorism, the correct understanding of which is my goal.

64. H.J. Kraemer, *ibid.*, pp. 15-29.

65. *Ibid.*, pp. 17-21.

66. The tendency to read the Platonic dialogues as pure literature can go to such extremes as we find, for instance, in V. Tejera, *Plato's Dialogues One by One* (New York, 1984), who wants to read the Platonic writing only "dialogically," that is, as "rhetorical," "poetic," "satiric," and "dramatic" theater.

67. A.N. Whitehead, *ibid.*, p. 39.

68. Whitehead's mind, and perhaps to a degree Russell's, belong to the notable exceptions to the general rule that European "philosophers" have traditionally been slavish laborers of such masters as dogmatic theology, scientific technology, and political ideology of the Left or the Right. Nietzsche would be another exceptional case representing the German speaking world, while Bergson (before his conversion to Catholicism) or Sartre (after his liberation from Catholicism) could function as representatives of the French speaking world. But, to say it again with stress, the exceptions are rare and relatively recent voices of protest.

69. That is to say, footnotes to the Biblical exegesis rather than to Hellenic Platonism, and to dogmatic theology, which is based on Scriptural revelations, rather than to dialectic philosophy of the type advocated by the Platonic Socrates.

70. In this respect, medieval and modern "philosophers," as well as contemporary practitioners of "the linguistic analysis" of the language of science, are virtually indistinguishable. They all use "philosophy" in order to serve a "Higher Authority," that is, Religion and Science respectively. It is expected that "the truth" will be given either by "divine inspiration" or by the "scientific method," and that the function of the so-called "philosopher" is to provide assistance for the logical clarification and coherence of the respective "revelation." Thus ancient "Lady Philosophy," the supposed queen of the sciences, has been reduced to the status of a handmaid of one Mistress or other (that is, *ancilla theologiae* or *ancilla scientiae*), which is regrettable.

71. Thus, the theologians seem to falsify both, the sincerity of simple faith of the believing heart, and the dignity of philosophy.

72. F. Nietzsche, *Twilight of the Idols/The Anti-Christ*, R.J. Hollingdale, tr. (New York, 1985). Consider some of his aphorisms: "Are there any German philosophers?—people ask me abroad. I blush" (p. 60); "Who has not pondered sadly over what the German spirit could be! But this nation has deliberately made itself stupid, for practically a thousand years: nowhere else are the two great European narcotics, alcohol and Christianity, so viciously abused" (p. 61); "Among Germans one will understand immediately when I say that philosophy has been corrupted by theologian blood. The Protestant pastor is the grandfather of German philosophy, Protestantism itself is its *peccatum originale*. Definition of Protestantism: the half-sided paralysis of Christianity—and of reason ... One has only to say the words 'College of Tuebingen' to grasp what German philosophy is at bottom—a cunning theology ... Kant's success is merely a theologian's success: German integrity was far from firm and Kant, like Luther, like Leibniz, was one more constrain upon it ... Kant, this fatal spider, counted as the German philosopher—still does ... The erring instinct in all and everything, *anti-naturalness* as instinct, German *decadence* as philosophy—that is Kant!" (pp. 121-122).

73. That is, the same fruit of knowledge (*gnosis)*, which the Biblical God had forbidden the faithful folks to eat from (*Genesis*, 2).

74. I will write *logos* with a small letter, to remind you that Socrates and the Hellenic his friends were interested in the human *logos*, in its double sense (as discursive and intuitive reason), as opposed to Divine *Logos* of the Christian and Islamic revelations.

75. *Philebus*, 28c.

76. Hence the relevance and the need for such a philosophy today. For more on this see the last essay of this collection.

77. May God (or, more precisely, the forgotten Goddess of wisdom, Athena), enlighten and save them from this indignity.

78. In this respect, Orthodox Christianity, which is represented by tiny Greece in the Leviathan of the European Union, can perhaps play a positive role. Strong spirituality, connection to classical modes of thought, highly cultivated aesthetic appreciation, expressed ecological concern, democratic leaning (in contrast to Papacy), prudent distance from power politics, are characteristics of Orthodox Christianity. These and a healthy immunity to two chronic handicaps, which have plagued Catholicism and Protestantism respectively, that is, scholastic legalism and puritanical fundamentalism, may show that Hellenized Orthodox Christianity can still help the European Union. It can perhaps even "save it" from becoming enslaved once again to ecclesiastical dogmatism, by keeping an open mind with regard to free scientific inquiry and unfettered philosophic speculation about the nature of all things, physical, political, spiritual, and even divine, especially the latter, because they can easily be abused.

79. For the textual context of the aphorism itself, see note no. 1 above, where the entire passage was quoted.

80. The three volumes of *Principia Mathematica* were published in the years 1910-1913. One may regret that the cooperation did not continue. The combination of Whitehead's profundity of thought and Russell's clarity of mind and lucidity of style could have finally produced a European philosophy worthy of its name. For both men, despite their bias towards science, were freer from the other two "Masters" of European minds, that is, fanatic theology and political ideology.

81. Wittgenstein was probably the link for Russell's connection to the Vienna Circle and analytical program. Although Russell had shown some respect for Wittgenstein's early work, the *Tractatus Logico-Philosophicus*, he was rather disappointed by his friend's later work, the *Philosophical Investigations*. Socrates would have been disappointed by both works and with the entire movement of *Logical Analysis* with its pathetic narrowness of mind and dryness of style and use of language. Let me give you a sample of the kind of philosophy to be found in the *Investigations* (Paragraph 197): "Don't I know, then, which game I want to play until I have *played* it? Or are all the rules contained in my act of intending? Is it experience that tells me that this sort of game is the usual consequence of such an act of intending? So is it impossible for me to be certain what I am intending to do? And if that is nonsense—what kind of super-strong connection exists between the act of intending and the thing intended? Where is the connection effected between the sense of the expression "Let's play a game of chess" and all the rules of the game?—Well, in the list of rules of the game, in the teaching of it, in the day-to-day practice of playing" (Anscombe's translation).

82. In fact, the subtitle of *Process and Reality* was *An Essay in Cosmology*. In this work, Whitehead attempted to provide the metaphysical foundations of a new theory about the whole Cosmos based on the latest findings of the natural sciences, especially Physics and Biology, in order to replace the old Newtonian theory.

83. *Ibid.*, p. 96.

84. *Ibid.*, p. 39.

85. Consider, for example, his comparative judgment on Newton and Plato, regarding the modern quantum theory: "Newton would have been surprised at the modern quantum theory and at the dissolution of the quanta into vibrations; Plato would have expected it. While we note the many things said in the *Timaeus*, which are now foolishness, we must also give him credit for that aspect of his teaching in which he was two thousand years ahead of his time. Plato accounted for the sharp-cut differences between kinds of natural things by assuming an approximation of the molecules of the fundamental kinds to the mathematical forms of regular solids. He also assumed that certain qualitative contrasts in occurrences, such as between musical note, depended on the participation of these occurrences in some of the simpler ratios between integer numbers. Thus he obtained a reason why there should be an approximation of sharp-cut differences between kinds of molecules, and why there should be sharp-cut relations of harmony standing out amid dissonance" (pp. 94-95).

86. The comments, which I will make in the rest of this section, will be limited to the contrast between Whitehead's views of the Cosmos and its Creator and the traditional Biblical stories of creation. We will leave out of consideration the other two great mysteries of Christian religion, the incarnation of the Son of God and the resurrection of the human body. For Whitehead, the Platonist, does not write, and would probably be ashamed to write, about these things. In this sense, he is different from the traditional Christian Platonist, represented by Augustine, regarding shame.

87. For a thorough discussion of Whitehead's conception of God and God's role in his metaphysics, see the excellent study by Ivor Leclerc, *Whitehead's Metaphysics: An Introductory Exposition* (Bloomington, 1975), especially Chapter 4.

88. At this point Whitehead quotes the familiar passage from Aristotle's *Metaphysics* 1072a 23-32, which describes the First Unmoved Mover (Aristotle's Supreme God) as an

"object of desire." Then, he proceeds to draw the similarities and differences of the two philosophical conceptions. There is no favorite reference to the "creation story" of *Genesis* in his book.

89. Some of us may think otherwise and may beg to differ on this essential point even with Whitehead who, in so many other ways, is a kinder spirit. This needs further elaboration and will become the theme of a work in progress with the tentative title, *The Passion of Hellenic Philosophy in Europe.*

90. More on this point in the last essay, "The Character of Hellenic Philosophy."

91. The fact that the Ottoman Islam failed to imitate the Arabs, the Byzantines, and the Europeans in this regard, is an historical tragic error from which the Turks have suffered in the past and will continue to suffer in their aspirations of becoming accepted by the Europeans. But they can take prudent measures to put an end to the traditional and deplorable mistrust of Hellenic philosophy. The project "Philosophy at Assos" is a hopeful sign in this regard.

92. See also on this the last essay of the collection.

93. In this connection, one is compelled to think that the failure of the socialist experiment of Marxist atheism in Eastern Europe will inevitably lead to the revival of fanatical Islamic and Christian monotheism. This, in conjunction with nationalism, can lead mankind back to the Dark ages again, unless the precious lessons of religious tolerance and diversity, as expressed by Hellenic polytheism and Platonic philosophy, are absorbed by students in the post-Cold War and post-modern world in transition.

94. *Phaedrus*, 279b. The Socratic prayer reads: "Dear Pan, and all the other gods who dwell in this place, grant that I may become beautiful within, and that the external goods which I possess may not conflict with the spirit within." (Given in a free translation.)

Chapter 3

Aristotle and Western Rationality

Introduction

The history of Ancient Hellenic philosophy is like the Hellenic pantheon. The names of Hellenic Gods have been replaced now by the names of Hellenic philosophers: Thales and Anaximander, Heraclitus and Anaxagoras, Parmenides and Empedocles, Xenophanes and Xenocrates, Pythagoras and Socrates, Plato and Aristotle, Zeno and Pyrrho, Epicurus and Epictetus, Aristippus and Antisthenes, Democritus and Theothrastus, Plotinus and Porphyry, Plutarch and Proclus. Of the twelve pairs, Plato and Aristotle is the most famous and influential pair. These two great philosophers respectively represent the loftiest spirit and the sharpest mind produced by a millennium of continuous philosophic activity in the extended lands of Hellas.[1]

There are, of course, historians of philosophy who emphasize the similarities between the two philosophers and, following A.N. Whitehead's characterization of the history of Western philosophy as nothing but "a series of footnotes to Plato," see Aristotle's philosophical writings as the first and probably the best footnotes.[2] On the other hand, those who want to stress the points on which, in their view, the two philosophers differ, face the question of how to evaluate the respective merit of Plato and Aristotle. For the latter group, the question may take any of the following forms of false, for the former group, dilemma: Of the two, which is better, the Platonic or the Aristotelian philosophy? What is metaphysically preferable, Plato's idealism or Aristotle's ousiological realism? Which is preferable in epistemic terms, Plato's mathematical rationalism and the deductive method, or Aristotle's empirical inquiry and the inductive method? Which is politically more promising, the political utopia of Plato or the pragmatic reforms suggested by Aristotle?[3]

In the interval of time separating us from the beginning of such questioning in late antiquity, the fortunes of Aristotelian philosophy, on the balance of the West's theocratic appraisal, have changed several times. At times, especially in the Middle Ages, the authority of Aristotle was held high, since he was perceived and praised as *the Philosopher* by Christian and Moslem theologians and "philosophers," typified by Thomas Aquinas and Averroes respectively. For reasons which were not simply or strictly philosophical, the followers of the two dogmatically apocalyptic, monotheistic and, therefore, naturally intolerant religions, thought that Aristotle had providentially provided the world with a complete philosophical system, ready for good religious service.[4] Thus, their theologians dogmatically claimed that *the Philosopher* had established by logic and pure reason the same "truths" which God, in His mercy for sinful mankind, had later fully revealed in divinely inspired books, the Bible or the Koran.[5]

At other times, especially during the Platonic renaissance of the fifteenth century and during the "scientific revolution" of the seventeenth century, Aristotle was anathematized by many and was apparently unjustly held responsible for Medieval Scholasticism and the concomitant scientific stagnation of the previous many centuries of Dark Ages. As a matter of fact, Europe had witnessed regression in science and philosophy, especially in *philosophia naturalis*, for more than a millennium, but Aristotle was hardly to be blamed for that misfortune.[6]

In more recent times, the name of Aristotle has been used in order to give a philosophical facade and to provide some kind of authoritative justification for what has been called a European "cultural myth." This myth incorporates "The idea that the culture of the West is distinguished from all other cultures in being rational."[7] It is also alleged that the deep roots of this "cultural myth" go back to Aristotle. So, he is connected to what is perceived by non-European scholars as two European vices, that is, *ratio* (or the calculating human reason, narrowly defined as a tool of the European will to unrestrained political power and profit); and *imperium* (again, in the sense of an imperialistic power of the colonialist type, as it developed in modern times).[8]

Assuming that this diagnosis is correct, it would seem to touch upon several culturally sensitive issues, which are in need of open discussion. For it charges, *inter alia*, that Aristotle's philosophy has been a divisive rather than a unifying force in modern history, by its alleged close connection to "Western rationality;" and it also questions the European claim to cultural superiority, which is allegedly based on reason and Aristotelian "rationality."[9]

For these reasons, and in order to make Aristotle's philosophy better understood, I would like to provide a brief but accurate account of the concepts of *logos*, (discursive reason) and *nous* (intuitive mind), and their respective functions in his method of dialectic. Dialectic was used in all the major works of the *corpus Aristotelicum*, in the philosopher's great effort to noetically grasp and philosophically explain the place of man in the cosmic order of things, and his search for *eudaimonia* or "wellbeing".

Since Aristotle's conception of human nature and its potential for virtuous activity, whether at the ethical and political or at the intellectual levels of excellence, has deeper roots in his ontology and ousiology, such a synoptic account will be useful. For it will provide an appropriate context for the correct evaluation of the ethical and political views of the Hellenic philosopher. Thus it will become clear that he is misunderstood by scholars in the West and in the East for different historical reasons. These will be elucidated as we proceed further into the discussion of our theme in these essays.[10]

The Scope of this Study

Specifically, by providing a new interpretation of the Aristotelian conception of man as rational and, more importantly, as noetic being, I shall attempt to show that Aristotle was a genuinely Hellenic and Platonic philosopher, that is, something more than a mere representative of European and "Western rationality."[11] Accordingly, in reading his various works, we should keep in mind that the basic concepts of logic, ontology, psychology, ethics, politics, and all areas of human experience, are expressed in words which are, as Aristotle often emphasized, *pollachos legomena* (that is, ambiguous and poly-semantic terms with more than one meaning). Such a reading will also provide us with the key to understanding Aristotle's philosophy correctly and evaluating it perhaps more judiciously. For his views on God and man, nature and *polis*, poetic and noetic activity, ethics and politics, personal virtues and the common good, domestic relations and political associations are, for him, all ontologically connected as parts of an organic whole held together by a kind of philosophic attraction and sympathy. This whole complex can be methodically explored with the effective method of dialectic as developed by the Platonic Socrates and perfected by Aristotle, *the Philosopher*.[12]

For Aristotle, and other Platonic philosophers, a search into any of the above mentioned subjects will inevitably lead to all the rest with which it is ontologically and methodologically connected. For instance, determining the ultimate ethical/political *telos* (that is, the end, aim, goal or good) of man understood as a political animal and citizen of a Hellenic *polis*, would call for an inquiry into the nature of man *qua* man (the what-it-is-to-be-human). This will lead to psychology, to ontology, to cosmology, to teleology and, ultimately, to natural theology. For Aristotle, "the good of man" is identified with the wellbeing of each citizen and all the citizens who, collectively, make up the political community of a free Hellenic *polis*, the classical city-state.[13]

Consequently, as Aristotle envisioned it, the organization of the Hellenic *polis* as a whole should make it possible for each and all of its citizens to actualize their potential as human beings naturally endowed with certain physical, psychic, logical, and noetic capacities. In this way, the naturally and culturally best among them would be able to rise to perfection.[14] This road, as is dialectically mapped by Aristotle, leads to the summit of human perfection and enlightenment. It is to be followed primarily by the genuine philosopher, the ideal citizen of a Hellenic *polis*, as he heroically traverses the ontological distance separating the man-goat (or satyr of Hellenic mythology and drama) from the man-god (or sage of Platonic philosophy).[15]

It will become clear, in the light of my advanced interpretation, that the Platonic Aristotle, like the Platonic Socrates[16] and like Plotinus later on, had a high opinion of the power of philosophy to perfect the human being. He was convinced that (working slowly upon the soul and mind of the ascending philosopher, who has climbed step by step the *scala amoris*), the true love of wisdom will bring in contact the human and the Divine. What is divine in us, the *nous* (the intuitive mind, the noetic light shining in the human *micro-cosmos*), and the *Nous* (the Intellect of the *macro-cosmos*), are of the same essence.[17] At such privileged moments of noetic contact and enlightenment, it would appear that the energized human intellect acquires both self-knowledge and knowledge of "the Other," the divine Noetic Being. Thus, man becomes beloved to the Supreme God,[18] the eternally active Intellect, which moves the cosmos by the irresistible power of its erotic attraction, as if in a rhythmic dance orderly and eternal.[19]

In this way, a kind of philosophic *apotheosis* seems to take place at the end of the long road of Peripatetic dialectic. At this point, *logos* (discursive reason) must yield to intuitive and superior power of energized human intellect (*nous*). There, the human being, conceived here as a living, sensible, reasonable, noetic, communal, political, poetic, and potentially divine being, becomes divine actually, suddenly, and even self-knowingly. Thus, philosophically perfected, the ideal citizen of the Hellenic *polis* becomes fully enlightened.[20] That is to say, the actualized and active human intellect suddenly grasps, as in a flash of self-awareness, the truth that in its very nature the human being is *homoousion*, that is, of the same essence or *ousia*, as Divine Intellect.

Following along the path suggested by Aristotelian dialectic, we can then see that the eternally energized Divine Intellect and the dialectically perfected (and, thus, noetically transformed) mind of the true philosopher are identified as being essentially the same. So, at the end, they are recognized as closely related beings, as two beloved friends.[21] This is the road to enlightenment, which my Platonic interpretation of Aristotle's philosophy will reveal fully in what follows. It may be called properly the Aristotelian *via dialectica*.[22]

In this new light, Aristotle's philosophy and the Platonic tradition to which it belongs, would appear to be closer to Eastern ways of thinking (especially the Indian), than to the narrowly defined "Western rationality." By this expression is usually meant the kind of calculative and manipulative *ratio*, which is in the service of *utilitas*. For it serves utilitarian, technological, and ideological goals, which characterize much of modern and post-modern philosophy in the West under various masks, such as: British "logical analysis," Baconian "scientific method," and Marxist "scientific socialism."[23]

In the same light, as a genuine Hellenic and Platonic philosopher, Aristotle will appear to be something very different, better and nobler, than the caricature of a "servant philosopher," into which he has been compressed in the West. For he has been presented alternatively but equally narrowly, either as the scholastic logician and rationalist thinker in service of dogmatic medieval theology, or as the empirical and analytic thinker in the service of technocratic modern science.[24]

This double portrait of Aristotle, whether Medieval or Modern European, clearly does not resemble the historical Hellenic philosopher in his dialectic fullness. For his philosophic mind wanted to accomplish all of the following diverse tasks: see noetically the entire *kosmos*; understand the form and the function of every kind of substantive being; grasp the *telos* of man as citizen of the Hellenic *polis* and his multiple creations; admire the eternal beauty of the Cosmos; and find in it the proper place for God (understood as the Cosmic Intellect) and man's noetic self. For this human noetic self or *nous* was seen as a microcosmic god in the making, being potentially present in the well-endowed human soul. Clearly, then, the Western picture of *the Philosopher* does not fit the acuity of Aristotle's dialectic in all its flexibility and complexity as displayed in his texts.[25]

It is this "other side" of Aristotle's Platonic philosophy that my thesis will attempt to bring to light and to revive because it is needed now, and will be needed even more in the near future than ever before. For, at the present, the global failure of the Marxist "scientific socialism," in the communistic *praxis* of the so-called "dictatorship of the proletariat" in its Leninist and Maoist versions, is an historical fact. With its collapse and as the dreadful divisions of mankind (along the familiar lines of tribal nationalism, monotheistic intolerance, and sectarian fanaticism) begin to re-surface globally,[26] the need to revive the lost spirit of Hellenic philosophy becomes apparent. The spirit of religious tolerance, philosophic pluralism, and Hellenic humanism is needed now and its need is felt deeply by sensitive souls and far-seeing minds.[27]

Let this suffice, as an introduction. It is now time to turn to Aristotle and the available textual evidence, which will help us substantiate this challenging thesis as outlined above.

Aristotle's Move from *Logos* to *Nous*

For anyone wishing to discover the roots of "rationality," as it is understood in the West, Aristotle would seem a reasonable *terminus a quo*. For, as we saw in the first two essays, European historians of philosophy believe that Hellenic philosophy, whose characteristic trait is assumed by them to have been the *logos* in the sense of discursive reasoning, reached its climax in the philosophies of Plato and Aristotle. They were closely related as teacher and student.[28] Besides, whatever little the Medieval Western World knew about Ancient Hellenic philosophy was related to parts of Aristotle's logic, the famous *Organon*.[29]

For such an inquirer, therefore, and for these reasons, the following questions are of special interest: Was Aristotle the "first cause" of the rising of rationalistic and technocratic science in Europe in the last few centuries, as has been alleged? Does "Western rationality," in the above-specified sense, really have its beginnings in Aristotle's philosophy? Can Aristotle's philosophy without distortion, and his dialectic method without misapplication, provide justification to claims of cultural superiority and hegemony that have been advanced by the European powers in order to justify their colonial exploitation of Africa, America, and Asia? Last, what do the terms "reason" and "rationalism" mean, and is Aristotle the root of "Western rationality?"[30]

The answer to these complex questions cannot be simple. It may be affirmative or negative depending on the sense which is attached to the word *ratio*, which was itself a clumsy attempt to render into Latin the poly-semantic Hellenic word *logos*. In the language and literature of Ancient Hellas, the word *logos* has as many meanings and shades of meanings, as Proteus has faces, forms, and shapes. Basically, it means meaningful or significant speech, that is, the richness of human (preferably Hellenic) language and the human mind with all its concepts, thoughts, feelings, and visions, which can be symbolically expressed orally or in writing by the power of this specifically human tool, the human *logos*.[31] In this broad sense, not only great Hellenic philosophers, but every human being, who is unimpaired and prepared to make careful and meaningful use of the innate *logos*, is naturally a *logical* and *rational* being.

As an epistemic concept, employed widely in modern theories of knowledge and epistemology and extensively discussed in the histories of "Western philosophy," rationalism is contrasted to empiricism and to intuitionism. Its method is called deductive because it supposedly moves from general, self-evident, and axiomatic principles to implications, which follow necessarily from such principles, if and when they are combined in proper syllogistic forms, according to specific logical rules of inference. In this sense, Pythagoras, Descartes, and Russell, for example, who were mathematicians and philosophers, are considered as "rationalists." They were willing to follow the hypothetical and deductive method of reasoning as the only correct way of obtaining reliable scientific knowledge. As pure rationalists, they did not trust the evidence provided by sense experience. In this respect, they differed radically from the empiricist philosophers, like Democritus, Epicurus, and Hobbes, for example. For the latter, the senses are the only source of trustworthy information about the real world which, for them, was identified with the sensible world.

Where, then, did Aristotle stand on this epistemological division? Was he a rationalist and "the root" of Western rationality, as some scholars and historians of philosophy have maintained? Or was he to be found in the opposite camp of the empiricists, where Kant, among others, had placed him?[32] It would be closer to truth to say that he was both an empiricist and a rationalist, because he was a dialectician with common sense. His common sense and his open mind allowed Aristotle to see that each side was correct in some specified sense, but neither had the whole truth. On this matter, as in many others, Aristotle was the antithesis of what is called a "dogmatist."[33]

Being critical of the dialectical deficiencies of the various previous theories of knowledge, Aristotle was able to simultaneously praise the senses and criticize empiricism.[34] He was also able to define syllogism and the deductive method used in mathematics but, at the same time, admit that induction and intuition played an important role in ascertaining the first principles and the major premises of valid deductions.[35] Above all, he was able to conceive of truth as being neither revealed dogma nor private property of any human being regardless of his philosophical accomplishments. On the contrary, for the open-minded Hellenic philosopher, the truth was a "common property" belonging to mankind as a whole. It was a kind of "commonwealth," to which all persons more or less contribute, even when they are in error, since others may learn how to avoid such errors and find truth.[36] The following statement is characteristic of this and reveals Aristotle's mind and method of inquiry:

> Now our treatment of this science [Ethics] will be adequate, if it achieves that amount of precision, which belongs to its subject matter. The same exactness must not be expected in all departments of philosophy alike, anymore than in all the products of the arts and crafts ... For it is the mark of an educated mind to expect that amount of exactness in each kind which the nature of the particular subject admits. It is equally unreasonable to accept merely probable conclusions from a mathematician and to demand strict demonstration from an orator.[37]

There is no need to add more passages like the above in order to make the point that dialectical flexibility, sharpness of questioning, and moderation of expression are characteristic of Aristotle's method.[38] He had learned from his teacher Plato and from Socrates the importance of dividing and defining, of clarifying and qualifying, of distinguishing and analyzing the terms involved in a given question or a proposed problem. With unsurpassed confidence and acuteness, he practiced the method of dialectic to the best of his ability in the service of truth and humanity. As a critical philosopher, Aristotle wanted to ascertain the facts in each case and "to save the phenomena." He also wanted to review "the received proverbial wisdom" of the many and the opinions of the few "wise men" and to suggest solutions, which might pass the test of time and, more importantly, the test of competent criticism and self-criticism in seeking consistently "the truth."[39]

The flexibility of Aristotle's dialectic method, which can embrace reasonable discussions of questions related to the foundations of the practical (for example, Ethics and Politics) and the theoretical sciences (for example, Physics and Metaphysics), is impressive. His honest search for human truth by human means, and the sharpness and openness of his mind are such that they have made Aristotle one of the best representatives of Hellenic philosophy. Carefully following the flexible, though slippery, path of dialectic, he succeeded in embracing the claims of empiricism and rationalism, as well as the claims of the intuitive and noetic vision (*noesis*).

Aristotle was able to accomplish this task as a philosopher because he did not limit human experience to sensations and sense data, as modern empiricists have done; nor to cogitation and rationalization, as modern rationalists did. For him, besides the basic realm of *aisthesis* (sense perception) and the realm of practical human *logos* (discursive reasoning, rational discourse, meaningful speech), there is the realm of divine *nous* (intuitive, intellective, immediate grasp of first and true principles; non-discursive reason, intellect, intelligence). The door to this realm opens, at certain privileged moments, to dedicated Hellenic lovers of wisdom, who may follow the long road of Aristotelian dialectic and inquiry to the very end.[40]

More significantly, for Aristotle as for fellow Platonists, the Hellenic philosopher considered as an intellect, which is engaged in theorizing about the cosmos and the nature of things, was not alone in this noble pursuit.[41] For them, the philosophically conceived cosmos was orderly, beautiful, and intelligently governed at the highest level by the Divine *Nous* (the eternally energizing and active Intellect, or Aristotelian God). For these philosophers, there was a plurality of other and lesser intellects too, including the one in us, in the human soul, the *nous*.[42]

Consequently Aristotle was simultaneously the philosopher who invented the syllogism, systematized logic for the Hellenes and, perhaps more than any other Hellenic philosopher, practiced and perfected the Socratic method of dialectic. Yet the same man did not hesitate to describe the cosmic God, the highest Intellect, in poetic language which would have pleased even a Hellenic poet, like Aeschylus or Pindar.

For Aristotle's God is noetically conceived as the inexhaustible source of pure noetic energy, which erotically attracts and harmoniously moves everything in the cosmos, as we will see in the next section. It is the Great Beauty, with which the entire cosmos seems to be in love. It is the Great Light and cause of enlightenment for the mind of the true philosopher in the triple Socratic manifestation. The first is identified as lover of Hellenic *mousike*,[43] that is, the practitioner of the art of poetic rhythm, harmonious sound, and audibly appreciated beauty. The second is identified as lover of Hellenic *eidetike*, that is, the practitioner of the art of visible patterns, symmetrical forms, and optically appreciated beauty. The third is identified as lover of Hellenic *dialektike*, that is, the practitioner of the art of logic, ordered form, principled life, rational discourse, intuitive grasp of principles, and noetically appreciated truth.[44]

Aristotle on Divine and Human Beings

The above perception and interpretation of Aristotle certainly differs from that of the scientific thinker and logician, with whom the Western world is accustomed. For it is framed around the Hellenic word *nous* (mind) which is not easy to translate into English.[45] Besides, the noetic affinity and friendship which exist naturally between (the philosophically conceived Aristotelian) God and the perfected human being (that is, the Hellenic philosopher who is engaged in noetic vision and understanding), are expressed by him in a strange language. It is more poetic, noematic, and enigmatic, than the logical discursive reasoning (*logos*), with which he is identified in Europe.[46]

I would like, therefore, to allow Aristotle to speak on behalf of his noetic philosophy and in support of my unorthodox thesis. He will provide us with sufficient textual evidence for the consideration and enlightenment of any nonprejudiced person regarding this Platonic aspect of Aristotle's philosophy and its potential political implications for the following triangle of relations: West/Hellas, Hellas/East, and East/West. Consider, therefore, the following three paradigmatic cases of Aristotelian texts, which point the way to Hellenic philosophic enlightenment.

A. *Ousiological Questions Lead Aristotle to Cosmic God*

We have said in the *Ethics* what the difference is between art and science and the other kindred faculties; but the point of our present discussion is this, that all men suppose what is called Wisdom to deal with the first causes and the principles of things; so that, as has been said before, the man of experience is thought to be wiser than the possessor of any sense-perception whatever, the artist wiser than the man of experience, the master-worker than the mechanic, and the theoretical kinds of knowledge to be more of the nature of Wisdom than the productive. Clearly then Wisdom is knowledge about certain principles and causes. Since we are seeking this knowledge, we must inquire of what kind are the causes and the principles, the knowledge of which is Wisdom ...[47] The subject of our inquiry is substance;[48] for the principles and the causes we are seeking are those of substances. For if the universe is of the nature of a whole, substance is its first part; and if it coheres merely by virtue of serial succession, on this view also substance is first, and is succeeded by quality, and then by quantity ... There are three kinds of substance—one that is sensible (of which one subdivision is eternal and another is perishable; the latter is recognized by all men, and includes for example, plants and animals), of which we must grasp the elements, whether one or many; and another that is immovable ... On such a principle, then, depend the heavens and the world of nature. And it is a life such as the best which we enjoy, and enjoy for a short time (for it is ever in this state, which we cannot be), since its activity is also pleasure. And thinking in itself deals with that which is best in it-self, and which is thinking in the fullest sense. And thought thinks on itself because it shares the nature of the object of thought; for it becomes an object of thought in coming into contact with, and thinking, its object, so that thought and object of thought are the same ... If, then, God is always in that good state in which we sometimes are, this compels our wonder; and if in a better, this compels it yet more. And God is in a better state. And life also belongs to God; for the actuality of thought is life, and God is that actuality; and God's self-dependent actuality is life most good and eternal. We say therefore that God is a living being, eternal, most good, so that life and duration continuous and eternal belong to God; for this is God.[49]

B. *Psychological Questions lead Aristotle to God Within*

Holding as we do that, while knowledge of any kind is a thing to be honored and prized, one kind of it may, either by reason of its greater exactness or of a higher dignity and greater wonderfulness in its objects, be more honorable and precious than another, on both accounts we should naturally be led to place in the front rank the study of the soul. The knowledge of the soul admittedly contributes greatly to advance of truth in general, and, above all, to our understanding of nature, for the soul is in some sense the principle of animal life. Our aim is to grasp and understand, first its essential nature, and secondly its properties ...[50] Hence the soul must be a substance in the sense of the form of a natural body having life potentially within it ... What has soul in it differs from what has not, in that the former displays life. Now this word has more than one sense, and provided that any one alone is found in a thing we say that thing is living. Living, that is, may mean thinking or perception or local movement and rest, or movement in the sense of nutrition, decay and growth. Hence we think of plants also as living [besides animals and human beings]... Certain kinds of animals possess in addition the power of locomotion, and still another order of animate beings, that is, man and possibly another order like man or superior to him, the power of thinking, that is, mind [*nous*] ... Thinking, both speculative and practical, is regarded as akin to a form of perceiving; for in the one as well as the other the soul discriminates and is cognizant of something, which is. Indeed the ancients go so far as to identify thinking and perceiving ... Thus that in the soul, which is called mind (by mind I mean that whereby the soul thinks and judges) is, before it thinks, not actually any real thing. For this reason it cannot reasonably be regarded as blended with the body ... And in fact mind as we have described it is what it is by virtue of becoming all things, while there is another which is what it is by virtue of making all things: this is a sort of positive state of light; for in a sense light makes potential colors into actual colors. Mind in this sense of it is separable, impassible, unmixed, since it is in its essential nature activity (for always the active is superior to passive factor, the originating of force to the matter which it forms). Actual knowledge is identical with its object: in the individual, potential knowledge is in time prior to actual knowledge, but in the universe as a whole it is not prior even in time. Mind is not at one time knowing and at another not. When mind is set free from its present conditions it appears as just what it is and nothing more: this alone is immortal and eternal, and without it nothing thinks.[51]

C. *Ethical Questions Bring Together the Two Divinities*

Every art and every inquiry, and similarly every action and pursuit, is thought to aim at some good; and for this reason the good has rightly been defined to be that at which all things aim. But a certain difference is found among ends ...[52] Now, since politics uses the rest of the sciences, and since, again, it legislates as to what we are to abstain from, the end of this science must include those of the others, so that this end must be the good for man ... But if happiness consists in activity in accordance with virtue, it is reasonable that it should be activity in accordance with the highest virtue; and this will be the virtue of the best part of us. Whether then this be the intellect [*nous*], or whatever else it be that is thought to rule and lead us by nature, and to have cognizance of what is noble and divine, either as being itself actually divine, or as being relatively the divine part of us, it is the activity of this part of us in accordance with the virtue proper to it that will constitute perfect happiness; and it has been stated already that this activity is the activity of contemplation ... Such a life as this however will be higher than the human level: not in virtue of his humanity will a man achieve it, but in virtue of something within him that is divine; and by as much as this something is superior to his composite nature, by so much is its activity superior to the exercise of the other forms of virtue. If then the intellect [*nous*] is something divine in comparison with man, so is the life of the intellect divine in comparison with human life. Nor ought we to obey those who enjoin that a man should have man's thoughts and a mortal the thoughts of mortality, but we ought so far as possible to achieve immortality, and do all that man may to live in accordance with the highest thing in him; for though this be small in bulk, in power and in value it far surpasses all the rest. It may even be held that this is the true self of each, inasmuch as it is the dominant and best part; and therefore it would be a strange thing if a man should choose to live not his own life but the life of other than himself. Moreover what was said before will apply here also: that which is best and most pleasant for each creature is that which is proper to the nature of each; accordingly the life of the intellect is the best and the pleasantest life for man, inasmuch as the intellect more than anything else is man; therefore this life will be the happiest.[53]

The above and similar passages of the Aristotelian corpus, if read in the context of his philosophy as a whole and in its relation to other Hellenic philosophies of nature and *polis*, provide a clear picture of Aristotle's conception of God and man, and their respective place in the cosmos. The kind of life of which man is optimally capable, as well as the communal and political arrangements, which would make possible the flourishing of such a life for the best qualified citizens, are recognized by Aristotle. They are not considered as the arbitrary recommendations or commandments of some divinely inspired and dogmatic prophet, but as the fulfillment of an entelechy, that is, as the *telos* (end), which is present in the human soul and human nature *qua* human.

For the same intelligent ordering principle, which pervades the entire cosmos, is also potentially present in the individual human soul. It can manifest itself in the rational structuring of various forms of natural and political associations, such as the family and the *polis*, as well as the perfected human life by *philosophia*. Accordingly, in order to understand Aristotle's *Politics* correctly, one should place it in the context of his *Metaphysics*, *De Anima*, and *Ethics*. I will try to do so, in a synoptic way, in the following section.[54]

Distinguishing Between *Ontology* and *Ousiology*

Aristotle's model of the cosmos is perhaps more complex than any of the other models, which were advanced by his predecessors from Parmenides to Plato. In fact, it is the antithesis of the Parmenidean absolutely immovable One Being. By Aristotle's time, the Parmenidean "theory of being" had been transformed by a series of revisions of the original formula either "It is" or "It is not." For

Parmenides the disjunction, "Being or non-Being," was an exclusive disjunction, for between the sphere of Being and the abyss of non-Being, nothing else could possibly be. Being was to be conceived and thought of as one whole, eternally immovable, and internally undifferentiated.[55] In the history of Hellenic philosophy, it was probably Anaxagoras who first set the two spheres apart, the "sphere of material being" apart from the sphere of pure *Nous*. Thus, matter and mind, that is, the material world and the noetic world, were distinguished. Like a powerful ruler, the Divine Mind or *Nous* ruled the material cosmos from afar.[56]

To simplify the process by which Plato attempted to correct and to complete the Parmenidean conception of cosmic Being, it may be said that in him we find each of the old divisions, Being and non-Being, but each of them is subdivided once again and made double. So we have two spheres of each, Being and non-Being. By mixing two of the divided spheres (one sphere of Being and one of non-Being) Plato was able to create the sphere of Becoming. This is interposed between the sphere of pure Being (the noetic world of Forms or Ideas, the model or paradigm of the cosmos) and the sphere of non-Being (formless matter). The sphere of Becoming, which is the world of sense experience, the copy, image, or icon, is thus the result of the mixing of certain images of the Platonic Ideas or Forms with that part of non-Being, which receives them, the Receptacle. The multiplicity of perceptible entities, which populate the visible cosmos[57] and the cosmos itself, were brought into being by the Platonic Demiurge.[58]

With this background in mind, we can see that Aristotle's conception of the cosmos differs significantly from those of his predecessors, although he borrows from them and builds upon their foundations. In a sense, the Aristotelian cosmos is like the Parmenidean sphere, since it is one, non-generated, indestructible, and eternal; but it is movable and ultimately moved by the Unmoved Mover (Divine Intellect). Thus, it is dynamically or organically unified whole, whose parts are functionally differentiated, but interactive and even partially interchangeable.

This conception avoids the fragmentary randomness of the Democretian model of cosmos, as well as the artificiality of the Platonic/Pythagorean model. Its orderliness is not explained in terms of chance (*tyche*) and necessity, as in the former; nor in terms of *techne* (art) and persuasion, as in the latter; but in terms of *physis* (nature), life, and *nous* (the active, intuitive, self-knowing intellect), as if it were a living being.[59]

However, the process by which Aristotle moved dialectically from *ontology* to *ousiology*, in his account of the cosmos, is rather complex and in need of further elaboration.[60] For, according to Aristotle, the Hellenic word for being (*to on* or *einai*) does not have only one sense; that is, it is not a mono-semantic word as it was for Parmenides. For it does not mean the "One-Being" in its uncompromising and aloof antithesis to non-Being. Rather it is predicated in many ways and, therefore, it has many different "categorical" meanings.[61] In Aristotle's view, it has as many meanings as there are kinds of things, which have categorically a claim to be, in some sense.

As a matter of fact, Aristotle specified as many senses of the word "being" as there are items enumerated in his tenfold list of categories.[62] The tenfold division of beings is simplified by radical reduction into a twofold division, substance and accidents (or properties). Under the latter are subsumed the kinds of beings, which belong to any of the other nine categories as determinations of substance or *ousia*. They are: being qualified (quality), being quantified (quantity), being related (relation), being in position, being in possession, being in place, being in time, being active and being passive. Aristotle has specified that the most important of the ten generic categories is the category of *ousia* (substance). On it all the other categories depend *ontologically*.[63]

So far so good, but for Aristotle the word *ousia* (substance), like the word *on/onta* (being/s), is also poly-semantic, that is, it can be predicated in many different ways, and by doing so it may refer to different entities. It may, for example, refer to the primary substances, the concrete individual entities, each of which is a composite of matter and form; or it may refer to secondary substances, that is, the species and the genera, which can be predicated of the respective primary substances "essentially."

Furthermore, even within the limited sphere of the individual primary substances, there are important subdivisions. In fact, it was the search for the most primary among the primary substances that led Aristotle to discover his God and the linkage between God and man *qua* man, that is, the human species in its essence or "essential being." In his view, the best specimen of man is the philosopher, that is, the man whose potential has been fully actualized by the acquisition and exercise of an excellent (that is, ethical, rational, and noetic) self. Thus traditional *ontologia*, the theory of being *qua* being and inquiry into the nature of reality, was transformed by Aristotle's dialectic into *ousiologia*, the theory of substance and inquiry into the nature of *ousia*.[64]

Accordingly, the Aristotelian cosmos is populated by a great number of primary substances (οὐσίαι), which are classified in terms of the following pairs of contraries: either perishable or imperishable, temporal or eternal, organic or non-organic, sensible or non-sensible, movable or immovable, mortal or immortal, and potential or actual.[65] To a concrete human being apply the first terms of each pair, the less valuable; to a divine intelligence apply the second and more valuable terms of each pair. God is thus conceived as a very special primary substance, unlike any other being, in that it is not composite, but simple. God is a living and eternally active Intellect (*Nous*), that eternally energizes other divine Intellects, and occasionally even the *nous* (intellect), which is potentially present in each human soul.[66]

According to Aristotle, therefore, the soul or *psyche* of man is a complex system of powers or faculties. These psychic powers range from nutritive and reproductive powers (which are actually shared by all living beings); to sensitive and kinetic powers (which are shared with other animal species); to logical powers (in the double sense of *logos*, as the capacity to reason and as articulate speech).

Best of all, though, are the intuitive or noetic powers of human soul, not only as a potential, but also as an actualized *nous* or intellect, which are shared with other divine intellects.[67]

By the stimulus of philosophy and the appropriate education (*paideia*), to be offered by the well-organized Hellenic city-state (*polis*) freely to its competent citizens in accordance with the principles of right reason (*orthos logos*), the human potential can be actualized and some human beings at least can flourish optimally. They can, thus, become enlightened personalities and god-like human beings, in so far as such optimal outcome is possible for the composite primary substance of human beings.[68]

Therefore, at the end of our analysis and by following the long and meandering road of Aristotle's dialectic, we have reached the place where the "end of man," understood as the ultimate ethical *telos* or goal, and the supreme human good are located. This is the well-ordered *polis*, as the result of the proper function of the difficult art of Hellenic politics, which Aristotle calls "the architectonic art."[69] The rest of our brief discussion will be devoted to this aspect of his philosophic theorizing.

Perfecting the Aristotelian Political Animal

The *raison d'etre* of the Hellenic *polis*, as Aristotle conceived of it, was the securing for all of its citizens the conditions not simply of life, but of "the good life," according to their respective merit. In this way, the optimal actualization of human natural and educational potential would be fully accomplished.[70] The citizens, who may entertain hopes of reaching such politically desirable peaks, would have to have extraordinary natural endowments, as well as an excellent or good *paideia* (education).[71]

An ideal citizen would have to be all of the following, in a complete course of life from childhood to maturity and to old age. First of all, he would have to be naturally well endowed with the necessary powers of the body, the soul and, especially, the mind. He would have to be educationally well trained, in music and gymnastics, acquiring a good physique, good habits, and the excellences of character and intellect. He would have to be personally well ordered, so that the soul would rule over the body wisely, and the rational part of the soul over the irrational part gently. The noetic part would enlighten the rational part of the soul, by providing the appropriate principles of thinking and acting virtuously. He would also have to be domestically well equipped with wife, children, servants, parents, and moderate property. Finally, he would have to be politically well organized with other friends and well disciplined, so that he can learn how to rule and be ruled with justice by his equals in turns.

At the end of his life, if all went well, he would have: (a) survived the just wars in defense of the *polis*; (b) seen his sons take his place in the hoplite ranks; (c) freed some of his domestic servants, if they could take care of themselves;[72] (d) dedicated himself (and perhaps his graciously aging wife) to the service of the many gods and goddesses of the city-state; and (e) occupied himself with philosophic *theoria* of the Supreme *Nous*, the magnificent cosmos, and the divine *nous* within the human soul.[73]

In this connection we may recall that, according to Aristotle, the nature of the ideal *polis* in the Hellenic sense of a city, which was also the center of a measurable state, is not artificial, conventional or simply man-made, as European political theorists have maintained following the "social contract" theory.[74] It is as natural as the union of male and female, the growth of the family tree, and the formation of a small village which, with the passage of time, may branch out and give birth to other small villages. When these villages of common ancestry would unite politically for better protection, exchange of goods, self-sufficiency, and the good life of virtue, a Hellenic *polis would* come "naturally," according to Aristotle, into being and so political life would begin.[75]

In his view, the defense, protection, and well-being of the naturally constituted political community necessitates the division of labor among males, in an analogous way as the survival and preservation of the human species has naturally necessitated the different roles of male and female, and those of father and mother.[76] Domestically, the wife was to play the role of "the queen" of the house. The man's main duty *qua* citizen was the politically assigned task of "protecting the family" as a whole and its property by the art of war, in times of war, and by the art of politics in times of peace.

These activities were to be undertaken in friendly co-operation with other citizens of equal political status as heads of families.[77] Since the art of war and the art of politics at that time were rather demanding, in terms of physical and mental powers, the males who could not measure up to prevailing standards were assigned the "servile role" of assisting in domestic production.[78]

The master/servant relation (as understood by Aristotle, and strange as it may sound to post-modern ears) was for the good of both parties involved. In this respect, it differed from the husband/wife and parent/child relations, which served exclusively the interests of the protected parties. Enslavement by force is to be condemned, in Aristotle's view, and so is "equality" among unequals. Equality among equals, that is, the citizens of a *polis*, and what he considered as "natural servitude," was approved.[79]

But it should be obvious that such thorny issues as natural slavery and political equality and inequality demand extensive treatment, which cannot be provided here. I shall attempt to offer only a few additional comments on some possible and reasonable contemporary objections regarding Aristotle's views on these sensitive issues.[80]

Possible Post-modern Objections to Aristotle

First Possible Objection. Aristotle's views on natural servitude and "slaves by nature" are bound to be offensive to sensitive contemporary ears as they were to some people in his time. They had declared that by nature all men are born free and that slavery, without exception or excuse, is by convention and against nature. Others at that time had tried to justify slavery as an outcome of war, in which case the vanquished lost unfortunately everything including their precious freedom.[81]

To take either side of this dichotomy and to stay with it without raising questions or asking for qualifications would have been uncharacteristic of Aristotle's mind. So, by following his standard method of dialectic and by applying it to the question of slavery, he searched for a possible "mean" between the two stated extreme positions. Aristotle was able to reject the universal, at that time, custom of enslavement of the prisoners of war, and the custom of hunting and selling for profit men, who were born free and capable of taking care of themselves.[82]

However, given the natural growth of the *polis* out of the villages and the families; and the necessity of the division of labor in any community working together towards common goals, Aristotle concluded that some defective men would have to depend on other men for their survival. For the survival of a free community was dependent on the ability of its citizens to defend its freedom, but the natural endowment of some were not up to the demands of martial and political arts. These men, then, as naturally incompetent, would be better off if they were to serve the domestic needs of the warrior-citizens who would, thus, have more needed leisurely time to fully dedicate themselves to the service of the common good of the city-state as a whole.[83]

Furthermore, in a serious sense, according to the Aristotelian understanding of human nature and political life, no man is totally free, independent and self-sufficient, unless he turns into a god or a wild beast.[84] Within the family, naturally, children are dependent on the parents, who serve their needs with dedication. The servants may obey the orders of their master or mistress but, in turn, they may also control other servants for more efficient production. The citizen-warrior who, as head of his family, may play the role of ruling over his servants despotically, over his wife gentlemanly, and over his children royally, must learn to obey too. The officer in the battlefield, the magistrates in the assembly of the people, and practical reason and the laws of a *polis* had to be obeyed by all citizens. In this sense, master and servant become relative terms within the political community, whose common good was to be served well by a just organization of all of its component parts.[85]

Second Possible Objection. Aristotle's preference for hierarchical social/political structures, which are apparently dominated by males in the roles of fathers, warriors, and civil-office holders, is again bound to be objectionable today when the women's movement and other equal rights movements are in fashion. These movements and their respective political claims are the inevitable outcome, Aristotle would say, of the modern tendency to make the individual, as opposed to the family, the fundamental unit of the state and the consequent political organization of contemporary states.[86]

On the contrary, Aristotle's organic conception of the *polis*, allowed each of its citizen to represent not just himself and his interests as an individual citizen in the assembly of the citizens, who were equal *qua* citizens in democratic states and had equal political rights. Rather he represented the common interest of the extended family, whose legal head he was and was recognized as such. The family unit, we may recall, ordinarily would include wife, children, elderly parents, servants, and other relatives, whose natural incapacity had reduced them to the status of "servitude."[87]

Aristotle, of course, was well aware of the ambiguities and the controversies surrounding the demand for political equality. Now, equality among equals in certain respects is one thing, but equality among naturally and educationally unequal men is quite a different matter. Aristotle dialectically found fault with both of the following claims: the Democratic claim that citizens must be equal in every respect, since they are equal in terms of political freedom as citizens; and the Oligarchic claim that their share in political power should be unequal because their property holdings are not equal.[88] Aristotle thought, correctly it would seem, that neither wealth nor high birth, but Hellenic *arete* (that is, ethical and intellectual excellence and capability of contributing to the common good more than the other citizens) should be the only criterion for fair distribution of political offices and honors to meritorious, but otherwise equal, citizens.

The ability to serve the commonwealth well, for Aristotle, should count more than other considerations. For even if all citizens are born equal as human beings, the fact remains that their capacity for virtuous activity is differentiated not only culturally, but also naturally, as is their physical capacity to run the marathon and their intellectual competence to solve mathematical equations. In other words, Aristotle was in favor of the rule of the best, in terms of natural endowment, as well as educational and cultural achievement among the politically equal citizens of a democratic *polis.* This is the true etymological meaning of that meaningful and beautiful Hellenic word *aristokratia.*[89]

Third Possible Objection. Aristotle's division of men into Hellenes and Barbarians is also bound to be objectionable these days when the "barbarians," as the Hellenic and philosophic poet Cavafy has said, are hard to come by, or even to be found in the horizon, much to the despair of the "decadent" European man.[90]

Several things should be clarified in this connection. To begin with, every group of men, which managed to acquire historically recorded civilized life, like the Egyptians, the Chinese, the Hebrews, the Indians, and many other nations, thought of themselves, and still think of themselves, as somehow superior to other outsiders. The Ancient Hellenes were no exception to this "politically incorrect," but general and ancient rule.

According to Herodotus' report, the Hellenes probably learned this distinction, as so many other things, from the Egyptians.[91] At any rate, in Aristotle's time, because of the political struggle of the Hellenes against the Persians, the latter were invariably identified as "barbarians" in comparison with the Egyptians, whom they had enslaved, while the Hellenes encouraged them in their resistance to the Persian Despotism. Also, to Hellenic eyes the Persian people, which had put up with such Despotism for so long and the Asiatic peoples who did not resist the Persian tyranny as vigorously as the Egyptians and the Hellenes, looked like human beings, who were born to be slaves.[92]

Consequently, Aristotle thought that these people would be better off if they were to serve the well educated citizens of an ideally organized Hellenic city-state, where the hope for freedom was always present to slaves, especially the domestic servants, of any nationality who had proved that they were slaves by misfortune rather than by nature. To Aristotle, as a philosopher, the world as a whole would probably be a better place to live, if it were to be ruled by gentle, intelligent, and sensitive Hellenic lovers of wisdom rather than by some boorish and wild barbarians. By reason of possession of the above noble qualities, it seemed reasonable to Aristotle that such civilized rulers would be guided by proper *paideia* to adopt sooner or later the Hellenic ethical ideal of moderation, moving away from the double vice of excess.[93]

Fourth Possible Objection. The fact that in Aristotle's *polis*, even under ideal conditions, few persons will be able to reach the highest point of virtuous activity and intellectual development, will also be found objectionable these days. For contemporary politics seems to be more attuned to the feelings and the flattery of the masses than it was at that time, the Golden Age of Hellas. How, then, are the many to be saved? Is there any "immortality" for them? There are no simple answers to such difficult questions. Like the wise Platonic Socrates, in all probability Aristotle would say that immortality in some sense is open to all human beings, as well as other living beings, by the natural process of reproduction.

In some other loftier sense immortality is a privilege of the gods, who enjoy eternally a pure noetic life, and of very few mortals who have succeeded in making themselves god-like. This they may have achieved at the end of a life spent in virtuous activity and service to their political community and in search for the unclouded truth. Their good deeds and their honors will survive their death; and, if the gods would welcome any mortals to their blessed company, the perfected philosophers would have a better chance than any other mortal beings.[94] This would seem fair enough.

But the concern with the "after life" may be beside the point. For Aristotle was politically interested in this life, not in the next, for the simple reason that in "the next life," the meaning of "life" would change radically and, among other things, there will not be any need for politics.[95] Even so, for Aristotle the life of virtue, here and now, is worth living for the sake of that which is best in us and divine, that is, *nous*. As the body is more valuable than the cloak, so is the soul more valuable than the body; and as the thinking and ruling part of the soul is more valuable than the irrational and obedient part, so is the noetic and theoretic life more valuable than the political life.[96]

Hence, as far as it is possible, as many people as possible should strive for this kind of life because it is the best for the citizens. For Aristotle, the citizen of the Hellenic *polis* is potentially a divine being. He is really the noetic mind or *nous*. If anything, this is the divine presence in every human being harboring a precious human *psyche*.[97] I do not think that there can be many people who would honestly object to such a humanistic and noble ideal as this one, to which Aristotle's dialectic method has given the clearest possible Hellenic articulation. Let this then suffice.

Fifth Possible Objection. Aristotle's identification of the human *telos* with the activity of ethically and noetically perfected citizens, and his attempt to ontologically connect the supreme good for civilized human beings with the noetic activity of the Divine, is also bound to sound "ridiculous" to the sophisticated ears of post-modern thinkers. It would make no difference whether these "thinkers" are Marxist atheists, Nietzschean nihilists, desperate existentialists, neo-pragmatic relativists, or sophistical deconstructionists. Even empathetic theists of the type that, at our time, tends to be seriously devout and fundamentally fanatical (whether they call themselves Christian, Jewish, or Muslim peoples of the Book) will find Aristotle's conception of God, and his tolerant and playful polytheism, unprofitable. To them, his theoretic approach to ethical problems would be too intellectual, too offensive to monotheistic sensibilities, and too insufficient in emotional power to arouse the masses to fight fanatical holy wars and "crusades." What can one possibly say in defense of Aristotle's philosophic humanism against such powerful objections coming from these two extreme camps, the atheists and the theocrats?

First of all, we should perhaps keep in mind that Aristotle was an Ancient Hellenic Philosopher, which means that he was able to philosophize freely and to follow, like the Platonic Socrates, only the self-limiting authority of human *logos* wherever it might lead. Now, it is true that, for the representatives of the above mentioned movements and schools of thought, the characterization "ancient Hellenic philosopher" would be, in all probability, a liability rather than an asset, as it is for the unbiased students of the history of Hellenic philosophy. For the above mentioned "thinkers" tend to believe that we (post-Hellenic modernists) are better off materially and, therefore, spiritually too, than peoples of any previous epoch, because of our "revealed religion" or our "technological progress" or, most likely, because of both of these great blessings.

To continue this litany, since Aristotle lacked the "light of revelation" and the tools of modern technology, he could not possibly have been correct (so "the argument" would run) in his assertions on such serious matters as the nature of God, the nature of reality, and the nature of man. Especially he was in ignorance of "the original sin" and the ultimate salvation "by grace." But, on the other hand, the "sophisticated thinkers" of our times may suspect the bitter truth that either "God is dead" or, if he is still alive and well somewhere, he couldn't care less about human beings and their destiny. Alternatively, theists may insist that God exists and is definitely only "One God," and as despotic and arbitrary as only a Medieval Bishop or an Oriental Monarch could be.

In our sophistication *we* "post-modernists" have also learned that "reality" and "truth" are really man-made; that man has no nature; and that *a fortiori* there cannot be an ethical *telos* appropriate for human beings other than the momentary preference for this or that variety of bodily pleasure and political expediency. Alternatively again, for those who have no stomach for such tough to digest post-modern "truths," there is always available the consolation of God's revelation. For God in his mercy has made clear the one and only "true way" of salvation by grace through faith in a Savior or some sort of divine testament or revelation. Historically, there has been a trinity of such for the Europeans in the last two millennia: the Jewish Old Testament of the Holy Scriptures was in time replaced by the Christian New Testament of the Holy Bible, to be superseded by the Islamic (Newer) Testament of the most Holy Koran.

Now, if one were to wonder whether Aristotle would have been more impressed with the *mania* of atheistic nihilism of the proletarian type, or with the *moria* (folly) of apocalyptic theism of the religious type, the latter would seem to have a better chance. As an ancient Hellenic philosopher, Aristotle was aware of all the atheistic, agnostic, relativistic, and sophistic tricks and fallacies, to the refutation of which he had devoted the last treatise of his *Organon*. Since, however, Aristotle (384-322 BC) lived about four centuries before the advent of Christianity, and a whole millennium before the Hegira (622 AD), he was completely unaware of the human vulnerability to the peculiar monotheistic *monomania*.

In the hands of a few shrewd (semi-Hellenized) Jews of the *diaspora*, with help from some decadent (semi-barbarized Hellenes) of the Graeco-Roman times, this monomania turned the pious Jewish superstition regarding a tribal god and the myth of his "chosen people" into a fanatical force of major proportions. In time, it proved to be capable of controlling the hearts and the minds of millions of Muslim and Christian women and men for thousands of years in every continent, including Europe and even Hellas, the land of Olympian gods and Hellenic philosophers. Hence derives the great "passion" of Hellenic philosophy in the Christianized and de-Hellenized Europe.

At any rate, as Hellenic philosopher, Aristotle would be neither afraid nor ashamed to follow *logos* (discursive reason) and *nous* (intuitive intellect) in his dialectic search for truth about the essential beings of the cosmos, which included human and mortal beings, as well as divine and immortal ones. Having found many faults in the theories of his predecessors, Aristotle had learned the lesson of humility and did not claim infallibility. His open-mindedness and acuity led him to choose, like Platonic Socrates, what he judged to be philosophically the more satisfying of the two basic options. At that time they were the Democritian option with its materialistic ontology and mechanistic etiology, and the Pythagorean or Anaxagorean option, which provided ample room for a noetic ontology (or, rather, the Aristotelian *ousiology*) and teleology.

Although he respected the former for its consistency, Aristotle chose the latter as the better theory to account for all the facts of reality and for the whole spectrum of human experience leading from *aisthesis* (sense-perception) to *noesis* (intuitive grasp, intellection), through *logos* (discursive reasoning) and following the *via dialectica*.

In so doing, Aristotle was not simply following the steps of the Platonic Socrates and Plato, his beloved teacher of philosophy, but also his own inner personal conviction, I would suggest. This was probably based on his experience as a mature dialectical philosopher, a man who had realized the value of both human *logos* and *nous* as a separate, that is, non-material and immortal entity, potentially present in the human soul (or, rather, the Aristotelian *psyche*). That is the core of my thesis.

Conclusion

In the light shed by our synoptic analysis of the Aristotelian road to enlightenment, we may now see clearly the nobility of this Hellenic conception of the human *telos* and his ability to assign to human beings a privileged place in the cosmos, mediating between gods and beasts. Above all, his readiness to acknowledge man's affinity and potential friendship with the philosophically conceived God (the Divine Intellect that erotically attracts and noetically governs the cosmos) is apparent here. Evidently, he made a heroic philosophic effort to conceptually grasp the entire cosmos, in all its multiplicity of accidental and substantial beings, including the complex human being and the divine *ousia*. In his attempt to provide a reasoned account of all human experiences (aesthetic, logical, noetic, ethical and political), Aristotle succeeded in developing a comprehensive system of rational thought. This system naturally reached beyond the Western "rationality" of discursive reason (*logos*), moving towards the noetically intuitive *nous*, and even towards the intelligible and divine realm of *Nous.*

Because of this solid basis, there is no doubt that Aristotle's system is one of the most complete and influential philosophical systems, which the Hellenic minds produced. For our synoptic discussion has shown that the reasoned account of the Aristotelian road to enlightenment (*via dialectica*) is based on sense experience (*empeiria*) and discursive reasoning (*logos*). But it, significantly, includes the intuitive and self-validating activity of the mind, that is, the respectively (eternally and temporally) energized intellects of God (*Nous*) and of man (*nous*). Thus, the conventional gap separating the human and the divine realms of intelligent activity, as well as the gulf allegedly dividing the East and the West culturally, has been here dialectically and satisfactorily bridged.

In this important sense, then, Aristotle would seem to have been something more than a mere "rationalist," simple, cold, and dry. If this be so, I would like to think that I have done my "peripatetic duty" of defending Aristotle against the unfair charges of those who like to dump on him the accumulated intellectual and other waste of the Western world in the last two millennia. Neither Aristotle, nor any other Platonic and genuinely Hellenic philosopher, would have approved of what the Modern European man, in his greedy desire for profit and his demonic will to power, has made out of Hellenic *philosophia*, forced to serve theocracy and technocracy, sometimes together.

For, in the eyes of the Ancient Hellenes, genuine philosophers (as opposed to Sophists) were supposed to contemplate the cosmic beauty, not to deform it by changing it. They were supposed to comprehend the cosmic order and to live in harmony with it, not to pollute it by exploiting it. Above all, they were expected to provide prudent suggestions for the appropriate organization of human affairs so that the free spirit of inquiry and the flourishing of the human life of excellence would become possible for the human being as citizen. This being was conceived as living, sensitive, reasonable, communal, political, noetic and, (potentially, but essentially), a god-like being.[98]

Hence the urgent need felt by the few philosophically minded persons in Europe and the West today to return to their primordial philosophic roots, which were pre-Christian and pre-Islamic. The Platonic Aristotle, like the Socratic Plato, and the Hellenic philosophy in general, perhaps can guide their steps towards this noble goal.[99]

Notes

1. In fact, it would be more than a millennium if we calculate its dates from Thales of Miletus (early 6th century BC), to the closing of the Hellenic schools of philosophy by Justinian, the Byzantine Emperor of the Christianized Roman Empire, in 529 AD, when it officially ended. By using Hellas and Hellenic, instead of Greece and Greek, which is more common in the West in spite of their pejorative connotations to Hellenic ears, I want to show due respect for the Ancient philosophers. They did so much to perfect philosophy, even if they did not claim to have invented the art of wondering and theorizing freely, as the first essay of the collection showed correcting the European view. The words Greece and Greeks will be used in reference to Modern Greeks and the Modern Greek State.

2. *Process and Reality: An Essay in Cosmology*, D.R. Griffin and D.W. Sherburne, eds (New York, 1978), p. 39. See I. Leclerc, *Whitehead's Metaphysics: An Introductory Exposition* (Bloomington, IN: Indiana University Press, 1975), perhaps the best exposition of Whitehead's difficult thought; L. Bargeliotes, *The Revised Subjectivism of A.N. Whitehead* (Athens, 1984); and the review of it in *The Greek Philosophical Review* 3, no. 8 (1986): 195-197. Consider also the second essay of the collection.

3. In the light of such questioning, the history of Western Philosophy can be pictured as a pendulum moving rhythmically from left to right and back again. Alternatively, it can

be seen as a dialectical process between two opposite poles provided by the perceived polarity between the Platonic and the Aristotelian modes of philosophizing, the ascending and the descending, as immortalized in the Renaissance painting by Raphael, "The School of Athens." However, in my view, there are fundamental differences between philosophy, as understood and practiced by the Ancient Hellenic philosophers, and Western or European "philosophy" as developed during the Middle Ages and in modern and post-modern times, some of which will be considered below.

4.   In this way, Aristotle's authority replaced the authority of Plato during the Middle Ages, because his Christian commentators believed that his philosophy was more congenial to the prevailing spirit of Catholic Scholasticism. But, in fact, neither of these Hellenic philosophers was compatible with the revealed dogma, whether Christian or Islamic, as Pletho clearly perceived. See also the fifth essay for more on this point.

5.   That is to say, the Holy Scriptures, which make up the Bible and the Koran respectively. Aristotle would have been surprised to hear of the strange coincidence of his dialectic and humanistic philosophy and the apocalyptic and theocratic revelations, which have historically inspired fanatical faith in the souls of so many peoples in the West and in the East. In Pletho's correct view, Aristotle would have rejected such misuses, by Christians and Moslems, of his philosophy for religious and theocratic purposes. As we will see, Aristotle intended his humanistic and dialectic philosophy for autonomous human beings, for citizens of democratic cities, for free spirits, and for minds without irrational fears and superstitions. See also *La 'De differentiis,' de Plethon*, B. Lagarde, ed., *Byzantium* 43 (1973): 312-343; and my "Pletho's Critique of Aristotle and the Revival of Platonism in the Italian Renaissance," *Skepsis* VIII (1997): 146-170, reprinted here, with some changes.

6.   For a recent appraisal of the changes in the concept of nature and the philosophy of nature, see Ivor Leclerc, *The Nature of Physical Existence* (New York, 1972), Parts 3 and 4; and A.N. Whitehead, *Science and the Modern World* (New York, 1967).

7.   Mukund Lath, "Aristotle and the Roots of Western Rationality," *Journal of Indian Council of Philosophical Research 9*, no. 2 (1992): 55-68. I am grateful to Dr. Daya Krishna, Editor of JICPR, who brought this article to my attention and published an earlier version of my essay in response to it in the *Journal of Indian Council of Philosophical Research 12*, no. 1 (1994): 49-78.

8.   M. Lath, *ibid.*, p. 55. According to Lath, this myth has been dressed up in "scientific garb," and vested with the authority of Sociology by such scholars as Max Weber and Claude Levi-Strauss. Thus, it has become "an unquestioned dogma," not only in the West, but also and regrettably, "among the 'educated' in other cultures too, who have been socialized into Western modes of thought."

9.   Having made the perceptive diagnosis, Lath could perhaps have proceeded to question whether the above hypothesis (or dogma of modern European imperialism) has, in fact, its roots in Ancient Hellas; and if so, whether it has, in fact, the sanction of Aristotle's philosophy and authority. Instead of following this critical approach, he has opted for something different. He thinks that, "The march of Western rationality is traced back to Greece, and sometimes specifically to Aristotle, often considered the prime mover, the major guru of Western rational thought;" and that "The contours, or the seeds, of the idea of demarcating societies on the basis of rationality and the notion of the West as a uniquely rational society, with all the prejudices and problems such a concept presents, is first articulated in Aristotle from whom it has entered later thought." So, it is understandable that he would wish to get to "the root" of the problem, as he claims, and resolve "the unresolved

tensions of Aristotle's scheme which still remain in Western thought." He also thinks that he can accomplish all that by a sociological interpretation of certain passages selected at random, mainly from the *Politics*, and without even suspecting that Aristotle's theory of human nature has much deeper ontological roots.

10. In a preliminary way it may be said that the Hellenic philosophers were autonomous and sincere in their seeking of truth as it pertains to the macrocosm and the microcosm. In this important respect, as will be argued in the sixth essay of this collection, the ancient Hellenic philosophers differ radically from their Western interpreters, whether they be medieval metaphysicians and theologians, modern sociologists and logicians, or contemporary deconstructionists and neo-pragmatists. For the latter appear to have been interested in playing some sort of word-game or in serving the revealed religious dogmas, or the dictated political dogmas of their respective sects or parties. They have shown no real interest in the free search of the human mind for truth from a purely Socratic love of wisdom and regardless of the personal pain, which such search may entail for the seeker.

This basic characteristic of Socratic philosophy is similar to Gandhi's *satyagraha*, that is, "the passionate adherence to truth," as P.T. Raju, *Structural Depths of Indian Thought* (Albany, NY, 1985), p. 547, renders this term. During his trial, Socrates told the jury that he was prepared "to die a hundred deaths" rather than give up the pursuit of truth and the philosophic way of life, as Plato reported: "Gentlemen, I am your very grateful and devoted servant, but I owe a greater obedience to God than to you, and so long as I draw breath and have my faculties, I shall never stop practicing philosophy and exhorting you and elucidating the truth for everyone that I meet. I shall go on saying, in my usual way, My very good friend, you are an Athenian and belong to a city which is the greatest and most famous in the world for its wisdom and strength. Are you not ashamed that you give your attention to acquiring as much money as possible, and similarly with reputation and honor, and give no attention or thought to truth and understanding and the perfection of your soul? And if any of you disputes this and professes to care about these things, I shall not at once let him go or leave him. No, I shall question him and examine him and test him; and if it appears that in spite of his profession he has made no real progress towards goodness, I shall reprove him for neglecting what is of supreme importance, and giving his attention to trivialities. I shall do this to everyone I meet, young or old, foreigner or fellow citizen, but especially to you my fellow citizens ..." (*Apology*, 29d-30b).

11. In this respect, that is, in his relation to "European philosophy," Aristotle is not different from Plato, as discussed in the second essay above, "Plato and European Philosophy." For a re-thinking of "rationality," "rational belief," and "rational decision making," along the lines of what is called neo-Utilitarianism and neo-Pragmatism, see Robert Nozick, *The Nature of Rationality* (Princeton, NJ, 1993).

12. In Aristotle's hands especially, the method of Socratic and Platonic dialectic became a powerful tool or *organon* of inquiry into any conceivable area or aspect of nature and culture. Compare this breadth of the Hellenic conception of philosophy with the sort of linguistic activity to which it has been reduced by the narrow-mindedness of contemporary analytical "philosophers," for whom philosophy has become an *ancilla linguae* (a handmaid of language) and a bad joke. For example, Ayer insists that: "What confronts the philosopher who finds that our everyday language has been sufficiently analyzed is the task of clarifying the concepts of contemporary science. But for him to be able to achieve this, it is essential that he should understand science ... What we should rather do is to distinguish between the speculative and the logical aspects of science, and assert that philosophy must

develop into the logic of science." *Language, Truth and Logic* (Great Britain: Penguin Books, 1972), pp. 201-202. While for Wittgenstein, "The problems arising through a misinterpretation of our forms of language have the character of *depth*. They are deep disquietudes; their roots are as deep in us as the forms of our language and their significance is as great as the importance of our language.—Let us ask ourselves: why do we feel a grammatical joke to be *deep*? (And that is what the depth of philosophy is)." *Philosophical Investigations*, G.E.M. Anscombe, tr., (New York, 1968), p. 47, (paragraph 111). Rudolf Carnap put it briefly; "The only proper task of philosophy is Logical Analysis," in Morton White's, *The Age of Analysis: Twentieth Century Philosophers* (Boston, 1955), p. 223.

13. To understand Aristotle's *Ethics* and *Politics* correctly, one should place it in the context of his *Metaphysics* and *De Anima*. For him, the same ordering principle pervades the cosmos in the form of divine *Nous*, and is present in the individual human soul, in the form of human *logos* (discursive reason) and of the human *nous* (intuitive intellect), and their manifestations in all forms of social organizations and natural associations. These include, naturally for Aristotle, the family and the *polis* as well. But even A. MacIntyre, who attempted to provide an open-minded approach to Aristotle's theory of virtue and its relevance to our society today, seems to have missed this important point. See, *After Virtue: A Study in Moral Theory* (Notre Dame, 1981), chapters 9, 11, 16, and 18; and my review of the book in *The Review of Metaphysics*, XXXVII, no. 1 (1983): 132-134.

14. Being an open-minded and clear-sighted philosopher, and not a revolutionary propagandist, Aristotle could see that only a few citizens of any given city-state would be able to rise to the top, even under democratic equal conditions of freedom and education, due to the other important factor, natural endowment. As a good biologist he appreciated this factor, while in our time it is overlooked in political declarations of "human rights." For Aristotle, the recognizable "rights" are those of the citizen, and are reciprocal and proportional to his actual or potential contribution to the common good of the city-state. See on this A. MacIntyre, *op. cit.*, Chapters 8-18; J. Waldron, ed., *Theories of Rights* (Oxford, 1984); M. Golding, "Towards a Theory of Human Rights," *The Monist* 52 (1968): 521-548; my "The Aristotelian Tradition of Virtue: The Case of Justice," in *On Justice*, K. Boudouris, ed. (Athens, 1988); and F.D. Miller, *Nature, Justice and Rights in Aristotle's Politics* (Oxford, 1995).

15. This, of course, was to be "the true philosopher," a god-like man among mere common mortals. By free, independent, and autonomous pursuit of the truth, and by an ethically impeccable life, the true lover of wisdom was expected to be able to give up the brutish ways of indulgence in self-centered pleasures of the flesh and to rise towards the stars or the Gods. Accordingly, for the Pythagoreans, between the mortal men and the immortal Gods, there was a third category of "being," represented by their teacher Pythagoras. For Plato (Symposium, 212a) and Aristotle (NE, 1177b-1178a), the true philosopher was the only mortal worthy of the company and friendship of the immortal Gods. For Epicureans, like Lucretius, he who would follow the precepts of Epicurus would live "like a god among men," for "man loses all semblance of mortality by living in the midst of immortal blessings." *Greek and Roman Philosophy after Aristotle*, J.L. Saunders, ed. (New York: The Free Press, 1966), p. 52. This noble conception of philosophy has been lost in the history of the so-called "Western philosophy" of the Christian Europeans. For more on this important point, see also the last essay of the collection titled.

16. The Platonic Socrates is different from the "Socrates" of modern and contemporary Western "philosophy," whether he derives of the hermeneutic or the analytical school, who

is virtually indistinguishable from the Sophists. For the Platonic Socrates has more love for divine wisdom and a "greater soul" than language analysts do and post-modernists can comprehend or appreciate. See, for example, V. Tejera, *Plato's Dialogues One by One: A Structural Interpretation* (New York: Irvington Publishers, 1984); G. Vlastos' *Socrates: Ironist and Moral Philosopher* (Ithaca, NY: Cornell University Press, 1991); and my review of the book in *Journal of Neoplatonic Studies*, vol. 1, No. 1 (1992): 133-141. Consider, for instance, how would the Platonic Socrates address the Sophists of his, as well as of our, time: "Do you think it a small matter that you [Thrasymachus] are attempting to determine and not the entire conduct of life that for each of us would make living most worth while?" *Republic* 344d (repeated in 352d). Again: "And, by the god of friendship, Callicles, do not fancy that you should play with me, and give me no haphazard answers contrary to your opinion. And do not either take what I say as if I were merely playing, for you see the subject of our discussion—and on what subject should even a man of slight intelligence be more serious?—namely, what kind of life one should live, the life to which you invite me, that of a 'real man,' speaking in the assembly and practicing rhetoric and playing the politician according to your present fashion, or the life spent in philosophy, and how the one differs from the other" (*Gorgias*, 500b-c).

17. In this light, it would seem that Aristotle's conception of the Divine is closer to the Eastern than to Western conceptions of God, that is, the Christian and Islamic versions of the intolerant and anthropomorphic Judaic monotheism. Consider, for instance, A.N. Whitehead's view on this point: "The Eastern Asiatic concept [of God is that of] an impersonal order to which the world conforms. This order is the self-ordering of the world; it is not the world obeying an imposed rule." In contrast to this, "The Semitic concept [of God as] a definite personal individual entity ... is the rationalization of the tribal gods of the earlier communal religion." *Religion in the Making* (New York: New American Library, 1926), pp. 66-67; also his *Process and Reality*, pp. 342ff.

18. That is to say, the noetically activated philosopher becomes a friend of God; see on this, Aristotle's *Nicomachean Ethics* 1177b-1178a, and compare it to Plato's *Symposium*, 212a-b. Clearly, on this important point, the two Hellenic philosophers were in agreement with each other and in disagreement with the Europeans.

19. As Aristotle put it almost poetically in the heart of his *First Philosophy* or *Metaphysics* (1072a 20-30): "There is, then, something which is always moved with an unceasing motion, which is motion in a circle; and this is plain not in theory only but in fact. Therefore the first heaven must be eternal. There is therefore something, which moves it. And since that which is moved and moves is intermediate, there is something, which moves without being moved, being eternal, substance, and actuality. And the object of desire and the object of thought move in this way; they move without being moved. The primary objects of desire and thought are the same. For the apparent good is the object of appetite and the real good is the primary object of rational wish. But desire is consequent of opinion rather than opinion of desire; for the thinking is the starting point."

Anyone who has ever experienced true love, will understand perfectly well Aristotle's deepest thought regarding the power of the noetically erotic "object of desire" to move by its beauty the entire heavens no less than the human heart and mind. That power cannot be other than the Divine Intellect or God. On this point, as in so many others, Aristotle remained to the end a true Platonist. In this respect, Porphyry was justified in writing the treatise: *On the Unity of Plato's and Aristotle's Philosophy*. See also Evangeliou, *Aristotle's Categories and Porphyry* (Leiden, 2nd edn 1996), p. 5.

20. The meaning of Aristotelian enlightenment lies precisely in that, by the ultimate divine contact, the maturing philosopher as a potentially noetic being is transformed into an actually noetic and god-like being, thanks to the power of the love of wisdom.

21. See cases A, B, and especially C, below. The point of my thesis is that, if we can show that this self-realization and *apotheosis* is the ultimate outcome even of the philosophy of Aristotle, considered as the most rigorous and scientific Platonist, then *a fortiori* we will have shown that the same holds in other "more spiritual" Platonists. Since in the Platonic tradition, as if in a great river, converge all the springs of Presocratic philosophical speculation; and given its longevity and influence on the development of Hellenic philosophy, it would be reasonable to take it as representing the Hellenic philosophical thought as a whole. Thus, Hellenic philosophy is brought closer to the eastern philosophical traditions than to the narrowly conceived Western "rationalism" and "philosophy." One could make the case that the same holds even for Epicureanism and Stoicism, at least in their ethical theories, and in spite of their materialistic conceptions of reality. But even if they were considered exceptions to the rule, this would not alter the fact about Platonism as being the mainstream of Hellenism.

22. This sounds very much like the "*Tat tuam asi*" of the Vedanta, as the Indian friends of wisdom would recognize. In other words, *via dialectica* is the Hellenic way of expressing the same truth as that which is captured by the wonderful Indian formula "That are Thou" (that is, you as *atman* and God as *Brahman* are essentially one and the same). As Sarvepalli Radhakrishnan put it: "The Upanishads speak to us of the way in which the individual self gets at the ultimate reality by an inward journey, an inner ascent ... The goal is identity with the Supreme." *Source Book in Indian Philosophy*, (Princeton, NJ, 1973), pp. 38 and 85. The same noble goal pervades the Hellenic philosophical tradition, from Pythagoras to Proclus, if correctly understood. Aristotle and Plato are two central figures of this honorable Hellenic tradition, as we said. For this reason two essays of the collection are devoted to them respectively.

23. The modern and post-modern European "philosophers," who have reduced Hellenic philosophy (the traditional queen of arts and sciences) to a "humble handmaid" of (technocratic) science and (political) ideology respectively, seem to follow on the steps of Medieval (Christian and Moslem) theologians, for whom philosophy had become another *ancilla theologiae*. The enslavement of Hellenic philosophy to such strange "Masters" in the West has transformed its original autonomous character to an almost unrecognizable degree. The echo of the name *philosophia* may sound the same, but the meaning is different for its joyous and free spirit has been lost. But it can be recovered.

24. By turning Modern Science, in the same way as the Medieval Theology, into a tool of controlling power, the Europeans, whether capitalists or socialists, have exploited the natural and cultural resources of the globe for profit and political power with disastrous results for humanity's future wellbeing on Mother Earth.

25. Aristotle, in this light, would appear to be very different from what we find, for example, in G.E.L. Owen's *Logic, Science and Dialectic*, M. Nussbaum, ed. (Ithaca, NY: Cornell University Press, 1986). What logicians of science and analytical "philosophers" do not seem to understand is that, for Aristotle and any genuine Hellenic philosophers, the concern with language and logic was only preliminary to more fundamental questions of philosophy such as, "How should we live?" Related to this Socratic question there was a cluster of questions of ethical, political, psychological, theological, ontological, and cosmological import: Who really are we and what does it mean to be human? What is the

good (or the best possible) life for human beings *qua* human? What is the good (or the best possible) organization of the city-state, in which the good life of its best citizens can be realized? What is our place in the cosmos and what kinds of beings does it contain? What is "Being" in general and how is it related to other beings? Is there anything divine in the cosmos and perhaps in us? What is divine, philosophically conceived, and how is the divine being related to cosmos and to man?

To perceptive students of Hellenic philosophy it would be clear that for Aristotle, as for the Platonic Socrates, a complete answer to any of these questions presupposed or implied specific answers to the other questions, with which it is connected. Ultimately, the connections would lead back to the fundamental teleological question of the human *telos*, and the kind of life which would help the philosopher, as the best specimen of the human species, to achieve the highest good for man. At least this is my thesis here.

26. To this list one may add America, where wrong-headed atheists, equally dogmatic monotheists (whether Christians or Muslims), and other gentler and kinder persons (who may be neither monotheists nor atheists) must learn to live together in peace. Hence our need for the help which Hellenic philosophy can provide. In the new light of my Platonic interpretation of Aristotle, the Aristotelian views on man, nature, cosmos, the divine, and their respective multiple relations, become relevant once again. By extension, so do the views of other Hellenic philosophers of the Platonic tradition, as well as the perspectives of other non-Hellenic traditions and cultures. Especially relevant would be the cultures of the East (India, China, Japan), which were relatively free from fanatical intolerance, technocratic arrogance, political ideology, theocratic hierarchies, and religious inflexible dogmas.

27. Consider, for example, A. Armstrong's judicious judgment. "This sort of monotheistic complacency is becoming more and more difficult to maintain as we become more and more vividly aware of other religious traditions than Judeo-Christian-Islamic, notably that of India ... The Greeks in the end found it perfectly possible to combine this with monotheism, to believe in God without ceasing to believe in the gods." "Some Advantages of Polytheism," *Dionysius* 5 (1981): 181-188; and "Porphyry's Criticism of Christianity and the Problem of Augustine's Platonism," *Dionysius* 13 (1989): 51-70.

28. Aristotle spent about twenty years in Plato's Academy from which he departed only after his beloved teacher's death. In spite of occasional criticism of specific Platonic doctrines on which he respectfully disagreed with his teacher, Aristotle remained a loyal Platonist to the end. Many miss this point because they tend to focus narrowly on points of difference between philosophers, which are there but make no real difference. When one looks at Plato and Aristotle, as the Hellenic philosophers of late antiquity looked at them, they appear to belong to the same school of philosophy, the Socratic tradition. In this light, my "new" interpretation of Aristotle is really ancient. It needs no apology. See also, *Aristotle's Categories and Porphyry* (Leiden, 2nd edn, 1996), pp. 1-14.

29. Even the "revolt against Aristotle," which led to the revival of Platonism in the fifteenth century and to the scientific revolution of the seventeenth centuries, was fought to a large extent with the weapons of Aristotle's logic and categories, transmitted to the West by the commentaries and translations of Boethius. See on this, *Aristotle's Categories and Porphyry*, pp. 164-181.

30. In the sense in which, for example, Descartes, Leibniz, and Spinoza are said to be rationalists; or even in the sense in which Bacon, Hobbes, and Locke may be called "rational" empiricists. Would Aristotle have felt at home, in the company of either of these

groups of Europeans? Not exactly, in my view, because he was a philosopher of a more versatile, flexible, noetic, dialectic, and non-dogmatic character. Aristotle was a Hellenic philosopher of the type which the Aegean and the Ionian seas used to produce in abundance until their waters were "polluted" by the spread of the "decadent" spirit of Christianity, as Nietzsche would have it. *Twilight of the Idols and The Antichrist*, pp. 55ff; also A. Nehamas, *Nietzsche: Life as Literature* (Cambridge, Mass., 1985); and my review of the book in *The Review of Metaphysics*, vol. XL, No. 3 (1987): 592-594. In his fury, Nietzsche extended the characterization "decadent" to the Platonic philosophy, perhaps because he, like so many other European thinkers, failed to distinguish between the two versions of Platonism, Hellenic and Christian, as discussed in the second essay.

31. According to Aristotle, "Spoken words are the symbols of mental experience, and written words are the symbols of spoken words. Just as all men have not the same writing, so all men have not the same speech sounds, but the mental experiences, which these directly symbolize, are the same for all, as also are those things of which our experiences are the images ... A sentence [*logos*] is a significant portion of speech, some parts of which have an independent meaning, that is to say, as an utterance, though not as an expression of any positive judgement." *De Interpretatione* 16a-b.

32. He was also a lover of *nous* (the intuitive mind), as we will see. In this light, Kant's judgment is incorrect: "In *respect to the origin* of the modes of 'knowledge through pure reason' the question is as to whether they are derived from experience, or whether in independence of experience they have their origin in reason. Aristotle may be regarded as the chief of the empiricists, and Plato as the chief of the noologists [which is Kant's neologism for rationalists]." *The Critique of Pure Reason*, N.K. Smith, tr. (New York, 1965), p. 667.

33. It must be credited to the rhetorical skills and ingenuity of Christian and Moslem theologians, who managed to persuade the medieval and much of the modern world that they had found in Aristotle's philosophy sufficient support for their respective revelations and the theocratic *dogmata*. Ironically, it was against this "Aristotle" that European thought rebelled in modern times. Since then, it has served faithfully Modern Technology and/or Political Ideology, instead of Medieval Theology. Sadly, philosophy has not as yet recovered its ancestral autonomy and dignity. In this sense, European "philosophy" is very different from genuine Hellenic philosophy. The sooner we grasp this historical fact the better off we will be philosophically in the future.

34. "All men by nature desire to know. An indication of this is the delight we take in our senses; for even apart from their usefulness they are loved for themselves; and above all others the sense of sight. For not only with a view to action, but even when we are not going to do anything, we prefer seeing to everything else." (*Metaphysics*, 980a 22-24, the translation is that of Ross). Aristotle proceeds to show how human understanding moves from sense experience to the reasoned accounts of the arts and sciences, to the noetic grasp of first principles and causes, and ultimately to the intuitive knowledge of Divine Intellect (*Nous*) and of the human inner self (*nous*). For him, as for Plato, God and man are essentially the same. This is, in a nutshell, my thesis.

35. "A syllogism is discourse in which, certain things being stated, something other than what is stated follows of necessity for their being so. I mean by the last phrase that they produce the consequence, and by this, that no further term is required from without in order to make the consequence necessary." *Prior Analytics*, 24b 18-22 (A.J. Jenkinson's translation). Compare it to conclusion of *Posterior Analytics* (100b 5-13): "Thus it is clear

that we must get to know the primary premises by induction; for the method by which even sense-perception implants the universal is inductive. Now of the thinking states by which we grasp truth, some are unfailingly true, others admit error—opinion, for instance, and calculation, whereas scientific knowledge and intuition [*nous*] are always true: further, no other kind of thought except intuition [*nous*] is more accurate than scientific knowledge, whereas primary premises are more knowable than demonstrations, and all scientific knowledge is discursive. From these considerations follows that there will be no scientific knowledge of the primary premises, and since except intuition nothing can be truer than scientific knowledge, it will be intuition that apprehends the primary premises— a result which also follows from the fact that demonstration cannot be the originative source of demonstration, nor, consequently, scientific knowledge of scientific knowledge ..."

36. "The investigation of the truth is in one way hard, in another easy. An indication of this is found in the fact that no one is able to attain the truth adequately, while, on the other hand, we do not collectively fail, but every one says something true about the nature of things, and while individually we contribute little or nothing to the truth, by the union of all a considerable amount is amassed" (*Metaphysics*, 993a 30-b 6).

Compare this thoughtful statement with the Indian wisdom as expressed in a Jaina saying: "Perfect truth is like an ocean: it is the Jina's omniscience; and all philosophical views are like rivers." Quoted by K.S. Murty, *ibid.*, p. 190. It is enlightening indeed to contrast these sensible eastern views on truth to the statements made by Kant, the most "critical" representative of European thought. Without irony the critical Kant has stated: "In this inquiry I have made completeness my chief aim, and I venture to assert that there is not a single metaphysical problem which has not been solved ... Metaphysics, on the view which we are adopting, is the only one of all the sciences which dare promise that through a small but concentrated effort it will attain, and this in a short time, such completion as will leave no task to our successors save that of adapting it in a *didactic* manner according to their preferences without their being able to add anything what so ever to its content. For it is nothing but the inventory of all our possessions through pure reason, systematically arranged. In this field nothing can escape us."

Thus spoke the author of the *Critique of Pure Reason* (p. 13). But a few years later G.W.F. Hegel was to prove Kant wrong in this arrogant claim and to beat him sorely in this especially German word-game which is called "metaphysics." For, as G. Lightheim says, in his introduction to Hegel's *The Phenomenology of the Mind* [*or Spirit*], (New York, 1967), p. xxi: "Kant's rather bleak rationalism in turn provoked a Romantic reaction—of this Hegel's *Phenomenology* may be regarded as an example, in so far as its author did not disdain the use of metaphor for purposes other than illustration." As expected *The Phenomenology* ends appropriately in German fashion at "the Golgotha of the Absolute Spirit" (p. 808), and the "imaginative idea" that: "The Divine Being is reconciled with its existence through an event—the event of God's emptying Himself of His Divine Being through His factual Incarnation and His Death" (p. 780).

It makes one wonder what would Anaxagoras or Epicurus say if they could read this kind of European "philosophy?" So much about "modesty" or "truth" as expressed in German Idealism and Rationalism representing the apex of "Western philosophy." See also G.W.F. Hegel, *Lectures on the Philosophy of Religion*, P.C. Hodgson, ed. (Berkeley, CA, 1988), p. 489; Part III, "The Consummate Religion," is revealing of the mind of this "European philosopher."

37. *Nicomachean Ethics* 1094b 13-28. Compare it to Kant's endeavor to make

Metaphysics a "science" of the same precision and exactness as Euclidean Geometry and Newtonian Physics. He would accomplish this task by the critical method of "pure reason" applied with "German thoroughness" to "the subject" as seen in the light of the "Kantian revolution," which again was patterned after the "Copernican revolution." See *Critique of Pure Reason*, pp. 13-25. At the end, however, Kant confesses humbly on page 29: "I have therefore found it necessary to deny knowledge, in order to make room for faith," (that is, faith in the existence of God, the freedom of the will, and the immortality of the soul, just as E. Gilson would have expected). His *Critique* ends with his declaration of faith in the three dogmas of his "moral theology" which cannot be demonstrated but is "postulated" as the demand of the Supreme Will: "Thus without a God and without a world invisible to us now but hoped for, the glorious ideas of morality are indeed objects of approval and admiration, but not springs of purpose and action" (p. 640).

In other words Kant, the philosopher of Protestantism, wants: "To make him [the Christian man] *fear* the existence of a God and a future life" (p. 651), the emphasis is not added. How alien is all this to the Hellenic philosophers, "the wonderful Greeks!"

38. Absent from Aristotle's thinking and writing are the dogmatism and the obfuscation, which characterises what has been coming out of Western Europe in the last few centuries under the homonymous term "philosophy." On this issue I will have more to say in the last essay of the collection.

39. The proverbial "*Amicus Plato sed magis amica veritas*" captures this trait of Aristotle's philosophical mind, which is Socratic, Platonic and Hellenic. It is also found in Indian thought and is best expressed by Gandhi's "passionate adherence to truth" (*satyagraha).*

40. The perfected philosopher, described in the *Nicomachean Ethics* (Book X) and *Politics* (Books VII-VIII), fits the Platonic pattern as developed in the *Republic* (Books II-VII). As human beings, (that is, as composite entities of body, soul, and mind), they must have been naturally well endowed and culturally prepared by the appropriate *paideia*, which they would have received as citizens of the Hellenic *polis*, through gymnastics and the musical or liberal arts. The more an actual city-state would approximate the ideal *polis*, as envisioned by Plato (for both sexes) and Aristotle, the greater the probability of the actualization of the philosophic perfection of its citizens would be.

41. I use "theory" here in the original sense of the Hellenic word, that is, to look and see, to have a view of something, to intuit, to contemplate. By engaging in intelligent *theoria* of the intelligible cosmos, the Hellenic philosopher was at home with nature and the world, unlike the contemporary "existentialist souls" of ex-Christian European thinkers, who feel at a loss in an "absurd world." I have in mind thinkers and writers such as, for example, Jean Paul Sartre, Albert Camus, Nikos Kazantzakis, and Martin Heidegger.

So, in order to bring the question closer to us, we may ask: What can Hellenic philosophy possibly mean to post-modern men and women, as they try to cope with "the absurdity" of their lives? Even if their lives are not always as "nasty, brutish and short," as Hobbes would have them be, they are certainly mortal and seem meaningless to many Westerners, including some "philosophers." As they drag their existential *angst* along a Sisyphus' pathway, life on earth, and the earth itself, looks to them like an "old bitch." And to think of it, it is the same earth which ancient poets, philosophers, and common people respectfully called "Mother Earth!" and "Sweet home!" It will emerge, from our discussion of Aristotle's road to enlightenment, that part of the suggested answer to the above question would relate to the double loss which Europe had suffered, that is, the loss of philosophical contact with (a) the divine spark in us (the *nous* within) and (b) the divine *Nous* in the cosmos. This would seem to have occurred, when the two "aberrations" of genuine Judaism, namely Christianity and Islam, introduced into the Mediterranean world, especially into Western Europe, the monomaniac monopoly of the One God and the myth of "the chosen people."

By reducing all the ancient gods and goddesses to one masculine God, Christian and Muslim theologians have, perhaps inadvertently but unwisely, pointed the way to the abyss of "No-God," which Marx, Nietzsche, Sartre and other post-Modern atheists and nihilists followed blindly, in their furious rebellion against the despotism of dogmatic Catholicism and the fanaticism of puritanical Protestantism in Europe. Hence, the need to rediscover and reconnect with our roots in pluralistic and polytheistic Hellenism, in polyphonic philosophy, and in the Hellenic emphasis on "harmony in diversity." For more on this present need, see the last essay in this collection.

42. The affinity of this Hellenic thought to Chinese and Indian philosophies is evident from passages like the following: "Silent, isolated, standing alone, changing not, eternally revolving without fail, worthy to be the mother of all things. I do not know its name and address it as Tao. If forced to give it a name, I shall call it 'Great';" "What is God-given is what we call human nature. To fulfil the law of our human nature is what we call the moral law." Lin Yutang, ed., *The Wisdom of China and India* (New York, 1942), pp. 596 and 845; and "The real which is at the heart of the Universe is reflected in the infinite depths of the self." S. Radhakrishnan and C. Moore, eds, *A Sourcebook in Indian Philosophy* (Princeton, NJ, 1973), p. 38. It would seem that the Aristotelian relation, between *Nous* and *nous*, is analogous to the Indian relation between *Brahman* and *atman*, of which the Upanisads speak. On this relation and the corresponding double intuitive knowledge (*vidya*), of human self and the Divine Self, the Vedanta system of thought is based. See, K. Satchidananda Murty, *Philosophy in India: Traditions, Teaching and Research* (Delhi, 1991), pp. 3-7. Professor Murty renders *vidya* as "science." But its meaning may be something more than this. A better translation would be "intuitive knowledge" or "intuition" to capture the meaning of "seeing" which is at the root of the Indian word *vidya*, as it is in the equally beautiful Hellenic and Platonic word *idea*. The same Ancient Hellenic word [*nous*], has also been used for something divine in us by Hellenic poets from Homer to Kazantzakis, whose magnificent *Odyssey: A Modern Sequel* (a poem of 33,333 lines), ends with the liberation of Odysseus' mind (*nous*) from the body thus:

"Then flesh dissolved, glances congealed, the heart's pulse
stopped and the great mind [*nous*] leapt to the peak of its
holy freedom, fluttered with empty wings, then upright through
the air soared high and freed itself from its last cage,
its freedom ..."

Book XXIV, lines 1390-1394 (Kimon Friar's translation).

43. The importance of music for the development of Hellenic philosophy, especially in its Pythagorean, Socratic, Platonic, and Neoplatonic lines cannot be overestimated. For these philosophers, music and harmony were always connected to mathematics, that is to theories of number (*arithmos*) and proportion (*logos*). A comparative study, which would consider Hellenic music, arithmetic, philosophy, and compare them with possible parallel developments of Indian music, mathematics, and the various philosophical systems, would be very interesting and welcome. I would not be able to do it here (or elsewhere for that matter); Dr. Lath's comments (*ibid.*, p. 60), regarding Aristotle's theory of music and

harmony and its political implications, seem interesting but inadequate. For more on number and harmony see C.A. Huffman, *Philolaus of Croton: Pythagorean and Presocratic*, Cambridge, 1993, pp. 54-77.

44. That is to say, all the first principles of "primary being," "indubitable knowing," and "virtuous living." For my thesis, this third road, the road of dialectic, *via dialectica*, which would culminate in a "noetic vision" of the whole cosmos, including God and man, and the end of man as a free citizen, was Aristotle's long peripatetic road to enlightenment. In all these aspects Aristotle, I would like to suggest, remained to the end a Platonist, that is, an enlightened pupil of Plato, a free inquirer, and an able practitioner of the philosophic method of dialectic.

45. Intelligence or intellect, in the sense of intuitive reason and noetic seeing, is perhaps the best rendering of *nous*, which I have tried to follow in these essays consistently. To avoid any confusion, I have simply transliterated this important word in most cases.

46. This is not to suggest that Aristotle the original logician, or Aristotle the empirical biologist, is not a legitimate aspect of the Aristotelian philosophic outlook. On the contrary they are, but they are not the only legitimate aspects, nor are they the most important aspects for the post-modern world which needs help to face its multiple crisis. That Aristotle and other representatives of Hellenic philosophic *logos* can provide such help, in this time of need, is the main point of my thesis.

47. The inquiry is what is known today as *Metaphysics* 981b 25-982a 6; but to Aristotle it was simply *First Philosophy*, since it dealt with the first principles or causes; see Evangeliou, *Aristotle's Categories and Porphyry*, pp. 59-92.

48. By applying his dialectical method and his theory of the categories Aristotle succeeded in transforming the traditional inquiry of being (or *to on*, ontology) into an inquiry of *ousia or* substance (*ousiology*). For Aristotle, *ousia* (that is, essential being), is the most important of the ten categories or "genera of being," because it captures the basic sense of the term "being," whose ambiguity allows it to become a predicate of different kinds of things. See Evangeliou, *Aristotle's Categories and Porphyry*, pp. 188-204.

49. *Metaphysics* 1069a 18-34; and 1072b 14-29. That Aristotle's conception of the Divine was very different from the despotic, dogmatic, moody, mean, jealous, and vindictive character of the Biblical Jehovah, who has influenced both the Christian and Islamic conceptions of God, is evident also from the following remarks: "That it [first philosophy] is not a science of production is clear even from the history of the earliest philosophers. For it is owing to their wonder that men both now begin and at first began to philosophize ... Evidently then we do not seek it for the sake of any other advantage; but as the man is free, we say, who exists for his own sake and not for another's, so we pursue this as the only free science, for it alone exists for its own sake. Hence also the possession of it might be justly regarded as beyond human power; for in many ways human nature is in bondage, so that according to Simonides 'God alone can have this privilege,' and it is unfitting that man should not be content to seek the knowledge that is suited to him. If, then, there is something in what the poets say, and jealousy is natural to the divine power, it would probably occur in this case above all, and all who excelled in this knowledge would be unfortunate. But the divine power cannot be jealous (nay, according to the proverb, 'bards tell many a lie'), nor should any other science be thought more honorable than one of this sort ... All the sciences, indeed, are more necessary than this, but none is better" (*ibid.*, 982b 11-983a 12).

50. This is the opening statement of the *De Anima* 402a 1-8. The other passages are

from Books II and III (the translation is that of J.A. Smith).

51. *Ibid.*, 430a 14-25. In a parenthesis, which I omitted, Aristotle explains why the active intellect in us, after its separation from the body by death, will have no memory of its earthly adventures. He states: "we do not, however, remember its former activity because, while mind in this sense is impassible mind as passive is destructible."

Like Platonic Socrates, Aristotle prudently does not say much on such a speculative subject as the destiny of the noetic part of the human soul after death. It was left to Christian and Moslem theologians (who found in the Holy Scriptures vivid descriptions of Hell and Heaven) to worry about the details. Presumably he thought that the Platonic philosophers (or other people who had a noetic experience and had become self-aware), would not need much explanation here, while no detailed explanation could enlighten those who did not have the enlightening noetic experience itself. As Plato said (*Timaeus*, 28C): "But the father and the maker of all this universe is past finding out, and even if we found him, to tell of him to all men would be impossible." Having told his "likely story," Timaeus concluded thus: "We may now say that our discourse about the nature of the universe has an end. The world has received animals, mortal and immortal, and is fulfilled with them, and has become a visible animal containing the visible— the sensible God who is the image of the intellectual, the greatest, best, fairest, most perfect— the one only begotten heaven" (*Ibid.* 92C).

52. This is the opening of *Nicomachean Ethics*, 1094a 1-4.

53. *Nicomachean Ethics* 1177a 13-18; 1177b 29-1178a 8.

54. In this way, a context will be also provided for a judicious appraisal of Dr. Lath's claim, regarding the close connection between Aristotle's rationality and Western philosophy.

55. A revision of Parmenides' model was made at the school of Leucippus and Democritus, who split the sphere of the Parmenidean Being into a multiplicity of "beings," *atoma*. These are the invisible, indivisible, perpetually in motion particles of matter, which move randomly in the *kenon* [void, empty space], collide and give birth to everything in the cosmos. Thus not only the absolute oneness of the Parmenidean Being has been replaced by a multiplicity of solid atoms, but also the Parmenidean non-Being has been compromised by becoming part of the "sphere of Being" as the void separating atoms. While Parmenides' "Being" had been of the same stuff as *Nous*, in Democritus' cosmos the minds and souls of human beings and gods are made of the same atomic matter in its more refine forms. Lucretius explains all this in *The Nature of the Universe, III*.

56. The Parmenidean identification of *einai* (to be, being) and *noein* (to think, thought), which was temporarily abandoned by Anaxagoras, reappeared in Plato. He incorporated Pythagorean insights into his ontology, and was able to introduce the most elaborate revision of Parmenides' doctrine. Thus, the way was prepared for Aristotle's move from *ontology* to *ousiology* with his conception of the Divine as "noetic substantive being," (that is, *Nous* and *Ousia*).

57. Actually, these are spatialized, temporized, magnified, dimensionalized, quantified, qualified, relativized, and realized, in the sense of being materialized, copies of Platonic Forms. The process by which the "materialization" of these Forms was supposed to take place became a target for Aristotle's critique throughout the *Metaphysics*, especially in Books A, M, and N.

58. According to Timaeus' "likely story," the cosmos is conceived as the only offspring of the unique metaphorical couple, Form (in the role of Father) and Matter (in the role of Mother), who are brought together by the Demiurge (as the cosmic matchmaker). As part of

the Platonic cosmos, human beings are also double, composed of body and soul (or matter and form, the hylic and the noetic parts, the maternal and paternal principles), with a different destiny after death for each of the two components.

59. Ontologically considered, the Aristotelian cosmos is a vast collection of different kinds of individual things and substantial beings, some of which are living. But it is not alive, in the sense in which the Platonic world of Becoming was alive as endowed with a soul, unless we restrict the meaning of "soul" [*psyche*] to its noetic function. For the Platonic model of creation, see the "likely story" told by Timaeus in the *Timaeus* and compare it with the Aristotelian model as presented in the *Physics*, *Metaphysics*, and *De Caelo.*

60. We can do no more than provide a *paraphrasis*, a summary account, of the involved dialectic or "peripatetic" process here.

61. To use Aristotle's favorite expression, it is a πολλαχῶς λεγόμενον, an ambiguous and polysemantic term.

62. See on this "The Plotinian Reduction of Aristotle's Categories," *Ancient Philosophy* 7 (1988): 147-162.

63. *Categories*, 2a 35-36. Here we read (in Apostle's translation): "Everything, except primary substances, is either said of a subject which is a primary substance or is present in a substance which is a primary substance."

64. Aristotle's *Metaphysics* is devoted to this ontological/ousiological inquiry and its philosophical implications. The *ontological* question of "what is being?" is changed into the *ousiological* question of "what is substance?" in the following way: "And indeed the inquiry and perplexity concerning what being is, in early times and now and always, is just this: What is a substance?" (1028b 4-6).

65. The central books of *Metaphysics* seek to explicate these contrasts in search for the most special kind of *ousia*, that is, the divine or God. On this see Joseph Owens, *The Doctrine of Being in the Aristotelian Metaphysics* (Toronto, 1963, 2nd edn); and compare it with Werner Marx, *The Meaning of Aristotle's Ontology* (The Hague, 1954).

66. See Cases A and B, above.

67. See Cases B and C, above.

68. Due to its composition, human nature is complex and limited in many ways. See also cases C and A, above.

69. For Aristotle, the sphere of "practical reason" is to be distinguished from the sphere of "poetical reason" as applied by craftsmen and artists, and from "theoretical reason" as used by scientists and philosophers for the development of scientific theories and of philosophic *theoria*. In its application, the practical reason appears threefold, as it may, alternatively, be concerned with the wellbeing of individual citizens (Ethics), the household (Economics) or the *polis* and the political community as a whole (Politics).

70. "When several villages are united in a single complete community, large enough to be nearly or quite self-sufficing, the state comes into existence, originating in the bare needs of life, and continuing in existence for the sake of a good life. And therefore, if the earlier forms of society [family and village] are natural, so is the state, for it is the end of them, and the nature of a thing is its end." *Politics* 1252b 27-32.

71. To the natural and educational goods of the body and the soul, the external goods of moderate property and wealth may be added. The latter more than the other goods are affected by luck. For a good discussion of the role of luck in Aristotle's ethical theory see, M. Nussbaum, *The Fragility of Goodness: Luck and Ethics in Greek Tragedy and*

Philosophy (London, 1986); and my review of the book in *Skepsis* I (1990): 210-216.

72. If the servants were of a "servile nature," which was the only type of servitude approved by Aristotle; and if they had learned by their service of a good man how to take care of themselves as well as of others, who were of a more servile nature than themselves; and if, of course, they wished to be freed, they could, then, be released and become free.

73. This would be a difficult task to accomplish, but it would not be impossible with the help of the appropriate political *paideia* as proposed in the last books of the *Politics*. Those who fail to see the philosopher as a citizen growing in a political environment are bound to argue about the compatibility of the theoretic and the practical life and their respective contribution to happiness. See on this, S. Broadie, *Ethics with Aristotle* (Oxford: Oxford University Press, 1991), pp. 366-438; J. Cooper, "Contemplation and Happiness: A Reconsideration," *Synthese* 72 (1987): 187-216; by the same, *Reason and Human Good in Aristotle* (Cambridge, Mass., 1975); and D. Keyt, "Intellectualism in Aristotle," *Paideia* (1978): 138-157.

74. Hobbes, Locke and Rousseau probably found in Plato's *Republic* (opening of Book II) the beginning of the theory of "social contract," which they helped popularize in the West. Needless to say, neither the Platonic Socrates nor Aristotle would take seriously Glaucon's hypothesis that there ever was such a political contract. Their insight into human nature and the nature of *Hellenic polis* helped them avoid this kind of blunder.

75. "Hence it is evident that the state is a creation of nature, and that man is by nature a political animal. And he who by nature and not by mere accident is without a state, is either a bad man or above humanity ... That man is more of a political animal than bees or any other gregarious animals is evident. Nature, as we often say, makes nothing in vain, and man is the only animal whom she has endowed with the gift of speech [*logos*]." (*Politics*, 1253a 1-10)

76. In view of the difficulties of giving birth, infant mortality, and child rearing at that time, it is not surprising that the female contribution to the state was exhausted by fulfilling the fundamental function of producing new citizens for the *polis*. If, instead of such primary need, the ancient city-states had a problem of over-population, and given his common sense, his open mind, and his favor for better education for all members of the community, Aristotle would have probably assigned additional political roles to the female portion of the population of the city-state. However, he would have in all probability objected to "same sex marriages" because of their sterility and unnaturalness in the eyes of the biologist philosopher.

77. Aristotle would have approved of Manu's lawful request: "Women must be honored and adorned by their fathers, brothers, husbands, and brothers-in-law who desire (their own) welfare" (III. 55).

78. As Radhakrishnan put it: "Each one has to perform the function for which his nature best suits him" (*ibid.*, p. 172). Aristotle, and the Platonic Socrates of the *Republic*, would agree with this statement, but for them, unlike Manu, the capacities of individual human beings are not to be determined by family and caste, but by nature and *paideia*.

79. These are the men to whom Aristotle (innocently would seem, though shockingly to some) refers as "natural slaves." This has become the target of criticism including that of Dr. Lath. In this connection, it should be considered that Aristotle's "servant by nature" may correspond to "the sudra," although he did not believe in a caste system, like the one legitimized by the law of Manu: "He was created by the Self-existent to be the slave of a Brahmin." Again, "A sudra, though emancipated by his master, is not released from

servitude; since that is innate in him, who can set him free from it?" *The Laws of Manu*, 413 and 414, quoted by Sarvepalli Radhakrishnan (*ibid.*, p. 189).

80. See also the last essay of the collection.

81. *Politics*, 1254a-1255a.

82. "But is there any one thus intended by nature to be a slave, and for whom such a condition is expedient and right, or rather is not all slavery a violation of nature? There is no difficulty in answering this question, on grounds both of reason and of fact. For that some should rule and others be ruled is a thing not only necessary, but also expedient; from the hour of their birth, some are marked out for subjection, others for rule ... But that those who take the opposite view have in a certain way right on their side, may be easily seen. For the words slavery and slave are used in two senses. There is a slave or slavery by law as well as by nature. The law of which I speak is a sort of convention— the law by which whatever is taken in war is supposed to belong to the victors. But this right many jurists impeach, as they would an orator who brought forward an unconstitutional measure: they detest the notion that, because one man has the power of doing violence and is superior in brute strength, another shall be his slave and subject. Even among philosophers there is a difference of opinion ... Hence, where the relation of master and slave between them is natural they are friends and have a common interest, but where it rests merely on law and force the reverse is true" (*Politics*, 1254a 17-1255b 15) .

83. We should always keep in mind the picture of "the city as a whole," when we evaluate either Aristotle's recommendations of political reform of the Platonic Socrates' ideal *politeia* as articulated in the *Republic* Books II-VII. See also the four essay of the collection "Aristotle's Critique of Plato's Polity."

84. *Politics*, 1253a 28-29. Even the divine intelligences, which control the heavenly spheres, depend on the ultimate activity of the Unmoved Mover. Even the noetically perfected philosopher, who is as self-sufficient as a human being may become, is in need of some friends to share with them the pure pleasures of *theoria*, which itself depends on the pure "being" of intelligible, noetic, and divine *ousiai*.

85. Aristotle predicted that, if the tools could do the necessary work by themselves, then the masters would not need the service of their servants, but the servants (if they are by nature servile) would still need the protection and help of their masters to cope with the demands of life. Life will never be easy for some people on this earth for some reason.

86. States, which are founded on such principles, tend to be not only appealing to our democratic feelings, but also inherently anarchic and, in the long run, become unstable.

87. Their kind of representation can be compared with that of a contemporary Senator or Congressman, who is supposed to represent the interests of his District or State respectively, although some seem to forget this "basic duty" as soon as they are elected.

88. Consider, for example: "All are agreed that justice in distributions must be based on desert of some sort, although they do not all mean the same sort of desert; democrats make the criterion free birth; those of oligarchic sympathies wealth, or in other cases birth; upholders of aristocracy make it virtue" (*NE* 1131a 25-30).

89. In Ancient Hellenic usage, *aristocratia* meant literally the rule of the best, both morally and intellectually best. It had nothing to do with money, at least in its philosophic usage.

90. See, for instance, the exquisite poem, "Expecting the Barbarians," in *C. Cavafy: The Collected Poems*, Rae Dalven, tr. (New York, 1976), pp. 18-19:

What are we waiting for, assembled in the public square?

The Barbarians are to arrive today ...
Why this sudden unrest and confusion?
(How solemn their faces have become.)
Because night is here but the Barbarians have not come.
Some people arrived from the frontiers,
and said that there are no longer any Barbarians.
And now what should become of us without any Barbarians?
Those people were a kind of solution.

91. See also the first essay in this collection.

92. "The Barbarians are of a more servile nature than the Hellenes," (*Politics*, 1285a 20); this clearly means that both the Greeks and the Barbarians, as human beings, are by nature non-free in many ways, as he has stated explicitly in *Metaphysics*, 982b 29.

93. "Those who live in a cold climate and in Europe are full of spirit, but wanting in intelligence and skill; and therefore they retain comparative freedom, but have no political organization, and are incapable of ruling over others. Whereas the natives of Asia are intelligent and inventive, but they are wanting in spirit, and therefore they are always in a state of subjection and slavery. But the Hellenic race, which is situated between them, is likewise intermediate in character, being high-spirited and also intelligent. Hence it continues free, and is best governed of any nation, and, if it could be formed into one state, it would be able to rule the world. There are also similar differences in the different tribes of Hellenes; for some of them are of one-sided nature, and are intelligent or courageous only, while in others there is a happy combination of both qualities" (*Politics*, 1327b 23-36).

94. "Hence if, as men say, surpassing virtue changes men into gods, the disposition opposed to bestiality will clearly be some quality more than human" (*NE*, 1145a 23-25); and Socrates' remarks in the *Symposium* 212a. For more on the possibilities of immortality for different kinds of lovers, see my "Eros and Immortality in Plato's *Symposium*," *Diotima* 13 (1985): 200-211.

95. See Case C, above. Aristotle does not speak of the immortality of the human soul as a whole, or even of the intellect as a whole. The "passive intellect" is perishable, and only "active intellect" is immortal or more accurately eternal. Wisely, though, he refrains from speculating about these eschatological issues in detail.

96. "But again it [*phronesis*] is not supreme over philosophic wisdom [*sophia*], that is, over the superior part in us, any more than the art of medicine is over health" (*Nicomachean Ethics*, 1145a 7).

97. See Case C, above.

98. An echo of the Hellenic and Aristotelian understanding of the close relation between philosophy and freedom is to be found in the following statement: "Philosophy is a means of education through and for freedom." *The Teaching of Philosophy* (Paris, 1952), p. 189; the same spirit echoes in the conception of "philosophy as seeking of *truth* and *freedom*." The Experts' Panel in Philosophy Report of 1978," (quoted by K.S. Murty, *ibid.*, p. 167).

99. The tragic case of Bosnia may be just the prelude of a much larger scale tragedy to unfold in the Balkans and Central Asia, in the remnants of the former USSR, and in the Middle East, where Islam and Christianity are bound to collide again as they have collided many times before. One could add Judaism, the elder sister of the three monotheistic religions, although there is a basic difference between it and its offshoots, Christianity and Islam. The traditional Hebraic monotheism and its pious myth of the "chosen people"

seemed innocent compared with its Christian and Islamic versions, in view of their fanatic and missionary zeal to spread the faith in the one God and the one Messiah or Prophet. The present day Zionism and its politics is a different matter.

PART 2
Critique and Character of Hellenic Philosophy

Chapter 4

Aristotle's Critique of Plato's Polity

Introduction

References to the Platonic *Dialogues* and critical comments on Plato's views on various themes of theoretical and practical interest are found in all the major works of Aristotle.[1] It was an important part of his method of inquiry to review his predecessors' doctrines on a given subject in order to determine what had been said well and what possibly needed improvement.[2]

In this respect, the *Politics* is no exception to Aristotle's rule of methodical research.[3] Here, too, we find dispersed comments on Plato's views, especially on that radical "communism," advocated half seriously and half playfully by Socrates in the *Republic*, as an effective means to the realization of the ideal city-state.[4]

It is my current purpose to examine Aristotle's criticism of the Platonic perfect *politeia* (polity), in order to determine the target at which he aims, his tactics of attacking it, and his reasons for doing it so vehemently. It will become clear from our discussion that Aristotle, much like Popper and unlike Randall, thought that Plato's proposal of political reform deserved a serious consideration.[5]

Even in his old age, Plato continued to consider the communal program, which as a mature philosopher he had advanced in the *Republic*, to be the best possible organization of the ideal state. This fact clearly indicates the strength of his convictions on this matter. It also provides us with a context of reading Aristotle's reservations about the desirability and practicality of the Platonic political plan, as well as his counter proposals for moderate political reform of the Hellenic *polis*.[6]

The Nature of the Problem

At the beginning of Book II of the *Politics*, Aristotle claims that it would be useful to consider both the existing states, which are well governed, and those theories about the ideal state, which are highly esteemed. Such consideration would help him to determine which is the best *polis*, either absolutely best, that is, under ideal conditions, or relatively to most peoples, times, places, and ordinary conditions.[7]

This claim provided Aristotle with the opportunity to launch a critique of Plato's provocative proposal regarding the guardians in the *Republic*; that is, the abolition of private property and even the abolition of private family life, including women, children, and servants, who were to be held in common. What provoked Aristotle most, and made him undertake a thorough critique of the central proposal of the *Republic*, was perhaps his concern about the limits of "unity," which is considered as a defining characteristic of both the Platonic ideal *polis* and the basic component of the Aristotelian state, the household.

Aristotle thought that the criterion of "excessive unification" of the state, as advocated by the Platonic Socrates in the *Republic*, assumed falsely that there were no significant differences between the well-ordered *polis* and the well-functioning household, and it should be limited. For him there was another and more important criterion for application here, that of "self-sufficiency." For his genetic conception of the state, this criterion should be the measure delimiting what is best for both the Hellenic city-state and its well-trained citizens.[8]

Specifically, according to Aristotle, members of a given city-state have three options regarding community and the sharing of the goods. They may have in common: (1) all things; (2) nothing at all; or (3) only some things, but not others.[9]

Having nothing in common goes against the essence of the city-state as Aristotle understood it and, therefore, the second option is not really an option, for the citizens must have in common at least the place where they live, if there is going to be a city-state at all. So, we are left with two alternatives: The citizens of a city may have all things in common, or only certain things in common and some other things separately.

Which of these two options of communal life is the better option was the question on which Plato's radicalism and Aristotle's traditionalism diverged. Aristotle considered the former as Plato's position, as expressed by the Platonic Socrates in the *Republic*,[10] and was determined to attack it on behalf of "common sense" and what was actually a common practice in Hellenic city-states at the time.

But should a well-ordered state have all things, as far as it may be, in common, or some only and not others? This was a serious political question, because the citizens of a given city-state might conceivably have wives and children and property in common, as Socrates proposes in the *Republic* of Plato. Which, then, is the better arrangement, Aristotle and other Athenian theoretical minds would ask, the present and the traditional condition, or the proposed new order of society?[11]

If it were to be striped from its dramatic embellishments, its irrelevant digressions, and its rhetorical devices, the *Republic*,[12] that ideally perfect *polis* built by Socrates and Glaucon in words, would appear to be faulty in several ways. At least to a critical mind like Aristotle's, it appears to be faulty in its coming into being and in its passing away. But above all it is faulty in its odd *status quo*, that is, as a close-knit community of good friends, determined to put into practice the Pythagorean maxim, "friends have all things in common."[13]

Accordingly, Aristotle's critique falls into three parts. He criticizes the Platonic Socrates for failing to take into consideration all necessary and sufficient elements of the state so that his utopia would not be incomplete, in the sense that it has room only for farmers, weavers, shoemakers, and builders.[14]

He also finds fault with the fictionalized scheme of change, by which the Platonic Socrates gets from the philosophical aristocracy of the perfect *polis*, to the city-state ruled by a heinous tyranny, by way of such progressively degenerated forms of government as timocracy, plutocracy, and democracy.[15]

Above all, Aristotle objects to Plato's proposal for radical political reform regarding the guardians' proposed "communal life." It is this part of his critique, which deserves special attention and will concern us in what follows. As we will see, it articulates some serious political differences between the two Hellenic philosophers and friends, regarding the means towards the common political goal, that is, the best possible life of man as citizen of the best organized *polis*.[16]

Community of Women and Children

In order for the Guardians of the perfected *politeia* (polity) to be able to dedicate their lives to the service and protection of the city-state from internal disorders and external attacks, the Platonic Socrates boldly proposed that they be freed from the cares and concerns of ordinary domestic living.

So, the Guardians of the *polis* were to be carefully selected and thoroughly educated philosophically. Their lives would belong to the *polis* than to themselves, and were to be completely regulated by philosophical reason for the common good from birth to death, both individually and collectively. Furthermore, the privilege of being a member of the ruling group in that ideal republic would have to be purchased at the price of sacrificing, at the altar of the communal good, the common pleasures of family life and the possession of private property.

More importantly, since the Guardians would monopolize the use of weapons and the means of military power, according to this proposal, they were to keep their hands clean from using gold and silver.[17] In Plato's vision, they would be the key factor for securing the unity of the city, if they were so trained as to perceive their political function as a higher mission to serve the ends of the state virtuously, while abstaining from the attractions of material goods and bodily pleasures.[18]

In other words, the Guardians were to be a new type of man, transformed by proper education and dedicated to the service of the city-state for the sake of the common good. Their disciplined and ascetic way of life would not be envied, while the common folks would be allowed to enjoy private property, family life, and profit seeking lawfully.[19] This arrangement would keep the *polis* balanced.

At least that was Socrates' dream as revealed in the *Republic*. In Aristotle's judgment, behind Socrates' proposal of total communal life for "the guardians" lies the desire to secure "the greatest possible unity of the whole city" (1261a 15). This would be accomplished by shaping the state on the model of a well-ordered and enlarged family.

Aristotle considers questionable both the desirability and the practicality of the Platonic Socrates' proposal, that is, the assumption that the supreme good of the city-state is to be identified with its perfect unity, and the means by which he proposed to achieve such political goal. His pessimism, regarding this point, and his criticism of the Platonic ideal stems from his different conception of the nature of the civil society.

We may recall here that Aristotle's conception of the nature of the city-state was that of an aggregation of villages which, in turn, are aggregates of households. These are composed of individuals having specific functions, as husbands and wives, parents and children, masters and servants. Thus he was able to argue that "unity" naturally decreases, as one gets from the concrete individual to family, to village, and finally to the city-state as a whole, while the self-sufficiency increases proportionally. In this light, Socrates' desire to build a city with "the greatest possible unity" appeared to Aristotle as contrary to the nature of the state, which would be destroyed by too much unity.

As Aristotle saw this problem, the largeness of the city-state, in conjunction with the fact that its composition necessarily includes a variety of distinct elements (that is, farmers and artisans, traders and merchants, solders and rulers, teachers and priests), would determine it specifically. This would differentiate it from both the tribe and the military alliance the members of which differ only numerically (1261a 22-24).

In addition to this, consideration of the criterion of self-sufficiency, which is greater in the city-state than in the household or the individual, would lead Aristotle to conclude that the Platonic policy of unifying the city-state in excess must be faulty by definition. But, in fairness to Aristotle, we have to admit that he does not say that a state should aim at the exact opposite of Plato's ideal, that is, to as little political unity as possible. Rather, he seems to be concerned with what he thought was Plato's "excessive" emphasis on unity and order at the expense of freedom and diversity.

When he states that Plato's ideal polity aimed at molding the whole city-state into one, like Aristophanes' portrayal of the pathetic lovers in the *Symposium*, the stress falls on the words "one" and "whole."[20] But this stress would be unfair to Plato who distinguished the producers and craftsmen from the auxiliaries and guardians of the city. His ideal of perfect unity, with its communal meals and other means by which Plato sought to bring it about, referred only to the latter, and not to the city as a whole.

Furthermore, Aristotle correctly implies that, in their collective use, the words "all" and "mine" lose the intensity of feeling, which is associated with them in their proper and individualistic usage. For, "Just as a little sweet wine, mixed with a great deal of water, produces a tasteless mixture, so family feeling is diluted and tasteless when family names have so little meaning as they have in a constitution of the Platonic order" (1262b 17-20).

Aristotle also speaks of "watery friendship" and concludes with the famous aphorism: "It would be better to be a cousin in the ordinary sense than a son after the Platonic fashion" (1262a 13-14). Such comments sound reasonable because they express a common sense view of familial feelings and attitudes, but as criticism of Plato's proposal for radical political reform, by means of transforming human nature through philosophically guided *paideia*, seem to miss the point.[21]

The Platonic Socrates' reply to this criticism would be that to apply to carefully selected and properly trained guardians of the ideal city the feelings, concerns, and prejudices of ordinary people is not entirely fair. For they were supposed to be, both by conception and by education, a new type of man, who would have successfully passed the strict test of rising above the sentimentality of the common folks in order to make it to the top of the Platonic political hierarchy.

They were supposed to rule and be ruled in accordance with reason and virtue. What Aristotle says about the feelings of attachment to persons and objects, as being depending on subjective feelings and property relations, may apply very well to the Athenian or the European bourgeois. But, under ideal conditions, it would be inapplicable to men like the Guardians of the Platonic polity who, owing to their excellent training and philosophic *paideia*, were to be athletes of virtue.

Another difficulty, in the proposal of having the wives in common, would be the inherent inability to conceal the identity of children in light of the fact that, in Aristotle's view, some females in the animal kingdom tend to produce offspring extremely similar to their sires. He mentioned the notorious Pharsalean mare of the legend in this regard, and the fact that there were African tribes where the women were held in common, but "the children born of such unions can still be distinguished by their resemblance to their fathers" (1262a 20-21).[22]

The same criticism would hold with regard to transference of children from one rank to the other and the potential danger of quarrels among the persons involved in this transaction.[23] Aristotle's argument incorrectly again assumes that the Platonic guardians would feel, think, and behave just like ordinary people of the petty bourgeois type. But this probably would not be the case, if we accept that education has the power to mould the human soul, and that the proposed Platonic program of *paideia* had its chance.[24]

Aristotle is also concerned about such crimes as assault, homicide, slander, and so on, which, he thinks, are more offensive to human sensibilities, when they are perpetrated against close relatives and they demand special purification rites. He observes that: "Such offenses must happen more frequently when men are ignorant of their relatives than when they know who they are; and when they do happen, the customary penance can be made if men know their relatives, but none can be made if men are ignorant of them" (1262a 30-32).

This is typical of his tactics in criticizing Plato's proposal. He assumes that, human nature being what it is, nothing would really change even in the Platonic polity, and that men will continue to go on living and "sinning" as usual.[25]

Community of Property

With regard to the abolition of private property, Aristotle has many objections to Platonic Socrates' proposal of complete communism. He makes a distinction between ownership and the use of property, each of which can be held either in common or privately. Thus the following threefold scheme is obtained:

1. Common ownership and common use;
2. Common ownership and private use;
3. Private ownership and common use.[26]

Of the three alternatives, Aristotle focuses his discussion on the first and third options. He considers the one, that is, common ownership and common use, as the Platonic view, but he declares that private ownership and common use, as had been practiced in some Greek city-states, is preferable.[27]

In view of the strict prescriptions of the *Republic* (416d-417b), it is difficult to see the Guardians of the Platonic *polis* as owners of anything, other than their virtue and the will to serve the common good. At any rate, Aristotle argues vigorously against the community of property and in support of private property, provided that it is "adorned by custom and the enactment of proper laws." Thus it would combine the merits of both systems and ensure the common use of the privately owned property:

> Property should be in a certain sense common, but, as a general rule, private; for, when every one has a distinct interest, men will not complain of one another, and they will make more progress, because every one will be attending to his own business. And by reason of goodness, and in respect of use, "Friends," as the proverb says, "will have all things in common." (1263a 25-30)[28]

Aristotle's first argument in defense of private property is not on pragmatic, as one might expect, but on ethical grounds. It is not based on efficiency and higher productivity, but on the intensity of pleasure, which the ownership of private property generates, and the opportunity of virtuous activity, which it affords. Aristotle states that "to think of a thing as your own makes an inexpressible difference;" and that "a great pleasure is to be found in doing a kindness and giving some help to friends, or guests, or comrades" (1263b 5-7).

But the Platonic Socrates, even if he would have agreed with Aristotle's evaluations, would have probably retorted that to think of the whole city as your own is certainly a source of much greater pleasure than to think of a piece of dry land and a pair of old mules.

Accordingly, it is curious to claim, as Aristotle does, that the virtuous activity of liberality would be thwarted among people who are not landowners, as if virtue were to be measured quantitatively rather than qualitatively. It is equally absurd to claim, as Aristotle does (1263b 10-14), that community of women would entail the sacrifice of the virtue of temperance by rendering adultery impossible, as if the Platonic city would not be full of temptations for the guardians. Being athletic, handsome, and stalwart, the guardians would have to guard themselves from the lascivious advances of the ladies of the producer class, who would have every reason to attract their attention.[29]

There are passages in Aristotle's criticism, in which he clearly acknowledges the seductiveness of Plato's political proposal. Consider: "All the writings of Plato are original: they show ingenuity, novelty of view, and a spirit of inquiry. But perfection in everything is perhaps a difficult thing" (1265a 10-13).[30]

Aristotle also disagreed with Plato's view that the source of all social evils is *akoinonesia* (absence of communism); for he considered *mochtheria* (wickedness) as a more probable cause (1263b 15-25). Even if we are inclined to side with Aristotle here, we must not forget that Plato was well aware of the deficiencies of human nature and, for this reason, he placed all his high hopes on life-long education in music, gymnastics, mathematics, and philosophy.[31]

In this light, Aristotle's surprise as expressed in the following passage would have surprised the Platonic Socrates: "It is therefore surprising that one who intends to introduce a system of education, and who believes that his ideal will achieve goodness by means of this system, should none the less think that he is setting it on the right track by such methods as he actually proposes, rather than by the method of social customs, of mental culture, and of legislation" (*ibid.*).

This line of criticism clearly indicates the contrast between Aristotelian realism and Platonic idealism, even at the level of practical politics, which perhaps had other and deeper roots.[32] Another telling Aristotelian criticism is that, in spite of his talk of unification, Socrates makes two out of one city-state, by sharply dividing the rulers from the ruled. So it is possible that the following situation may emerge: "the guardians being made into something of the nature of an army of occupation, and the farmers, artisans, and others being given the position of ordinary civilians" (1264a 25-27).

This situation and the fact that Plato's farmers control their holdings will make them insubordinate, in Aristotle's view, especially at the time, when the quota of their produce would have to be turned over to the guardians for their consumption. To amend this Platonic shortcoming, Aristotle proposed, in his ideal state, that farmers and artisans should not be part of the best city-state.[33]

Aristotle also charged that in Plato's polity the politically correct principle "to rule and be ruled in turn" has been abolished. This is only partly true though. For one thing the young guardians are ruled at first, and then they themselves rule, if and only if they are able to pass the strict tests of ethical and intellectual excellence successfully. It is true that farmers and artisans have no share in government. But it is doubtful whether they would wish to rule in a Platonic ideal city-state, which provided for the rulers neither pay nor pleasure.[34]

A last comment of Aristotle's must be mentioned before we close this discussion, because it is indicative of his political pragmatism. Believing that "almost all good things have been discovered," he pointed at Plato's innovations as historically unjustifiable. Thus he stated that: "We are bound to pay some regard to the long past and the passage of the years, in which these things would not have gone unnoticed if they had been really good" (1264a 1-3).

Aristotle was wrong in assuming that, politically speaking, all good things had already been discovered in the past, especially at the moment when his pupil Alexander was attempting something very new and radical. The philosopher would not have approved of Alexander's dream, the fusion of the Hellenes and the Persians in a grand *cosmopolis*, which was to overshadow the old city-states.[35]

However, Plato would have probably agreed with Aristotle's assertion here, in which case he would have to argue that his proposal of total communism was not an innovation. For it had been in practice in the very distant past not only among primitive African peoples, but also among the Athenians and even the Atlantians.

I would like to suggest that some passages of the *Timaeus* and the *Critias* would make better sense if they were to be read from this perspective. That is, as Plato's attempt to "prove" that the ideal *polis*, just as Socrates and Glaucon had dreamed of it in the *Republic*, with its abolition of family life and private property, had its roots in the Attic soil, and the sanctity of Athens' distant but glorious past.[36]

Conclusion

In conclusion, it is evident from the preceding analysis and critical discussion that Aristotle considered as the core of Plato's ideal polity the proposal of communism in its double form, community of women and children and community of property for the guardians, to achieve the perfect unification of the city-state. Aristotle objected to these innovations and posed as a defender of common sense and the common Hellenic political practice at that time.

His arguments were intended to show not only the impracticability of Plato's proposals and their incompatibility with common political practices, but also their undesirability. He believed that, human nature being what it is, a political reform would have a better chance if it did not aim at realizing heaven on earth, but rather at a political "golden mean," by minimizing the existing political evils.[37]

It is indicative of Aristotle's common sense approach to the political problems of his time that he followed the *Laws* in drawing his own ideal state, which was designed to fit most people at most times under more or less normal conditions.

In so doing, Aristotle became in time the champion of constitutionalism. But neither his nor Popper's criticism of the *Republic* has diminished its appeal as an ideal designed to serve as a source of inspiration for aspiring educators and legislators. Those who refuse to play the role of the expert practitioners of the art of the probable and the practicable will always return to Plato's *Republic* for inspiration.

Notes

1. The list of such works would include the *Physics*, *Metaphysics*, *Ethics*, *De Anima*, *De Caelo*, *De Generatione et corruptione*, and the *Politics*. Aristotle's tendency to stress the points on which he differs from Plato can easily mislead one into thinking that the differences between the two philosophers are greater than their similarities; or that Aristotle progressively abandoned his Platonism. W. Jaeger has adopted that thesis in his *Aristotle: The Fundamentals of the History of His Development*, R. Robinson, tr. (Oxford, 1934), pp. 3-7, and 259-292. But C. Lord, *Education and Culture in the Politics of Aristotle* (Ithaca, 1982), pp. 23-28, is critical of Jaeger and provides the recent bibliography on Aristotle's *Politics*.

More judicious than Jaeger's claim I find the view of the ancient historians of Philosophy, such as Porphyry, who maintained that Aristotle and Plato belong to the same school of thought in spite of their occasional differences. On this see my *Aristotle's Categories and Porphyry* (Leiden, 1988), p. 5, note 24. H.G. Gadamer seems to agree with Porphyry in *The Idea of the Good in Platonic and Aristotelian Philosophy*, P.Ch. Smith, tr. (New Haven, 1986), p. 4.

2. Knowing that the criticism of his teacher could be easily misunderstood as deriving from a spirit of sophistical contention rather than love of the truth about the ideal state, Aristotle took care to reveal his intention clearly (1260b 27-36). We read there: "Our purpose is to consider what form of political community is best of all for those who are most able to realize their ideal of life. We must therefore examine not only this but other constitutions such as actually exist in well-organized states, and any theoretical forms which are held in esteem; that what is good and useful may be brought to light. And let no one suppose that in seeking for something beyond them we are anxious to make a sophistical display at any cost; we only undertake this inquiry because all the constitutions with which we are acquainted are faulty." *The Basic Works of Aristotle*, R. McKeon, ed. (New York, 1941). As for the truth, in this and other philosophical matters, Aristotle's view was that: "No one is able to attain the truth adequately, while, on the other hand, we do not collectively fail." *Metaphysics*, 993a 32-33.

3. I have discussed the question of Aristotle's method and its relation to the medical sciences more extensively in "Aristotelian Ethics and Medicine," in *Philosophy and the Sciences*, L. Bargeliotes, ed. (Athens, 1988).

4. References to the *Republic* are found in 1261a 6, 1291a 11, 1293b 1, 1316a 2, 1342a 32; Aristotle also mentions the *Laws* in 1264b 27, 1271b 2, 1274b 9; and the *Statesman* in 1262b 12.

5. See K. Popper, *The Open Society and Its Enemies, I: The Spell of Plato* (Princeton, NJ, 1971), especially Chapters 6-9, which are devoted to "Plato's Political Programme." Also J. Randall, *Plato: The Dramatist of the Life of Reason* (New York, 1970), especially pp. 28-29 and 161-171. There we read comments like this: "To the audience for whom the *Republic* was originally written, it must have been a sustained piece of Plato's dramatic irony, a magnificent defense of the Athenian ideal against the Spartan." If so, one would be forced to say that either Aristotle was not included in that audience, or that he spent twenty years in Academy without learning how to appreciate even Platonic and Socratic irony. The sophisticated skepticism of Randall, of course, would not have any difficulty choosing between the two alternatives, since he doubts whether there was an Academy and whether Plato taught anybody anything during his long life. In this respect, Randall's presentation of

Plato and his relation to Aristotle is perhaps as misleading as G. Vlastos' presentation of Socrates and his relation to Plato. See his *Socrates: Ironist and Moral Philosopher* (Ithaca, NY, 1992); and my review of it in the *Journal of Neoplatonic Studies* I (1992): 133-141.

6. The *Laws* are devised for the "second best" state, where the rule of law will replace the rule of the enlightened philosophers. In what follows, I will concentrate on Aristotle's critique of the *Republic* and the communal organization of the life of the guardians as advocated by the Platonic Socrates. I will leave for another occasion his criticism of the *Laws*, as well as his dependence on that work for his version of the perfected city-state through education, as developed in Books VII and VIII of the *Politics*. Note also that Aristotle, in his criticism of Plato, does not seem puzzled at all by the question of how to read and interpret a Platonic *Dialogue*. The importance which contemporary scholarship attaches to this "hermeneutic question" is illustrated by the contributions to *Platonic Writings and Platonic Readings*, Ch. Grisworld, ed. (New York, 1981).

7. In order to show that there is still room for improving upon the proposed ideals (which he would try to fill in Books VII and VIII), understandably in Book II Aristotle focuses on the theories about the best state and the presumed best of the existing states. Since he found them faulty in many ways, he could reasonably claim that: "We only undertake this inquiry because all the constitutions with which we are acquainted are faulty" (1260b 35-36).

8. "When several villages are united in a single complete community, large enough to be nearly or quite self-sufficing, the state comes into existence ... For what each thing is when fully developed, we call its nature, whether we are speaking of a man, a horse, or a family. Besides, the final cause and end of a thing is the best, and to be self-sufficing is the end and the best" (1252b 27-35).

9. In *Republic*, 453a 1-5, Plato raises the same three possibilities regarding the common traits of the male and the female natures: everything in common, nothing in common, some things in common and others not.

10. This is not true without qualifications. The communal stipulations were intended only for the guardians of the Platonic polity, which is a comparatively small segment of the population.

11. *Politics*, 1261a 2-7. For Plato's proposals for community of property, women, and children, see Books IV and V of the *Republic*, especially 423e-462b. Plato's call for a radically "new ordering of the *polis*" was destined to appeal to all sorts of reformers, revolutionaries, and visionary philosophers of the left and the right. And this regardless of whether they agreed or not with the specific Socratic proposals of restructuring the city-state in search for the perfect political regime, in which philosophers might feel at home. But, unlike the Platonic Socrates, these modern imitators forget that one has to reform him-self first from within, before he can reasonably claim the right to reform other peoples' lives, let alone the state and the society as a whole (*Republic*, 591e).

12. It is a characteristic of Aristotle's penetrating mind that he can summarize in less than ten sentences that which took Plato ten books and other scholars multiple volumes to convey. Consider: "In the *Republic*, Socrates has definitely settled in all a few questions only; such as the community of women and children, the community of property, and the community of the state. The population is divided into two classes—one of husbandmen, and the other of warriors; from this latter is taken a third class of counselors and rulers of the state. But Socrates has not determined whether the husbandmen and the artisans are to have a share in the government, and whether they, too, are to carry arms and share in

military service, or not. He certainly thinks that the women ought to share in the education of the guardians, and to fight by their side. The remainder of the work is filled up with digressions foreign to the main subject, and with discussions about the education of the guardians" (1264b 29-41).

13. In *Republic*, 424a 1-2, this is presented as a proverb, κατά τήν παροιμίαν. Socrates repeatedly reminded his interlocutors, Adeimandus and Glaucon, of the wisdom of this saying and its importance for the erection of the perfect city. But Aristotle doubts its power to transform human nature so radically as Socrates would like to believe. He thinks that he can achieve the same good end by other and more humane means, such as virtue and the principle that recommends "common use of privately owned property." Hence his criticism of the Platonic/Socratic proposal.

14. Evidently this remark refers to the "first ideal city," which was characterized by absence of war and luxurious living, and which seemed to Socrates' shocked friends as being "fitting for pigs" rather than human beings. *Republic*, 369a-372b.

15. *Republic*, Books VII and IX.

16. On this goal and on the emphasis which they place on παιδεία and αρετή, the two philosophers were in agreement as noted.

17. Part of their education was aiming at instilling in the guardians the belief that their souls were made of divine metals, so that they should not be tempted by golden and silver coins. The Platonic Socrates correctly insists on this point because it is the heart of the matter. His critics, ancient and modern, seem to miss this important point: "Gold and silver, we will tell them, they have of the divine quality from the gods always in their souls, and they have no need of the metal of men, nor does holiness suffer them to mingle and contaminate that heavenly possession with the acquisition of mortal gold, since many impious deed have been done about the coin of the multitude, while that which dwells within them is unsullied" *Republic*, 416e-417a.

If any one wishes to reform the education or the political system of a state in hope of improving them, s/he would do well to heed Socrates' teaching.

18. Socrates' point here is that political power and wealth should not be in the same hands, if there is to be stability in the state. The wisdom of this insight can cure many civil evils even today.

19. We should not forget that the Socratic recommendations for community of women, children, meals and houses, are intended only for the guardians of the state who are a minority. The majority would continue to enjoy all the pleasures of private property, private homes, meals, wives, and children. Sacrifice of these goods is a necessary condition for rising in the state hierarchy, while desire of these pleasures would be sufficient reason for demotion of guardians who had not absorbed the Socratic lesson of virtue here.

20. *Symposium*, 191a-192b. The hint is Aristotle's, 1262b 12, and indicates that he had a greater sense of humor than a reading of his logical treatises might falsely suggest.

21. I think that Aristotle's assumption that even in the Platonic city only the "form," or structure, would be different, while the "material," the human element, would remain the same, is the root of much of his dialectical criticism of Plato. It would seem that Plato, not withstanding his Sicilian adventure, placed a greater trust in the power of *paideia* to shape the soul of man to divine perfection. Although the history of two and a half millennia has proven that Aristotle was right, ideally our hearts side with Plato in hope that some day his dream may come true.

22. This is an interesting comment indicative of Aristotle's polymathy and concern with Africa, which was called Libya by him and the Greeks. He certainly knew much about Carthage and its form of governments which he praised together with the Spartan and the Cretan as the best actual constitutions, "justly famous" 1273b 27. He also showed great respect for Egypt, its science and ancient civilization (1286a 13, 1329a 40-b 35).

23. Socrates knew that, unless the guardians of the city were well educated in the necessary virtues which would allow them (a) to drop from their ranks those whose soul had lost the quality of gold, and (b) to raise up from the lower ranks those whose soul had shown signs of divine quality, the perfect city would not last.

24. Books VII and VIII of the *Politics*, which are dedicated to the education in his version of the best state, indicate that Aristotle himself had hanged great hope from the peg of *paideia*, even if his was not as great as Socrates' trust.

25. In this regard, Socrates' arrangements become utterly absurd. But when Adeimandus, *Republic* 420B, complained that the strict requirements left little happiness to the guardians of the city, Socrates' response was: "We wouldn't be surprised if leading that kind of life made them the happiest of men, even though our object in founding the city wasn't the exceptional happiness of any one class, but the greatest possible happiness for the whole city."

26. The fourth alternative, "private ownership and private use," is excluded from consideration on the basis that some kind of sharing of the land is a prerequisite for the existence of any state.

27. Aristotle's defense of private property has recently attracted renewed attention, which perhaps is related to the collapse of the Soviet style socialism, although it has its own disinterested appeal. On this see, R. Mayhew, "Aristotle on Property," *Review of Metaphysics* 46, no. 4 (1993): 803-831; F.D. Miller, "Aristotle on Property Rights," in *Aristotle's Ethics*, J. Anton and A. Preus, eds (Albany, NY, 1991), pp. 227-247; and T. Irwin, "Aristotle's Defense of Private Property," in *A Companion to Aristotle's Politics*, D. Keyt and F. Miller, eds (Oxford, 1990); and by same author, "Generosity and Property in Aristotle's *Politics*," in *Beneficence, Philanthropy and the Common Good*, E. Paul et al., ed. (Oxford, 1987), pp. 51ff.

28. Aristotle's love of the golden mean is evident here as it is in his ethics, for which see my "A Paradox in the *Nicomachean Ethics*: The Mean Which Is an Extreme", *Mind and Nature* IV (1979): 8-17. The paper was based on my A.M. Thesis: "The Meaning of the Mean in the *Nicomachean Ethics*" (Emory University, 1976).

29. But Aristotle is correct in saying that the Platonic Socrates said too little about the other classes of the *Republic* and their relationship to guardians (1264a 30-33).

30. "Such legislation may have a specious appearance of benevolence" (1263b 15-16). But Aristotle wanted to suggest that, when the question is about ideals, there is always room for improvement, which is the point of his critique of the Platonic polity.

31. That is, the Socratic "right kind of education" (*orthe paideia*) (*Republic*, 423E).

32. This might be the outcome of the metaphysical disagreement of the two philosophers regarding the ontological status of the Ideas. Aristotle discussed them in *Metaphysics I*, in *Ethics I*, and elsewhere.

33. *Politics*, 1328b 34-41. This recommendation would come as a surprise to those who want to see Aristotle as a liberal democrat, in contrast to the conservative Plato.

34. Their only compensation for the service to the state regarding its external, and internal security, is to receive their modest ratios of food and drink, not in money but in

kind. For: "Their food, in such quantities as are needful for athletes of war sober and brave, they must receive as an agreed stipend from the other citizens as the wages of their guardianship, so measured that there should be neither superfluity at the end of the year nor any lack" (416e). One may wonder how many of our rulers would wish to rule under the Socratic specifications, which were tougher than Spartan.

35. As a result of these profound changes a new era was born the Hellenistic as opposed to Hellenic. Aristotle had many talents, but "political foresight" was perhaps not one of them.

36. Especially, *Timaeus*, 20e-27b. One is tempted to speculate that perhaps the critical discussion, which the *Republic* received in the Academy with Aristotle in the role of the protagonist, prompted Plato to moderate his politically radical views in the *Laws*. Aristotle followed this path prudently, in his version of the best polity (Books VII-VIII).

37. In this respect, Aristotle anticipated much of the criticism, if not the great pathos, of K. Popper and his desire for measured and only "piecemeal" political reform.

Chapter 5

Pletho's Critique of Aristotle's Novelties

Introduction

For the Greek-speaking world and the renascent Europe of the fifteenth century, Georgios Gemistos, better known by his Hellenized name Pletho, was the distinguished Platonic philosopher whose criticism of Aristotle and Averroes greatly contributed to the revival of Platonism.[1] As a philosophical tradition with distinctive and recognizable characteristics, the New Platonism or Neoplatonism was shaped by the thought of Plotinus and the contributions of his pupil Porphyry, Iamblichus and Proclus, to mention only three Platonists of the third, fourth, and fifth centuries AD, respectively.[2]

These prolific writers succeeded in reviving the philosophy of Plato, enriched by many Aristotelian and Stoic elements, so that a potent Neoplatonic synthesis was formed.[3] The efforts of these Platonists were guided also by their goal of defending Hellenism. By this term they meant the Hellenic tradition of religious tolerance and philosophical pluralism under attack from the advancing barbarism. This threat, especially in the form of intolerant and fanatical monotheism, in their view would destroy the traditional fiber of the Greco-Roman world from within, perhaps more effectively than the external attacks of the barbarians.[4]

In this respect, Porphyry of Tyre was the most characteristic representative of Neoplatonism. As a philosopher, he accomplished two important tasks: a reasoned reconciliation of Plato and Aristotle in his erudite commentaries on the *Categories* and other Aristotelian and Platonic works;[5] and a detailed critique of the Christian faith in his celebrated treatise, *Against the Christians*, in fifteen books.[6] Thus, because to Porphyry's influence, for the next three centuries Aristotle and Plato were to become friends once again, while Neoplatonism itself became and remained the main opposing intellectual force to the rapidly growing Christian Church and its monotheistic religious intolerance.[7]

Accordingly, it is no accident that Pletho's effort to revive Platonism once again, more than a thousand years after Porphyry is strikingly Hellenic and anti-dogmatic in its tone.[8] What is rather surprising is that, unlike Porphyry who had tried to reconcile all forces of Hellenism, including Aristotle, against their common enemy, the irrationalism and fanaticism of a "barbarous faith," Pletho found it necessary to turn his criticism against Aristotle as well. This may seem puzzling, but the puzzle has an explanation. For by the fifteenth century, and owing to the labors of such commentators as Averroes and Aquinas, Aristotelianism had become "a handmaiden of theology (*ancilla theologiae*), as represented by the two related and revealed doctrines of the Koran and the Bible respectively.

This may also explain the fact that Pletho opened his influential short treatise *De Differentiis* [9] with allusions to the "bad judgment" of the Arabs and Latins. In their eagerness to serve the revealed dogmas directly or indirectly, they were ready to believe that Aristotle was in harmony with the Holy Scriptures more than with Plato and, therefore, to honor him more than his teacher.[10] Especially the Latins were so effective and persisting in their dogmatism that, in Pletho's view, even notable Greek clerics, like Scholarios, the future Patriarch of Constantinople after its fall to the Turks (in 1453) had been misled by them.[11]

My purpose in this study is to identify and briefly discuss the major points on which Aristotle differs from Plato, in Pletho's judgment, by critically presenting his main arguments, which are invariably favorable to Plato, because of the perceived imbalance in favor of Aristotle in the Latinized West. In spite of this kind of bias, which is not unexpected in this context, it will become clear from our discussion that, by pointing out some fundamental differences between Plato and Aristotle, Pletho's critique accomplished three important philosophical tasks.

First, it revived the debate about the respective merit of Plato and Aristotle and, by extension, the distinct philosophic traditions of Platonism and Aristotelianism, more than a thousand years after Porphyry had tried to settle the issue; and it did so independently from any religious affiliation, Christian or Moslem.

Second, it injected the Renaissance movement with a strong dose of Platonism which, to a certain degree, determined the development of science and theology in the West for the subsequent centuries; but, ironically, it was Ficino's Christian version of Platonism and not Pletho's Hellenic version, which prevailed at the end.

Third, it initiated the process of liberating Aristotle from the uncomfortable embrace of Christian and Islamic Scholasticism. For Pletho showed that, in spite of their differences as philosophers, Aristotle's appropriate place was next to Plato in the sunny sky of Hellenic philosophical *logos*, and far away from the nebulous apocalyptic *gnosis*, both Biblical and Koranic, and its rhetorical elaborations by trained theologians.

In the preface of the short treatise titled *De Differentiis*, Pletho regrets that his contemporaries would admire Aristotle more than Plato, while the ancient Greeks (and the Romans) had wisely honored Plato above all other Hellenic philosophers. In Pletho's opinion, this change of attitude towards the two Hellenic philosophers was primarily effected by the influence of Averroes.[12] From the fact that this commentator had advanced the doctrine of "the mortality of the soul" (which he incorrectly attributed to Aristotle), Pletho concluded that Averroes could not have been as great a philosopher or as good a commentator on Aristotle as his admirers in the West believed. Yet, Averroism was very fashionable in Italy at that time.[13]

So, for the sake of the remaining few admirers of Plato and in order to set the record straight, Pletho undertook to critically discuss the points on which Aristotle disadvantageously differed from Plato. The ten areas of difference, which Pletho identifies and addresses respectively, in the ten chapters of his book, are the following: cosmology, theology, ontology, logic, psychology, ethics, art, causality, motion, and the theory of Ideas.[14]

In each of these areas of difference between the two philosophers, he thinks that Plato holds the correct doctrine and adduces many ingenious arguments to support his thesis and to refute Aristotle's many innovative, but erroneous claims.

In what follows, I intend to examine critically and to present here only a sample of these arguments, sufficient to show both Pletho's method and the target of his sustained critique of Aristotle, as well as the multiple misunderstandings of the Philosopher's thought in the West.

Innovations in Theology and Ontology

To begin with, Pletho asserts at the opening of his treatise, in reference apparently to the "likely story" of the *Timaeus*, that Plato recognized God and spoke unequivocally of Him as the Demiurge, that is, the maker, father and king of this magnificent cosmos. But, being well aware of the important Platonic distinction between the intelligible and the sensible realms of reality, Pletho is cautious in his assertion. He indicates that the Supreme God is the demiurgic cause (*aitia*) of the intelligible world "directly" and of the sensible world "indirectly." For the former served as the model (*paradeigma*) for the latter, which is a mere image (*eikon*), depending on the other for its being, that is, ontologically.[15]

Pletho further observes that, in contrast to Plato, Aristotle is silent about the creative function of God. Hence the dilemma: Either Aristotle thought of God as the demiurgic cause of all things, but omitted it from his writings, in which case he was not a very careful philosopher. Or he did not think of God in terms of demiurgic cause, in which case his philosophy is deficient, in that it lacks the best doctrine (*kalliston dogma*). In either case, in terms of theology, Aristotle compares poorly with Plato. So, in Pletho's judgment those who thought that Aristotle's philosophy was in concord with the (Biblical or Koranic) "creation stories" did not have a sound understanding of the philosopher's doctrine at all.

He adduces the following arguments to show that the second horn of the above mentioned dilemma is actually the case. First, it is very unlikely that a philosopher, like Aristotle, who busied himself with such trivial matters as "embryos and oysters," would have failed to address the issue of the "creative function" of God, if he had thought that God had such a function.

Second, it is the case that Aristotle pokes fun at the philosophers (presumably the Pythagoreans) who admit "generation of numbers," on the ground that it is impossible to speak about coming into being (*genesis*) of that which is eternal (*aidios*).[16] Since, however, the eternity of the Cosmos is his attested doctrine, it follows that any talk about its coming into being and its "Creator" would be inconceivable for Aristotle, the Philosopher.

In Pletho's view, this argument also indicates that Aristotle erroneously held that "coming into being" and "generation in time" follows necessarily upon "causal generation," which is not the case. For, as Plato had shown, the soul is un-generated in terms of time (*chronos*), while in terms of cause (*aitia*) it is not so.[17]

Pletho was aware, of course, that Aristotle spoke of his Supreme God, the Unmoved Mover, as the originator and provider of a *telos* (final end) for all cosmic movements and processes.[18] However, he insists that one should not confuse the cause of motion (*kinesis*) and the cause of being (*einai*), for the two are distinct and the former presupposes the latter.

Besides, in Pletho's view, Aristotle had been unfair to his own Supreme God, even by his own rule of *analogia*, which demands that honor be distributed analogously and proportionally to merit.[19] For, clearly, Aristotle's First Unmoved Mover differs from the other planetary "movers" only so much as the outermost sphere differs from the other heavenly spheres. But this superiority, Pletho claims, is not worthy of the Supreme God, who is exalted above all others. This important point Avicenna, who followed Aristotle's astronomical theories, was able to see.[20]

So much, then, about God and creation in Aristotle's philosophy, and its deficiency compared with Plato's. Next in order comes the question of ontology. The celebrated theory of the "homonymy of being," of which Aristotle boasted, in Pletho's view, as being his wonderful discovery provided the first target. To better understand what is involved here, something must be said about "homonymy."

As specified by Aristotle, two beings or entities are called "homonyms" (*homonyma*), if and only if they have in common only the name, but not the definition corresponding to the name. For example, a man and the statue of a man may both be called "animal." But, if we were to define what "animal" means in each case, we would give "essentially" different definitions. This specific characteristic distinguishes homonyms from synonyms, which have in common the name and the definition corresponding to the name.[21] For example, a man and a horse may be called "animal," and in this case both the name and the definition, that captures the essence of the thing in question and corresponds to the common term "animal," will fit nicely both entities, man and horse.

Now, given the important ontological distinction, between the intelligible and the sensible worlds and their relationship of asymmetrical dependence (like that of a picture to the original), the Platonists had to be careful here. They had always argued that each kind of thing is only "in a homonymous way" called after the Idea or Form, in which it participates. Since the intelligible Ideas are really real beings and the sensible things only images, reflections or copies of them, it follows that they have in common only a minimal likeness. For Aristotle, on the other hand, the individuals of a given species admit not only the same name but also the definition corresponding to the name, which would make them a case of *synonymy* (and not of *homonymy*).[22]

In addition to this problem, there is another and more striking difference between the Platonic and the Aristotelian conceptions of "being" and of beings. For the Platonists, the Ideas share equally in being, since they all derive from one source, whether it is identified with Intellect, God or the ultimate Good.[23] Being is conceived as the genus (and thus the generator) of all real beings in the sphere of the intelligible. Consequently, it can be predicated of them "synonymously."

Aristotle vehemently opposed the doctrine of "synonymy of being." For him, "being" is *pollachos legomenon*, that is, it has as many meanings as there are distinct ontological categories.[24] So, "being" cannot be a genus, strictly speaking, because no genus can be predicated of its *differentiae* (as opposed its *species*), while that would have to be precisely the case regarding the predication of "being." It follows from this that the term "being" cannot be predicated *synonymously*, as the Platonists maintained. But, for Aristotle, this does not constitute a case of simple *homonymy* either. It is rather a special case of what he technically called predication "*aph' henos kai pros hen*," that is "from one and towards one."[25]

The Aristotelian Homonymy of Being

Returning to Pletho now, we may observe that, first of all, he ignores the above technical distinction and assumes that in Aristotle's view being is predicated in a "homonymous" way. Then he proceeds to question the basis of the Aristotelian conception of being as homonymous. If the homonymy of being is based on the fact that there is a gradation (a more and a less) of participation in being, this would be a weak basis, in Pletho's view. For, although milk is not as white as snow, no one would call them "homonymous" because of this variation in degree.

The same holds, in Pletho's view, if one were to assume that the distinction between "prior and posterior" provides the basis for the claim of the homonymy of being. For the case of numbers, which are, sequentially, "prior and posterior" would disprove such a claim. Numbers, in Pletho's view, admit both name and definition, which is the characteristic of "synonymy." Similarly, with the priority of elementary simple bodies and other bodies, which are composite and derivative from them, without ceasing to be equally substances (*ousiai*).

In addition, the fact that unity (*to hen*) is "reciprocally predicated" of being (*to on*), does not make being homonymous either, as "capable of laughter" and "capable of locomotion" are predicated, respectively and reciprocally, of man and animal, without rendering them "homonymous."

Furthermore, it is not correct that "genuine" genera are not predicated of their *differentiae*, as Aristotle had suggested. For if, for example, we consider "the rational" (instead of "rationality") as the proper *differentia* of man, it becomes evident then that the genus "animal" can be predicated of "the rational", since by the expression "the rational" what is implicitly understood is, of course, "animal."

Be that as it may, the impossibility of the Aristotelian position can be made manifest by another consideration. If it were the case, as the Platonists maintain, that the multiplicity of beings derives ultimately from one source, it would be absurd if these beings had nothing in common. And if they do have something in common, what could that be other than their "being?" But if "being" is only in a homonymous way predicated of them, as Aristotelians maintain, it cannot stand for this essential communality. It would seem, then, that Aristotle, who castigated "polyarchy" and praised, with Homer, "monarchy," unwittingly introduced "anarchy" in his ontology, by not allowing "being" to be one in genus, as genuine Platonists do. According to Pletho, this unnecessary ontological innovation has also affected the Aristotelian logic, to which he turned next.

As expected, Pletho objects strongly to Aristotle's distinction between primary and secondary substance; to his identification of the former with the particular and the latter with the universal; and to his contention that the particulars are more important than the universals, that is, species and genera. This doctrine seems to Pletho to turn Platonism, for which the parts exist for the sake of the whole and the many for the sake of the one (and not vice versa), literally upside down. It also proves Aristotle inconsistent in that he insists on considering epistemic knowledge as being of "the universal" rather than the particular, in spite of "the ontological priority," which he (in a non-platonic manner) attributes to the particulars.[26]

It is equally objectionable, presumably because it is not genuinely Platonic, that Aristotle considers the universal and the particular as being analogous to matter and form, respectively. For Pletho, the opposite is true. The Idea or Form as something whole, he thinks, cannot be found in the particulars, which are included in it and which partake of it in accordance with their place in the ontological hierarchy. Besides, the universal is stable and perfect, while the particulars, in their coming into being, constant change, and final passing away, lack this kind of stability and perfection.[27]

Some other points, which Pletho considers false, include Aristotle's logical assertions that "two contradictory statements can both be true if they are undetermined;" that "the sensible object is prior to sense perception;" and that "the conclusion always follows the minor of the premises." These points of Pletho's arguments have been extensively discussed recently, so we may pass them over and pass on to psychology, which is the next point of difference between Plato and Aristotle discussed by Pletho here.[28]

Innovations in Psychology, Ethics, and Cosmology

Once again, Pletho found it necessary to point out some basic tenets of Neoplatonism. Thus, we are told that, of the three hypostases (One, *Nous* or Intellect, and Soul), the One is Absolute Unity, in the sense that neither potency (in the sense of potentiality) nor act, nor even being is discernible in it. In the Intellect being and act are discernible, but potency is lacking. Only in the Soul can all three characteristics be discretely found, that is, being, act, and potency.[29]

This means, *inter alia*, that the human soul as part of the Cosmic Soul contains the knowledge of all things only potentially and that it can move from one thought to another, so that Aristotle was incorrect in asserting that the soul is immovable (*akinetos*).[30]

It is true that the soul does not move locally. However, in his assertion evidently Aristotle does not refer to locomotion, but to motion and change in general. Besides, this assertion does not seem to be in harmony with Aristotle's other doctrine, according to which the human mind changes from the state of thinking to that of non-thinking and vice versa. Since, then, for Aristotle, the being of the human mind coincides with its activity, when it ceases to be active, it would seem that it also ceases to be, and it comes back into being again as soon as it is energized.[31] The point is that all these mental changes cannot leave the soul intact.

As for Aristotle's sustained objection to Plato's conception of knowledge as "recollection," it seems to Pletho to be inconsistent with the other Aristotelian claim that the human mind is prior in time to the body. But if the mind existed prior to the body, it must have been active, since nothing could possibly prevent it from being active; that means that it must have had knowledge, which it apparently lost "at the shock of birth," and must recover. But such a recovery of forgotten knowledge is precisely what Plato and Platonists called "recollection."[32]

The worst aspect of Aristotle's psychology is that, though he speaks of intellect (*nous*) as immortal (in *De Anima* and *Metaphysics*), he does not make good use of this doctrine where it is needed most, in his *Ethics*.[33] In Pletho's view, such a doctrine is conducive to virtuous activity. Not only this, but Aristotle also states that there is "no good for man" after death which, to genuine Platonists like Pletho, is simply shocking. For if there is something immortal in man, it must be identified with the real man, and death can mean only the liberation of the immortal part from the bonds of mortal body, as Socrates had made clear in *Phaedo*.

Aristotle once again has been found guilty of inconsistency here, according to Pletho's analysis, which proves him inferior to his teacher, Plato. He must be also held responsible for giving grounds, through his inconsistencies, to Alexander of Aphrodisias, to Averroes, and many others for maintaining even "the mortality" of the human soul (*psyche*).

Regarding Aristotle's ethical theory, Pletho has two main objections, which seem to place it in the worst possible light. One of his objections relates to the doctrine of ethical excellence understood as a "mean" or middle state (*mesotes*) between two extremes; the other questions Aristotle's identification of the human end (*telos*) not with what is noble (*kalon*) or good (*agathon*), but with pleasure, albeit theoretical or philosophical pleasure (*hedone*).[34]

Pletho thinks that Aristotle, in the first place, did not clearly specify which "mean" did he have in mind, the qualitative or the quantitative.[35] However, from his examples of reasonable and foolish fears, Pletho was able to conclude that

Aristotle, contrary to Plato, determines what is to be feared and what not in terms of "quantity" rather than "quality" and morality. For example, fearing a really fierce thing such as the thunderbolt would be a reasonable fear, for Aristotle.

But, Pletho points out that such fear is unreasonable for the following reasons. First, it is nor shameful (*aischron*) to be bolted out of this life by means of receiving a thunderbolt on the head, for what is not in our power escapes the ethical dichotomy of praise or blame-worthy. Second, the rareness of such an event makes the probability of its occurrence for a particular human being so unlikely that any fear of it would be "pathological." Third, the realization that there is nothing one could do to avoid receiving the thunderbolt on his head renders the fear of it the "least fearful fear."[36] For the Platonists, on the other hand, "the shameful is horrible" always and regardless of its "smallness or largeness," since they measure these things only qualitatively, and not quantitatively.

Furthermore, Pletho has some difficulty with the notion of *mesotes*, which can be easily abused, for it can be made to apply even in the case of "the-all-bad man" (*pammochtheros*) who is the opposite of "the-all-good-man" (*kalos kai agathos*).[37] Playing the Devil's advocate here, Pletho points out that a man who would desire both all good things and all bad things could claim to follow the path of *mesotes*, since half of the things he desired were good! To put it in another way, by pursuing opposite things in a manner which is opposite to the appropriate (that is, desiring those things, which one should avoid, and avoiding those things, which one should desire), "the-all-bad-man" would appear to be both the opposite of "the-all-good-man" and, like him, to be in the desirable state of *mesotes*!

Sophistical as these remarks may sound they should not be dismissed off hand, because they indicate difficulties involved in the Aristotelian ethical doctrine of "the mean," which has puzzled ancient and modern commentators alike.[38] As for Aristotle's identification of the human *telos* with theoretical pleasure, Pletho thinks (blurring here the distinction between "eudemonism" and "hedonism"), that Epicurus learned the doctrine of ethical hedonism from him, since he also places the pleasures of the mind higher than those of the body.[39] Pletho objects strongly to the combination of contemplation (*theoria*) and pleasure (*hedone*), and their identification with "the good."

He further claims that, for the conjunction T & H (*theoria* and *hedone*) to be true, at least one of the terms T or H (and strictly both) must be truly good. Now, if it is T or H, then Aristotle should have proclaimed that either contemplation or pleasure is the good. But if both T and H are good, then there must be a common factor, which makes them both good, that is, the Idea of the Good itself, as Plato and Pletho maintained, without this leading necessarily to infinite regress.[40]

Next, Pletho moves to cosmology in order to criticize Aristotle's unnecessary innovation, that is, the introduction of ether as the fifth element, besides the traditional four elements (earth, water, air and fire), which Plato had accepted as sufficient for a complete cosmological account.[41] It was Aristotle's purpose of explaining the perpetual motion of heaven (*aeikineton*), which necessitated the introduction of a new and imperishable cosmic body (the fifth element), whose natural motion is circular, the only type that is capable of continuing perpetually.

Pletho agrees with Aristotle on the point that everlastingness would imply circularity, but he argues extensively that fire, which is perpetually in motion, could serve Aristotle's purpose well. That fire seems to move upward in a straight line down here on earth may be explained, in Pletho's view, as a consequence of its being out of its natural place. But nothing would prevent it from assuming its natural circular motion, as soon as it had reached its natural place at high.

His main point, in this connection, is that the conception of an imperishable body is an Aristotelian novelty (*kainotomia*) and it is distasteful to Pletho. For no body *qua* body is or can be imperishable. The imperishability of the cosmos as a whole is due not to its possession of a special kind of body, but to the presence of a great Soul, whose incorporeal and immortal nature is naturally incorruptible.[42]

Pletho also finds unacceptable two other Aristotelian doctrines regarding the stars and the sun. That the stars are animated, according to Aristotle, is something Pletho could live with. But that the cause of their motion should be attributed not to their respective souls, but to the heavenly spheres which carry them, as Aristotle apparently maintained, makes Pletho wonder whether the souls of the stars differ at all from the souls of "the oysters." If not, then he would like to know whether such souls were worthy of those luminous and everlasting beings.[43]

As for the claim that the cause of the sun's heat is its motion, Pletho is skeptical observing that, if that were so, the moon which moves (and is much closer to Earth) would have similar effects, but it has none. Like the theory of the "fifth element," therefore, this is a mere Aristotelian novelty. In Pletho's view, it is not worthy of further consideration.[44]

Critique of Aristotle's Theories of Art and Cause

Pletho takes exception with Aristotle's dictum that even "art acts without deliberation," in support of his doctrine that teleology could be extended to natural processes, without the risk of conceiving nature as a deliberating agent.[45] Contrary to this, Pletho asserts that deliberation is what characterizes human art most distinctly, since the artist always aims at something mentally preconceived. And since art imitates nature, as Aristotle himself maintained, Pletho concludes that nature must possess the same trait in a much greater degree.[46]

Besides, being God's institution, nature cannot possibly be without reason, strictly speaking. In the eyes of Pletho, Aristotle made as little use of his God, regarding the explanation of natural phenomena, as did Anaxagoras of the Mind (*Nous*) to the disappointment of the Platonic Socrates.[47] Plato, on the other hand, had a clear notion of art, which he divided into human (for the artificial things) and divine (for the natural beings). Both make use of reason, Pletho argues, though man is like a novice compared to God, who is the matchless author and architect, as Pindar said.[48]

Next, Pletho attacks Aristotle's position on the question of determinism. In order to make room for man's deliberation and freedom, Aristotle argued against the first of the following two axioms, from the combination of which logically follows, in Pletho's view, that everything happens by necessity. The two premises are: "It is necessary that every effect must be brought about by a cause;" and "every cause effects whatever it does by necessity."[49]

The thrust of Pletho's approach to this problem is that Aristotle contradicts himself because he maintains that "the moved, whatever that may be, is moved by a mover, and on the other hand, that not every happening has a cause," as if motion were not a kind of happening. For Pletho every happening and every motion has a determining cause, and this is adduced as the strongest argument leading thoughtful men to God, whom they identify with the hidden cause behind phenomena, the explanation of which escapes them.[50]

Furthermore, man's deliberation, which Aristotle considered as the principle (*arche*) of action, is seen by Pletho as a proximate cause (*aition*) only, since human deliberation and action are co-determined by the pre-existing "surrounding environment."[51] Pletho also points out that the basic Aristotelian doctrine, which claims that the actualization of a potentiality demands another actualized entity to effect the change, will be weakened, if the possibility of something happening without a cause be allowed to hold. Aristotle is shown again to be inconsistent.[52]

In a short paragraph which constitutes Chapter Nine, Pletho takes exception with Aristotle's view that motion (*kinesis*) is not double and, therefore, homonymous, but one and the same in both the mover and the moved, as expressed in *Physics*.[53] Contrary to this, Pletho asserts that motion is in fact a double actualization of a double potentiality, that is, of that which has the capacity to move something, and of that which has the capacity to be moved by something. The one is potentially active and the other potentially passive, till they come together. Then the process of actualization of their respective potentialities begins. When actualized this double potentiality appears to Pletho not as one actuality, as Aristotle claims, but as double. The two distinct actualities may be labeled the actualized-active-potentiality and the-actualized-passive-potentiality, respectively.

To the possible Peripatetic objection that this so-called "active potentiality" would have to be inactive, while waiting for its actualization, Pletho responds by comparing it to the Unmoved Mover, whose ability to move other beings leaves itself unmoved, that is, not acted upon. He thus provides justification for the need of two separate Aristotelian categories, the acting and being acted upon, which Plotinus, in his critique of Aristotle on this point, had tried to subsume under a single heading.

Stating once again that his purpose is not to cover all the differences, which separate the two philosophers, but only the most fundamental, Pletho proceeds to the last and most important difference, to which he devotes the major part of his treatise. This is the Platonic theory of Ideas and Aristotle's merciless critique of it.

Our purpose was to give only a sample of his criticism in order to illustrate his aim and his method of criticizing Aristotle. Since our discussion so far would have accomplished both of these tasks, we can afford to be brief in considering this last dividing issue between Plato and Aristotle, as Pletho's critical mind saw it.[54]

Critique of Aristotle's Critique of the Theory of Ideas

Pletho first corrects two erroneous Aristotelian statements regarding the origin of the theory of Ideas and their relations to images. Firstly, contrary to Aristotle, who had charged that the introduction of the Ideas was a Platonic innovation, Pletho claims that they had been used earlier by the Pythagoreans and Timaeus especially. Secondly, the Ideas are not synonymous, as Aristotle claimed, but homonymous, to the sensible and perishable things, which imitate and participate in them. Since the intelligible and the sensible realms of being are incommensurable (*asymbleta*), their ontological relation is analogous to that of Lysander and his statue, in which case homonymy is clearly involved.[55]

Next Pletho addresses Aristotle's argument against the multiplicity of Ideas in its triple form: (a) that there must be Ideas of whatsoever is an object of epistemic knowledge; (b) that there must be Ideas of negations; and (c) that there must be ideas of perishable and man-made things.[56] To these arguments Pletho responds, after a short exposition of the Platonic position by following three strategies.

First, he draws a distinction between the Forms (*logoi*), as they are found eternally in "the Soul" and as they are temporally exemplified in the multiplicity of the sensible things, since the former, unlike the latter, are limited. Secondly, he argues that negations depend on assertions for their being and, thus, are caused by the same cause, that is, the Forms. Thirdly, he specifies that in the Idea of "man" are included, and can be reasonably accounted for, all man-made objects as well.

The same argument holds against the postulation of Ideas for all kinds of accidents of this world which, in Pletho's view, are the result of convergence of many accidental causes (*synodos aitiōn*). Only for each kind of sensible substance and their essential characteristics (*prosonta*), are there Ideas or paradigms in the intelligible realm. Pletho insists on this point and takes the opportunity to sketch once again the hierarchy of that realm with the (absolute) unity of the One, the (bifurcated) unity of the Intellect, and the (tripartite) unity of the Soul.[57]

Pletho's reply to Aristotle's argument that the Idea of number must be absurdly prior to the Dyad is rather short. Aristotle seems to confuse here the Idea of number, which is unitary and therefore prior to Dyad, and the quantified numbers, of which the dyad comes first.[58]

Pletho can also easily dispense of Aristotle's next argument, which is stated: "Since the Ideas are not participated accidentally, it necessarily follows that, if they are participated, there will be Ideas of substances only."[59] That might be so, according to Pletho, if the distinction between substance and accidents were exclusive. However, the Platonists, between substance and accidents placed what they called "substantial qualities" which, although inseparable from substance, are not identical with it, and are participating in Ideas.[60]

As for the Aristotelian "third man" argument and the infinite regress to which it leads, Pletho argues that the similarity between prototype and copy is due to the former, as the example of Lysander and his statue mentioned above clearly indicates. Therefore, in Pletho's view, there is no real need to postulate a third Form in order to account for their relation. This would stop the "infinite regress" before it even started.[61]

Perhaps the most serious objection, which Aristotle raised against the Platonic Ideas, is that they contribute nothing either to the change of things, which come into being and pass away, or to the motion of the imperishable heavenly bodies.[62] This kind of objection would seem reasonable, Pletho claims, coming from Aristotle who attributed to God only the kinetic cause and overlooked the "poetic" or generative cause. For other Platonists, however, the Ideas cause the sensible things to be, as well as to move, and to be like the Ideas, which each of them exemplifies. Thus, by knowing the paradigm one has a better grasp of the copy as well. If so, it would follow that, contrary to Aristotle's claim, the Ideas contribute significantly to the being and the knowing of the sensible things of this world.

Furthermore, the hierarchy and gradation of the Platonic ontology can account for two more of Aristotle's objections. He had objected that there would be more than one paradigm for each kind of being, in the sense that there will be Ideas of species as well as genera and higher genera, and so on. Besides, one and the same entity may appear alternatively as a paradigm and as an icon depending on its place in the ontological hierarchy.[63] In Pletho's view, these points would follow logically from the ontological presuppositions of the theory of Ideas, and give no cause for alarm.

Pletho next turns the accusation that Platonists like to introduce unnecessary causes against Aristotle, by charging that it was he who introduced odd novelties, such as the "fifth body." Furthermore, he is accused of having brought the *eidos* (form) down to the sensible things by making it dependent on them, instead of them being dependent on it, as Plato had maintained.

So, if anyone is to be blamed here, it should be Aristotle, who did not have a kind word for any of his predecessors including Plato.[64] To make clear to the reader Plato's superiority, Pletho concludes his treatise by giving, once again, a good summary of the basic tenets of Platonism. But we can stop here, without following the Renaissance Platonist further into this list and its new adventures.

Conclusion

Even from this brief account, it is clear that Pletho's message to the renascent Europe was radically novel. Aristotle, as Pletho presented him to the Europeans, was incompatible with their religious faith in God, in miraculous creation, divine providence, and any serious concern about sinful human souls. Pletho's portrait of Aristotle resembled neither the Averroist nor the Thomist portraits of him.

By raising Aristotle above all other philosophers, including Plato, while working on a scheme to make him acceptable to religious communities, these commentators thought that they were rendering good services to their faiths, by dressing them up in philosophical garments. It is evident from his extensive argumentation that Pletho's intention was to demolish these scholastic edifices by emphasizing a tendency in Aristotle to argue, at certain times, as a philosopher who is too much this-worldly, mechanistic, and even a-theistic. The last epithet should be understood in the sense that he makes too little use of his God in his cosmology. But, above all, Pletho wanted to make sure that Aristotle is placed in his proper place, that is, after or next to Plato, but not above him, and certainly not in any company of Christian or Muslim "saints."

In Pletho's judgment, Aristotle went astray any time he deviated from the right path of Platonism. His silence about God's generative causation; his daring doctrine of the homonymy of being; his novelties in logic; his complex psychology; his quasi-teleological physiology; his mechanistic cosmology; his rather meaningless doctrine of "the mean;" his acceptance of fortune; his view of non-deliberating art; his confused account of motion; and his irreverent criticism of the theory of Ideas were questionable. This list had convinced Pletho that Aristotle, in spite of his sharp mind and strenuous effort, did not really improve much on the legacy of his great teacher, Plato.

To Pletho the time seemed ripe for another of Plato's revivals. Pletho would recommend the reading of Aristotle, whose works are replete with many and good Platonic doctrines. But he sincerely thought that the time had come for Platonism to flourish again in Europe and the West this time, since Greece and the East, unfortunately, were about to ender the long and dark period of Turkocracy.

It is true that Pletho's critique of Aristotle sounds at times too negative, hyperbolic, minute, sophistic, and antagonistic. But we should not forget that his polemical purpose was to shake up the European peoples from their Scholastic lethargy of a millennium. As the revival of Platonic studies in the School of Mystra and the Platonic Academy at Florence attests, Pletho's efforts were significantly fruitful.[65] His case, therefore, can serve for us as a paradigm of what is needed in our troubled times, too.

Notes

1. For Pletho, his relation to Platonism and his philosophy in general, I refer to: F. Masai, *Plethon et le Platonisme de Mistra* (Paris, 1976); and his "Le probleme des influences byzantines sur le platonisme italien de la Renaissance," *Bulletin de l'Association G. Bude* 12 (1953): 82-90; P. Kristeller, "Renaissance Aristotelianism," GRBS 6 (1965):

157-174; K. Oehler, "Aristotle in Byzantium," *GRBS* 5 (1964): 133-146; E. Moutsopoulos, "Byzance et l'hellenisme medieval," *Bulletin de l'Association G. Bude*, (1960): 389-396; L. Bargeliotes, "Pletho as a Forerunner of the Neo-Hellenic and Modern European Consciousness," *Diotima* 1 (1973): 33-60; S. Runciman, The Last Byzantine Renaissance (Cambridge, 1970); N.B. Tomadakis, "Γεώργιος-Γεμιστός Πλήθων," *Συλλάβιον Βυζαντινών Μελετών και Κειμένων*, 2 (1966), 151-159; J. Hankins, *Plato in the Italian Renaissance* (Leiden, 1991), especially Part III; and the most comprehensive study of C.M. Woodhouse, *George Gemistos Plethon: The Last of the Hellenes* (Oxford, 1986).

2. For the specific contributions of these Philosophers, see A.H. Armstrong, ed., *The Cambridge History of Later Greek and Early Medieval Philosophy* (Cambridge, 1967); and R. Wallis, *Neoplatonism* (New York, 1972).

3. *Vita Plotini*, 14. In *Plotinus, Enneads*, A.H. Armstrong, ed. (7 vols. Cambridge, Mass., 1978-1988), vol. 1.

4. I have discussed this more extensively in "Plotinus' Anti-Gnostic Polemic and Porphyry's *Against the Christians*," in *Neoplatonism and Gnosticism*, R. Wallis and J. Bregman, eds (Albany, NY, 1992).

5. For a complete list of his works, see J. Bidez, *Vie de Porphyre* (Hildesheim, 1964), Appendices, p. 67ff; and Evangeliou, *Aristotle's Categories and Porphyry* (Leiden, 1988), pp. 1-14.

6. *Porphyry Against the Christians: The Literary Remains*, R.J. Hoffmann, tr. (Oxford, 1994); *A*. Harnack, Porphyrios *'Gegen die Christen,'* 15 Bucher, (Berlin, 1916); A. Hulen, *Porphyry's Work Against the Christians* (Scottdale, PA, 1933); M. Anastos, "Porphyry's Attack on the Bible," in *The Classical Tradition*, L. Wallach, ed., (Ithaca, NY, 1966). Consider also the second essay of this collection.

7. The conflict officially ended in 529 A.D. when Justinian closed the philosophical schools. See also E.R. Dodds, *Pagan and Christian in an Age of Anxiety* (Cambridge, 1965); and R.L. Wilken, *The Christians as the Romans Saw Them* (New Haven, 1984).

8. Pletho sought the revival of the Empire by proposing radical political reforms and the return to Hellenic polytheism. On this see H.F. Tozer, "A Byzantine Reformer, Gemistus Plethon," *JHS* 7 (1886): 353-380; and L. Bargeliotes, *Η Κριτική του Αριστοτέλους παρά Πλήθωνι* (Athens, 1980), especially pp. 1-24.

9. This is the short title by which the treatise is known. The complete title in a literal translation would be, *On the Points on Which Aristotle Differs from Plato*.

10. B. Lagarde, *Le "De differentiis" de Plethon d'apres l'autographe de la Marcienne, Byzantium* 43 (1973): 312-343; reprinted in *Platonismos kai Aristotelismos kata ton Plethona*, L. Bargeliotes, ed. (Athens, 1987); all references and quotations will be to this edition (abbreviated as *DeD*) by chapter and line.

11. *Patrologia Graeca*, 160, pp. 979-1020. About the controversy between Plethon and Scholarios regarding Aristotle's merit see Woodhouse, *George Gemistos Plethon*, pp. 215-307; and L. Benakis, "Plethonos'*Apocrisis*," *Philosophia* 4 (1974): 348-349.

12. It is not clear whether Pletho had any previous knowledge of Averroes' influence on the Italians, as *the* outstanding commentator on Aristotle's philosophy. But there is no doubt that his visit to Florence in 1438-1439 had provided him with an excellent opportunity to become informed about this and other developments in the West. His firm stand and his verdict on this matter, in favor of Plato's priority and superiority in terms of philosophical merit, prepared the way for the revival of the Platonic Academy in Florence a few years later.

13. It is indicative of Pletho's reputation that, in spite of his anti-Christian attitude, he was invited to participate in the discussions on the union of the Churches at Ferrara/Florence in 1438-39. His visit to Italy in his old age and his meeting with the Italian Humanists provided Pletho with the opportunity to lecture on the respective merit of Plato and Aristotle. Hence the genesis of the *De Differentiis*. For details on this, see Woodhouse, *George Gemistos Plethon*, pp. 136-188.

14. The tenfold division of the treatise, which will be followed here, corresponds to Lagarde's edition cited above. Woodhouse follows a different system of numbering the paragraphs, *George Gemistos Plethon*, pp. 192-214.

15. I have dealt with the importance of this distinction for Plotinus in "The Ontological Basis of Plotinus' Criticism of Aristotle's Theory of Categories," in *The Structure of Being: A Neoplatonic Approach*, B. Harris, ed. (Albany, NY, 1982), pp. 73-83.

16. *Metaphysics*, 1091a 12-13.

17. Pletho compares *Phaedo*, where the soul is presented as having no beginning (*aganetos*) in time, with *Timaeus* where it is considered as "*genete*" in terms of demiurgic cause (*ibid.*, 15-18).

18. *Metaphysics*, 1072b 3-4; and *GC* 335b 24-29.

19. *NE*, 1131a 30-b 24.

20. This is Pletho's only reference to Avicenna and it is complimentary, unlike his view of Averroes' competence as an Aristotelian commentator, with which he had opened his treatise.

21. *Categories*, 1a 1-15. Also, J.P. Anton, "The Aristotelian Doctrine of *Homonyma* in the *Categories* and its Platonic Antecedents (part I)," *JHP* 6 (1969): 315-326; and part II, in *Essays in Ancient Greek Philosophy*, J.P. Anton and G. Kustas, eds. (Albany, NY, 1972); and Evangeliou, "The Problem of Homonymy of Being in Aristotle and Pletho," in *Πλατωνισμός και Αριστοτελισμός κατά τον Πλήθωνα*, L. Bargeliotes, ed. (Athens, 1987).

22. *Categories*, 1b 10-15. This is a fundamental difference between Plato or Platonism and Aristotle. For Porphyry's attempt to reconcile them, see Evangeliou, *Aristotle's Categories and Porphyry* (Leiden, 1996), pp. 60-66.

23. For Plotinus and other Neoplatonists, the Platonic Ideas are not outside of the divine *Nous*. See *Enneads* V. 5; and A.H. Armstrong, *The Architecture of the Intelligible Universe in the Philosophy of Plotinus* (Cambridge, 1940).

24. *Metaphysics*, 1004a 20-31; 1026b 2-4; 1077b 17-19, and so on.

25. *Metaphysics*, 1003a 33-34. For a discussion of this kind of ambiguity, see G.E.L. Owen, "Τιθέναι τα φαινόμενα," in *Logic, Science and Dialectic*, M. Nussbaum, ed. (Ithaca, NY, 1986); M. Ferejohn, "Aristotle on Focal Meaning snd the Unity of Science," *Phronesis* 25 (1980): 117-128; D.W. Hamlyn, 'Focal Meaning," PAS 78 (1978): 1-18; and Evangeliou, *ibid.*, pp. 39-47.

26. In the *Categories* Aristotle emphasized the ontological priority of the particulars. Yet the epistemological priority of the universals is stressed in *Metaphysics* throughout, especially Book E. This inconsistency was exploited by Plotinus, before Pletho, in his critique of Aristotle, as I have shown in "The Plotinian Reduction of Aristotle's Categories," *Ancient Philosophy* 7 (1988): 147-161.

27. Plotinus had similar objections to Aristotle's ontology in *Enneads* VI. 1-3; see also Evangeliou, *Aristotle's Categories and Porphyry*, pp. 93-129.

28. See Bargeliotes, *op. cit.*, especially pp. 133-145; and Dummett's comment:

"Pletho's view is, indeed, sound on a *de dicto* interpretation of modal statements. He was, however, so anxious to show Aristotle wrong on every count that he failed to consider whether there might not be another interpretation on which, in this matter at least, he [Aristotle] was right," *ibid.* pp. 65-70.

29. This is a concise and precise characterization of what differentiates the three Hypostases from each other. See also Evangeliou, *ibid.*, pp. 130-143.

30. For Aristotle's criticism of the various theories of the soul, see *De Anima*, 403b-411b.

31. These and similar absurdities follow, in Pletho's review, from the Aristotelian tenet regarding the soul's immobility. Pletho's biting irony may sound odd to us but we should keep in mind that they served him well in his goal to diminish the influence of Averroes' version of Aristotelianism on the Italian Renaissance. For the role of Aristotle's conception of mind (*nous*), as a linkage between the divine and the human beings, see the third essay of the collection.

32. For *anamnesis* see *Phaedo*, 73c-71d; and *Memo*, 82b-85b.

33. Pletho seems to overlook such passages as *NE*, 1173b 33, where the *nous* "within us" (the active and intuitive mind) and *athanatizein* (the possibility of immortality) are clearly connected.

34. This is unjustifiable in view of Aristotle's statement, "It seems therefore that pleasure is not the Good." (*NE*, 1174a 13-14). What perhaps misled Pletho was Aristotle's claim that pleasure, like seeing, is complete at any given moment and it does not take time for its completion.

35. Again, Pletho bypasses the many qualifications, which clarify the definition of ethical excellence or virtue as the mean (*NE*, 1107a).

36. In expressions like "he who is afraid of the thunderbolt fears the least fearful fear," Pletho seems to combine pun and irony effectively" (*DeD*, V. 30-31).

37. Again Pletho in his polemical mood pays no attention to Aristotle's warning that it is absurd to search for "the golden mean" in that which is an extreme (*NE*, 1107a 17-22).

38. In *The Meaning of the Mean in the Nicomachean Ethics* (M.A. Thesis, Emory University, 1976), I have discussed the difficulties of interpreting Aristotle's ethical doctrine of *mesotes* correctly.

39. Unlike others who have misunderstood him, Pletho recognizes Epicurus' distinction between bodily and intellectual pleasures and his expressed preference for the latter.

40. In Pletho's view, it is the Idea of the Good, which causes both contemplation and pleasure to be good. The so-called "third man argument" would not really arise, in his view, if we keep in mind that the relation between an Idea and its copies is like that between Lysander himself and his many statues. About these no sane person is in doubt as to which is the cause of what.

41. Since the *Epinomis*, 984b, mentions five elements including ether, Pletho would have to consider it as non-Platonic.

42. Porphyry, *Sententiae ad intellegibiles ducentes*, E. Lambert, ed. (Leipzig, 1975), provides a description of the incorporeal; and *Select Works of Porphyry*, T. Taylor, tr. (Guilford, 1994).

43. This is another example of Pletho's abusive irony, but here he has a point. For if the stars have souls but cannot move, then they will be less like animals and more like trees.

44. In his abhorrence of uncalled for novelty, Pletho follows Plotinus who also thought

that in Plato the whole truth had come to light. See the opening paragraph of *Ennead* VI.2.

45. *DeD*, VII. 32-40. Pletho quotes from *Physics*, 199b 26-30, with a change of the word *kinoun* (moving) to *poioun* (making) presumably for its better application to productive art in general (*poiesis*).

46. In *Physics*, 194a 21, Aristotle stated that "Art imitates nature," but (in 199a 15) he added an important qualification.

47. *Phaedo*, 97a-98d.

48. "*Aristotechnes*," the Greek word used by Pindar and quoted by Pletho here, means literally "the best craftsman or artist."

49. In Pletho's emphasis on determinism a Stoic influence may be detected.

50. Pletho's stress of the anti-religious implications of Aristotle's doctrines is consonant with his polemical purpose. It casts doubt on any attempt, whether Thomistic or Averroistic, to reconcile Aristotle's philosophy with Scriptural revelations.

51. *DeD*, VIII. 28.

52. Pletho's strategy is to refute Aristotle by Aristotle, that is, by discovering and playing up the inconsistencies in his doctrines.

53. *Physics*, 202a 15, "Hence there is a single actuality of both alike [mover and movable]." But (in 202a-b), qualifications of this position are discussed, which Pletho overlooked.

54. Almost half of the treatise is devoted to Aristotle's criticism of the Platonic Ideas and deserves more thorough treatment than the limited space of this study permits.

55. Given Pletho's advocacy of the empire's reform on the Spartan model, his choice of Lysander in his examples, instead of Socrates and his statue, is understandable.

56. *Metaphysics*, 990b 12-15, "For according to the arguments from the existence of the sciences there will be Forms of all things of which there are sciences, and according to the 'one over many' argument there will be Forms even of negations, and according to the argument that there is an object for thought even when the thing has perished, there will be Forms of perishable things; for we have an image of these" (Ross's translation).

57. In *DeD*, IV. 35-38, the One, Intellect (*Nous*), and Soul (*Psyche*) are presented as "unities," with no differentiation at all (as in the case of the One), or one differentiation only (as in the case of the *Nous*), or two differentiations only (as in the case of Soul).

58. For Plotinus' similar views on this point, see Evangeliou, *op cit.*, pp. 102-105.

59. *Metaphysics*, 990b 22-28.

60. "The essential qualities" were supposed to bridge the gap between substances and accidents by providing an ontological basis for real definitions. Porphyry's *Isagoge*, E. Warren, ed. (Toronto, Ca, 1975), pp. 42-47, and Evangeliou, *ibid.*, pp. 60-73.

61. See, G. Vlastos' "The Third Man Argument in the *Parmenides*," *Philosophical Review* 63 (1969): 182-301.

62. *Metaphysics*, 991a 8-18.

63. A similar problem arises in *arbor porphyriana* about the subordination of species and genera. See Evangeliou, *ibid.*, p. 55.

64. Pletho apparently did not like Aristotle's comments, with which he closed his *Sophistical Refutations* (184a-b), on himself being the inventor of the syllogistic art without mentioning of Archytas or Plato.

65. Consider P. Kristeller's expert opinion: "Pletho did a good deal to awaken Platonic scholarship and philosophy in the Byzantine Empire during its last decades; and thanks to

Pletho's stay in Italy and to the activities of his pupil, Cardinal Bessarion, and of both Greek scholars devoted or opposed to him, this development had important repercussions in the West until and beyond the end of the fifteenth century." *Renaissance Thought* (New York, 1961), p. 53.

Chapter 6

The Character of Hellenic Philosophy

Introduction[1]

The appellation "Western" is, in my view, inappropriate when applied to Ancient Hellas[2] and its greatest product, the Hellenic philosophy. For, as a matter of historical fact, neither the spirit of free inquiry and bold speculation, nor the quest of perfection via autonomous virtuous activity and ethical excellence survived, in the purity of their Hellenic forms, the imposition of inflexible religious doctrines and practices on Christian Europe. The coming of Christianity, with the theocratic proclivity of the Church, especially the hierarchically organized Catholic Church, sealed the fate of Hellenic philosophy in Europe for more than a millennium.[3] Since the Italian Renaissance, several attempts primarily by Platonists to revive the free spirit and other virtues of Hellenic philosophy have been invariably frustrated by violent reactions from religious movements, the Reformation and the Counter-Reformation, and the bloody wars which followed their appearance in Europe.[4]

Modern science succeeded to a certain extent, after struggle with the Catholic Church, in freeing itself from the snares of medieval theocratic restrictions. Thus, it managed to reconnect with the scientific spirit of late antiquity and its great achievements, especially in the fields of cosmology, physics, mathematics, and medicine, which enabled modern science to advance further.[5]

But it seems that the mainstream European philosophy has failed to follow the example of science and to liberate itself, too. As in the Middle Ages, so in modern and post-modern times the "European philosophy" has continued to play the undignified and servile role of handmaiden of something. In addition to the medieval role of "handmaiden of theology" (*ancilla theologiae*), since the seventeenth century philosophy in Europe assumed the role of "handmaiden of science" (*ancilla scientiae*) and, with the coming of the Marxist "scientific socialism," the extra role of "handmaiden of ideology" (*ancilla ideologiae*).[6]

In this respect, the so-called "Western philosophy," as it has been historically practiced in Christian and partially Islamized Europe, is indeed a very different kind of product from the autonomous intellectual and ethical human activity, which the Ancient Hellenes named *philosophia* and honored as "the queen of arts and sciences."[7] However, as we stand at the post-cold war era, witnessing the collapse of Soviet-style Socialism and the coming of the post-modern era; as we look at the dawn of a new millennium and dream of a new global order of Freedom and

Democracy, the moment seems propitious for reflection. So we may stop and reflect upon our philosophical past as exemplified in the free spirit of Hellenic philosophy and its many misfortunes, that is, its great "passion" in Christian Europe in the last two millennia or so.[8]

From such a vantage point, it would seem imperative that the philosophic freedom and the concomitant religious tolerance, as experienced in the Hellenic, pre-Christian era in the Mediterranean world, be revived. Such freedom should be fostered in the post-modern world, if our fragile, global, and diverse cultural community is to be preserved and flourish in the dawning new third millennium.

In this connection, Hellenic philosophy and Neoplatonism, as a form of successfully revived Platonism in late antiquity, have much to contribute to the common goal of cultural preservation and global flourishing. Representing the last phase of activity of the free spirit of Hellenic philosophy in antiquity; and having played a key role in defending Hellenism against various forms of religious fanaticism, Platonism can again provide the impetus for the needed movement to restore global philosophy to its ancestral dignity and glory.

This task can be accomplished by reviving the Hellenic spirit of freely theorizing about nature and culture. Such revival would acknowledge no other authority but that of human reason in both its Hellenic forms, as *logos* and *nous*, (that is, discursive reasoning and intuitive seeing), and of rational action in its two aspects, as ethical and intellectual activity in accordance with *arete* or excellence.[9]

I would like, therefore, to take the opportunity to express some of my novel views regarding the question of the so-called "Western philosophy" and its alleged connection to and continuity with the free spirit of inquiry of ancient Hellenic philosophy.[10] In what follows, I shall provide evidence in support of the thesis that the appellation "Western" is a misnomer, as is uncritically applied to Ancient Hellas in general, and to Hellenic philosophy in particular. For, in the balance of "West vs East" and in this conventional and artificial division of the globe, it has historically inclined towards the spiritually more refined East with good reason.[11]

I shall also argue that the reason for which the Christian Europe and the Islamic World, as a matter of historical fact, did not develop schools of authentic philosophy comparable to the diverse schools of ancient and humanistic Hellas, is directly related to a terrible cultural misfortune. This calamity befell Europe and the World at large with the coming into being of the two aberrations of Judaism,[12] namely, missionary Christianity and militant Islam.[13]

These two monotheistic religions, perhaps because of their dogmatic theologies and theocratic proclivities, have been historically intolerant not only of other divinities, but also of the free spirit of Hellenic philosophy, as the Hellenes envisioned and practiced this discipline. That is to say, as a free and unfettered inquiry into the nature of all things, human and divine, in search for truth, beauty, goodness, and above all "human dignity" in life, a life worth living, and in death.[14]

A note of clarification is in order here. The expression "genuine philosophy," which will be used in this essay, is intended to capture the original sense, in which *philosophia* was understood by ancient philosophers during the millennium of free philosophic activity from Pythagoras to Proclus. For these men practiced Hellenic philosophy in two essential ways, which have been conspicuously absent from Christian Europe.[15] First, for the Hellenes philosophy was a free, unfettered, and intelligent search for the truth regarding nature and the nature of man. Secondly, for them philosophy was also an authentic way of life, which was ethically self-sufficient and active, in accordance with the two kinds of Hellenic excellence, the intellectual and the ethical *aretai*.[16]

In this respect, it would appear to a critical observer that Islam and Christianity have been primarily responsible for two grave sins against Hellenic *philosophia*, which can be identified briefly here. First of all, we have the strangulation of that unrestricted and free spirit of inquiry and that kind of autonomous ethical life, which had given birth to genuine Hellenic philosophy, as it developed in the pre-Christian and pre-Islamic Mediterranean world. This "sin" was committed by introducing into philosophical thinking the new authority of "sacred books" and "scriptural revelations." The errors were multiplied due to the demand that such revelations and strange writings should be accepted on faith as "the word of God."

Then, we have the fact that, like the Islamic world, Christian Europe (including Orthodox Greece)[17] has failed to produce a school of philosophy comparable to ancient Hellenic philosophy. Comparable, that is to say, with the Hellenic philosophy's autonomy, dignity, playfulness, and its self-sufficiency for the good life of free persons. Surely, there are many "philosophic homonyms," that is, entities bearing the name of "philosophy," but lacking the definition of its essence.

These European "homonyms" of genuine Hellenic philosophy, in essence, are for the most part nothing but dogmatic and scholastic theologies in disguise and in perennial "servitude." They are invariably in the service of some theocratic tyrant, like the Pope, the Caliph, the Holy Roman Emperor or the Turkish Sultan.[18] They have also served for some time (about three centuries now) fashionable scientific theories (Newton's and Darwin's), or fashionable European political ideologies, such as Communism, Capitalism, National Socialism, and Fascism.[19]

So, at the dawn of the twenty-first century, the time may seem right for a possible revival of genuine *philosophia*, especially the revised Platonism which, as the last representative of Hellenic philosophy, was able to preserve in some measure its autonomy, dignity, and diversity. It can, therefore, serve as a linkage for our World, in its transitional search for a New World Order, to reconnect with the Hellenic roots of its great philosophic past in order to move to a greater, that is, philosophically brighter and freer future of humanity.[20]

The Ambiguity of the Appellation "Western"

In the expression "Western philosophy" two ambiguous terms are connected closely and repeated so frequently that the confusion generated by such infelicitous juxtaposition of these words seems to cry out for clarification. Regarding the first term "Western," one would be taxed to point out, in the globe which revolves round the sun and makes day and night, where on Earth the East stops and the West begins. Even if we were to follow the conventional wisdom and allow that Iceland and England are definitely in the West, while Korea and Japan, for example, are definitely in the East, where shall we rightfully place median countries like Greece and India? Both are to the East of the first pair, but to the West of the second pair. Hence our problem arises. One may suppose that the problem can be easily solved by comparing these two countries directly to each other, in which case it can be said that India is definitely in the East and Greece in the West relative to each other. But the situation is more complex than it appears.

For, even if the Indians were to go along with this solution, I suspect that the Greeks would have great difficulty accepting it for the following simple reason. Geographically Greece belongs to Eastern Mediterranean. Since ancient times, it occupies the tiny peninsula and the beautiful Aegean Sea where three continents meet: Africa, Asia, and Europe. This fact perhaps explains why the Ancient Hellenes conceived of the strange notion that the center of the World, "the navel of the Earth" as they used to say, was right there in the middle of Hellas, at one of the peaks of Parnassus.

It was there, at the holy shrine of Delphi, where Dionysus, the god of music and dance, rested from his long journey from India through Asia and Africa, according to ancient legend, and was welcomed by his brother Apollo, god of light and reason.[21] In this symbolic way, the conventional "East and West" dichotomy was harmonized for the Hellenes. From the harmonious union of the Apollonian and the Dionysian element, the Classical Hellenic civilization emerged as ripe fruit of the spirit and took its rightful place among the other civilizations of the great rivers: the Nile, the Euphrates, the Indus, the Ganges and the Yangtze.

In terms of geography, then, the Modern Greeks, like their ancestors or like any sensible people, may think of themselves as Westerners when they face towards the rising sun, but when they turn around and face the setting sun they consider themselves as Easterners or, at least, as non-Westerners. Even if we turned to history for assistance, we would find that it provides no greater help than geography for the correct characterization of the place of Hellas and Hellenic philosophy: Western or Eastern? In terms of history (from the time of the rise of Rome to political power in the third century BC to the Italian Renaissance in the fifteenth century), Classical and Hellenistic Hellas (and even Byzantine Christian Empire) invariably identified itself with the culturally more refined East. This was in conscious opposition to the Latin West which, to the Hellenic eyes of the time, appeared simply as synonym of barbarity.[22]

When the Roman Empire was divided in the end of the fourth century (395 AD), the division created again the Latin or Western and the Greek or Eastern Roman Empires. Ironically, it would seem, history was to repeat itself in the eleventh century (1054 AD), when a schism occurred in Christendom between the

Catholic Church which was, not surprisingly, Latin and Western, and the Orthodox Church which was, again not surprisingly, Greek and Eastern.[23] These historical considerations tip the balance of placing both the Ancient Hellas and Christianized Greece definitively toward the East in the artificial division of the globe between "East and West."

But this is not the end of the story. Since the Crusades, and more so with the rise to prominence of European powers (France, Spain, England, and Germany),[24] the Christians of the North thought that they would gain some respectability if they presented themselves as "inheritors" of the classical world and its brilliant culture. They boldly claimed as their own not only the Latin, but also the Hellenic classical heritage which they began, at that specific time, to characterize as "Western," opposing it to the Eastern Orthodox and the Islamic world.[25]

It is true that some intellectually awakened people have remained skeptical on the applicability of the appellation "Western" to Hellenic philosophy and culture, and about the truthfulness of the European claim of an exclusive right to classical inheritance. However, Modern Europeans were successful in persuading almost the entire world that there is no real difference between themselves, in their role of colonial imperialists, and the creators of classical civilization and philosophy.[26]

The unfortunate result of the European aggressive activities in this regard has been that the Ancient Hellenes are uncritically identified as "Westerners" now. They are conveniently placed in the same basket with the British, French, Spanish, Dutch, and German colonialists of Africa, America, and Asia. This is done not only by the Europeans and their historians of "philosophy," but also by many African, Asian, and Latin American thinkers and native peoples, as they struggle for cultural identity and social reconstruction.[27]

This deplorable outcome is certainly unfair to the Ancient Hellenes; but it is also unjust to scholars in the African and Asian nations who, as a result of the European exclusive claim to the Hellenic heritage, do not readily perceive the falsity of such claim at their expense. Thus they deprive themselves of a valuable ally, the treasure of classical literary *paideia* and Hellenic *philosophia*, in their pedagogical, political, cultural, and intellectual endeavors. This historically ungrounded European claim is truly a tragic irony. It is, like the other claim to the one and true God, a monopoly of the worst possible kind.[28]

This being the case, the time has come for the truth to be told for those who have ears for it. Well, then, the achievements of the Ancient Hellenes, especially the Hellenic *philosophia*, do not belong exclusively or even primarily to the Christian Europeans or to Islamic Asians. Rather, they belong to the world at large and to mankind as a whole, especially to those remnants of pre-Christian and pre-Islamic traditions and cultures. With these cultures the Ancient Hellenes had many affinities, such as love of human wisdom, as opposed to dogmatic and "divine wisdom" to be found in some "sacred books;" and a tolerant worship of many divinities (gods and goddesses). This is contrary to the folly of masculine monotheism with its concomitant, misogyny, bigotry, and religious fanaticism.[29]

By working diligently and cooperatively those who value these old traditions of tolerance and wise diversity could bring about a revival of Hellenic philosophy, perhaps in America, the land of the free and the brave.[30] Let this, then, suffice regarding the ambiguity and the perplexities of the appellation "Western," when it is applied to Ancient Hellas and its brilliant *philosophia*.

It is time now to provide a more precise definition of Hellenic *philosophia* and to identify its representatives, as they have traditionally functioned in *theoria* and, more importantly, in *praxis*.

Hellenic Philosophy Delineated

The previous observations have shown that Ancient Hellas and the West have, historically and geographically, stood at opposite poles. Since philosophy is legitimately connected with Ancient Hellas, it would seem that the expression "Western philosophy," as used by European historians of philosophy to cover the historical period from the Presocratic philosophers to postmodernists, becomes problematic. Similarly, we will run into other sorts of problems, if we were to grant the Europeans their wish to remove Classical Hellas from the middle place, which it has historically, geographically, and culturally occupied between East and West, and South and North. There, it has stood for millennia as a beacon of bright light available to every part of the world seeking philosophic enlightenment.

Furthermore, if we were to allow the Northern Europeans to claim exclusively as their own the Hellenic Classical heritage, especially Hellenic philosophy which, by its very nature, has an ecumenical value and perennial appeal;[31] then, we would be doing a disservice to our students and to our children. For they deserve a better future, that is, a life with more Hellenic and humanistic *paideia*, and with less racial strife and religious bigotry.[32]

From these considerations a central question arises for the meditations that will follow. The question is this: Did Christian Europe, seen as an entity separate from Ancient Hellas, and narrowly defined as the barbarized part of the divided Roman Empire, produce any philosophers or philosophical schools, comparable to schools of Hellenic philosophy or to ancient Indian and to Chinese schools of philosophy?

This is an important and complex question, which cannot be answered with a simple and short answer. The nature of the answer would depend on the meaning to be assigned to the term *philosophia* which, like *demokratia*, is a very attractive Hellenic concept, but it has been much used and abused in the course of history by many European so-called "philosophers." These men, like the ancient Sophists, would like to appear rather than to be true philosophers.[33]

What, then, is genuine Hellenic philosophy, or *philosophia*? What is this attractive wisdom, with which the minds of authentic philosophers are said to fall passionately in love? What exactly did the Ancient Hellenes mean with this beautiful word *philosophia*, and how did they distinguish the genuine philosophers from the seeming "philosophers" of their time, whom they called sophists?[34]

In a broad sense, there is nothing mysterious about the inborn and burning human desire to philosophize. This urges us to learn by opening the eyes and the mind to the natural and the cultural world around us; by asking difficult questions both as teachers and students; and by trying, to the best of our ability, to articulate reasonable and honest answers to such difficult philosophical questions.[35]

But if we were to isolate specific criteria by which the authentic philosopher can be distinguished from his "homonyms," then, in the light of the history of Hellenic *philosophia*, we can specify as such criteria the two kinds of philosophic excellence, the intellectual and the ethical *aretai*.[36] According to this delineation of genuine Hellenic philosophy, one can say that a genuine philosopher is a person who is both noetically enlightened and an ethically self-sufficient and autonomous human being. This means that they have accomplished the following two important philosophical tasks.[37]

First, the genuine philosopher has thoroughly examined himself or herself. They have, for a long time, carefully observed the natural and the cultural world around them. They have diligently studied the works of other great minds and have freely discussed with friends the great questions of life; and, after prolonged and serious thinking, they have formed a cosmo-theory and/or a bio-theory, articulating an insight into the nature of things and human nature. So, they are able to give a reasoned account of these things and can teach others who may wish to learn, from such a lifelong experience in the pursuit of wisdom.

Secondly, the genuine philosophers do not only teach the acquired wisdom, but also and more importantly are able to practice the teaching in their own daily life. For they are willing to hold themselves to higher ethical standards than the ones which the society demands of the majority of the people, setting the value of philosophic freedom higher than life itself, and much higher than wealth and material goods of any kind. By so doing, the genuine philosopher naturally sets this lived *philosophia* as a "way of living" for the pupils and others persons who may wish to follow. Like Pythagoras and Socrates, Epicurus and Epictetus, Laotse and Confucius, Buddha or Gandhi, the true philosopher has become an enlightened person, a passionate lover of truth, a gentle teacher by word and deed, and a source of light to those who desire philosophical enlightenment in generations to come.[38]

This is, in outline, the noble portrait of "the ideal philosopher" as envisioned and occasionally realized by some of the Ancient Hellenes and other non-Western peoples, who were able to look at the cosmos, at their political institutions, and at their inner souls and minds as free human beings. That is to say, without the fetters of any dogma, least of all any ecclesiastical or religious dogma backed by the rhetoric and the sophistry of some "revealed" theology or, even worse, by the fear and the terror of some entrenched theocracy.

This being so, the crucial questions inevitably arise: What happened to this noble philosophical ideal in Christian Europe and the barbarized West? Why was the intellectual and ethical treasure of Hellenic philosophy lost? And, last but not least, can it be ever recovered, by the admirers of its beauty who mourn its loss?

Hellenic Philosophy and "European Philosophy"

Judging by the two above specified criteria, as set by the Hellenic philosophers,[39] it is doubtful that one will be able to find many or any of the so-called European "philosophers," who would be able to meet these criteria, especially the second. Let me explain my skeptical pessimism on this important point. By the criterion of noetically self-sufficient inquiry, any one who takes "on faith" divine revelations found in certain books of uncertain origin, and then uses "philosophy" to justify an imposed religious dogma on behalf of some established theocratic institutions, is disqualified from being called a philosopher. As the ancient Hellenic philosophers understood and used this honorable name, it does not befit such a person. Such devout person may be perhaps a good writer or a sharp advocate of the cause of their respective sect, but a genuine philosopher s/he cannot be according to the first Hellenic criterion of genuine *philosophia*.[40]

Similarly, by the second specified criterion of autonomous and self-sufficient life of ethical excellence, any one who believes in the efficacy of divine grace, (provided by baptismal ablutions in holy waters[41] or other sacraments of this kind), to produce and sustain a life of integral philosophic virtue, as Christians and Muslims traditionally have done, cannot be called a genuine philosopher. Such a person may very well be a good man or even a saint, but a philosopher, in the original sense of this Hellenic word *philosophia*, s/he will never be. For a genuine Hellenic philosopher is expected to rise to perfection by human means only and by self-conscious virtuous activity, even under the most adverse conditions.[42]

In this light, and considering the fact that Europe in the last two millennia has served various and dubious authorities, especially under the double yoke of Catholic scholastic dogmatism and Protestant puritanical fanaticism, it is not surprising that *philosophia*, in the Hellenic sense of the word, has not flourished. Genuine philosophers are conspicuously absent from this strange "theater" of the so-called "European philosophy."[43] Now, some may find it amusing, but it is sad to see how cautious the philosopher-theologians, and other thinkers of the Western European type, have been in their writings lest they contradict the received dogma of the respective sect and, thus, upset the ecclesiastical authority or hierarchy.[44]

The list of such persons is long and cannot be covered here in any detail.[45] It would certainly include Augustine, Aquinas, Bonaventure, and other theologians and Church Fathers; but also Descartes, Locke, Berkeley, Hegel, and many more European thinkers. For them, the purpose of "philosophizing" has been to either explicitly provide support for the Church doctrines, by using rhetorical techniques and philosophical argumentation; or, implicitly, to "make room" for the practice of faith, especially in its Protestant and Catholic formulations, which historically have dominated the Western European culture.[46]

It is true, of course, that in the last five hundred years or so, several attempts have been made to revive the spirit of free, autonomous, and self-reliable inquiry, but philosophically, as opposed to scientifically, they all have invariably failed.[47] For example, the hope that the opening of the Florentine Academy, during the Italian Renaissance in the fifteenth century, would lead to the rebirth of Platonic philosophy in its Hellenic version (as opposed to its Christian versions), was cut short. It was replaced by the Protestant Reformation coming, not surprisingly, from the Teutonic North.[48]

Moreover, "the Age of Light and Reason" of the late seventeenth and early eighteenth centuries, on which the French *philosophes* had build their dreams for a Europe freed from the religious oppressive dogma, ended with the formation of the Holy Alliance and the coming of Romanticism, German Idealism and obfuscation. Thus, once again, "Western philosophy" was turned into the handmaid of theology, this time of Protestantism, just as it had been an *ancilla theologiae* in Catholicism, during the long Dark Ages.[49]

These historical examples clearly indicate that up to the nineteenth century no genuine school of philosophy, in the above-specified sense, had appeared in the horizon of the Western world.[50] But the situation, significantly, has not changed much since that time, in spite of the multiplication of "-isms" coming out of Europe in rapid succession: Marxism, Existentialism, Atheism, Nihilism, and so on. The protagonists of these movements make some noise, but they seem to be only ephemeral phenomena. They can be fairly classified into five categories, of which none can pass the two tests of genuine *philosophia* as specified above. So, if we were to schematically categorize the European "philosophers" in descending order, according to the honesty, which they exhibit in their "philosophical" and literary works, we would obtain the following specimens:

First, there are those European thinkers who rebel against any established convention and demand the right to absolute freedom of thought and expression; Nietzsche, Russell, Sartre, and Kazantzakis perhaps belong in this category.

Second, there are the players of the familiar role of Western "philosophers," as providers of philosophical justification or respectability to ecclesiastic dogma; theist existentialists and devotees of phenomenology may belong in this group.[51]

Third, there are those who prefer to play the role of providing "philosophical foundations" for the grounding of scientific method and its methodically obtained truth; logical positivists and language analysts certainly belong in this category.[52]

Fourth, there are the players of the more radical role of serving the political ideology of "scientific socialism" and its issue "dictatorship of the proletariat;" faithful Marxists, Leninists, Stalinists and Maoists would fit well in this category.[53]

Fifth there are the experts of the old sophistical game of words, whom the Hellenes called "Sophists,"[54] but they pass as "philosophers" in Europe and the

West these days of extreme sophistication; deconstructionists, like Jack Derrida, and neo-pragmatists, like Richard Rorty, and many others would fit nicely here.[55]

But, be that as it may, things look a little more promising now. The complete collapse of communism; the disillusion of the hope that science will find the ultimate truth, by chasing the Platonic dyad of "Great and Small," as it becomes greater and smaller without end; and the end of the Cold War came earlier than expected.   Besides, the global "War on Terror" is a new and harsh reality. Paradoxically, all this has contributed to the possibility of a rebirth of philosophy.

The friends of Plato and Platonism, all true lovers of wisdom, are called upon to try again to restore philosophy to its ancestral autonomy, dignity, and glory. The task is noble and they may be more fortunate, than the Platonists of Florentine Academy or the Cambridge Platonists, for the common good of mankind as it is preparing to shape and to share the "global village" with its civil fragility.

Conclusion

In conclusion, and always from the perspective of Hellenic philosophy, the European terrain looks today, like the thing that it has always been, a wasteland. For, as we have seen, the nobility of Ancient Hellenic philosophy, as it was expressed in the unfettered freedom of inquiry and in the self-sufficiency of authentic ethical life for the philosophically minded, was lost in the West.

This occurred at the critical time of the barbarian invasions from the Teutonic North and of the revealed religions of "the Book" from the Semitic South. Messianic Christianity and militant Islam are the two faces of traditional Judaism, the mild and the wild. With their restrictive dogmatic theologies and oppressive theocratic political structures, they have historically appeared to the eyes and minds of Hellenic philosophers as twin forms of fanatic "barbarism," as we saw.

In this light, it would be benighted to present the history of so called "Western philosophy" as if it were a continuity in time, covering two and a half millennia of linear progression. For the gap, separating the Hellenic philosophers from Western "philosophers" (whether they may be called medieval theologians, modern positivists, Marxist/Leninist theorists, or post-modern deconstructionists), is too wide to leap over and too glaring to be overlooked. In the hands of these European "philosophers," what to the Hellenes had been *philosophia*, that is, the pure love of wisdom and the "Fair Queen" of arts and sciences, was turned successively (and shamelessly, one may add) into handmaiden of divinely revealed theology, methodically epistemic technology, and revolutionary political ideology.

In the eyes of Hellenic philosophers, these three alien Masters would constitute an "Unholy Trinity," which Hellenic *philosophia* has been forced to serve for the last two millennia in Europe and the West. This prolonged servitude and lack of freedom has transformed the character of Hellenic *philosophia*, and has produced what is called "Western philosophy." If closely observed, these two disciplines appear to have in common little else, other than the similarity of their names, which constitutes a classic Aristotelian case of *homonymia*. Hence the urgent need for the philosophically minded persons to return to their philosophical roots, which are pre-Christian and pre-Islamic, in search for a new inspiration for a possible revival of Hellenic philosophy and humanism in the new millennium.

The lesson to be learned, and the conclusion to be drawn by any person with an open mind and a sensitive soul, is that Hellenic philosophy, and Platonism in particular, does not belong exclusively to any specific group. Least of all does it belong to the Europeans, despite their unjustifiable claims to it. Rather it belongs to the world and mankind as a whole by reason of its perennial and humanistic virtues, including the freedom to theorize and the responsibility to perfect the human soul, following in the steps of Socrates and other Hellenic philosophers.

I am inclined to believe that perhaps, if we dig deeply enough in our human souls and cultural traditions, we shall discover that the roots of genuine philosophy (whether Hellenic and Mediterranean, Indian and Asian, Egyptian and African, or Native American), somehow connect in a common ground or underground.

This deep connection also points at the ascent towards a common ideal of philanthropic diversity, polytheistic tolerance, and political virtue, as the necessary preconditions of an authentic life of philosophic freedom and human dignity. Now, it would seem, more than ever before such a noble ideal is within reach and needed, for our unified global world and its fragile civility.[56]

Notes

1. The paper, in its present form, was presented at the XII International Conference on Neoplatonism and Contemporary Thought, which was organized by the International Society for Neoplatonic Studies in May 1995, at Vanderbilt University. A shorter version of it was published in the *Journal of Indian Council of Philosophical Research 12*, no. 2 (1995): 27-38. The thesis, presented in summary here, will be further developed in a work in progress, *The Passion of Hellenic Philosophy in Europe.*

2. Hellas and Hellenes have become for the Christian Europeans respectively Greece and Greeks, derived from the Latin *Graecia* and *Graeci*, which have had unpleasant connotations in the ears of the Ancient Hellenes, as well as the Modern Greeks who insist on calling themselves New Hellenes and their country Hellas.

However, Modern Greeks, in their eagerness to be accepted as partners in the European Union by Europeans, do not always seem to be aware of the difference or to mind the change of their ethnic name. So, I have retained both these names, which I have used consistently to refer to Ancient Hellenes and to Modern Greeks, respectively.

3. These noble ideals had been characteristically embodied in the lives and expressed in the theories of philosophers from Pythagoras to Plato, Plotinus, Porphyry, and Pletho.

4. The most promising, but sadly frustrated, was the movement to revive Hellenic philosophy in the fifteenth century, which was initiated by the great representative of Platonism, George Gemistos or Pletho. He opposed the Christianized and Islamized "European philosophy," for reasons which will become clear as we proceed further into this

thesis. See also the second essay; and C.M. Woodhouse's excellent monograph, George Gemistos Plethon: The Last of the Hellenes (Oxford, 1986).

5.   Many Europeans, who take pride in the achievements of modern science, seem to forget that many of the discoveries would have occurred perhaps a millennium earlier, had there not been a discontinuity of the Hellenic scientific and philosophical tradition. This was effected by the barbarian invasions and fostered by the theocratic organization and otherworldly orientation of the early Christian Church. If the terrifying eschatology of the Church, which proclaimed the approaching end of the world, is considered in connection with its inflexible dogma and its numerous ethical taboos, it can explain the paralysis imposed upon the European mind for more than a thousand years. At least philosophically, Europe has not as yet completely recovered from this great cultural calamity.

6.   It should be stressed that the three non-Hellenic masters of European "philosophy" (that is to say, dogmatic theology, technocratic epistemology, and political ideology) do not necessarily replace each other in the course of time. On the contrary, since the seventeenth century, many European "philosophers" have been willing and able to serve more than one master simultaneously. But the fact remains that it was in their long service to dogmatic theology (and the concomitant Christian theocracy in the West), that they acquired and passed on the bad habit of expecting "the truth" to be given to them ready made. The magic instrument for this transmission was initially "apocalyptic revelation" to be found in sacred books exclusively interpreted by the established hierarchy of ecclesiastical authorities. This kind of "magic" and the "bad habits" were transferred later to the "scientific method" of modern science, and even to the "scientific socialism" of Marxism.

Accordingly, these so-called "philosophers" became parasitic entities dependent upon the mentioned "Masters." They are used to do service work, instead of trying to find "the truth" for themselves and, then, live and die by it, as Socrates and other Hellenic philosophers had done showing the way to wisdom by living through it. In this important aspect, the two groups of philosophers, the Hellenic and the European, differ fundamentally from each other to such a degree that the term "philosopher" cannot apply to both of them in the same sense without equivocation; for it has become a mere "*homonymon*" (homonym), as Aristotle would say. However, this essential difference has been lost in the histories of Western "philosophy," which pass from Plato and Aristotle to Augustine and Thomas Aquinas, to Avicenna and Averroes (if these two are mentioned at all), to Descartes and Locke, to Hegel and Heidegger continuously. They do not even seem to notice the gap, which separates the ancient Hellenes from medieval and modern Europeans in their respective ways as philosophers. See, for example, *Hegel's Lectures on the History of Philosophy*, E.S. Handale and F.H. Simson, tr. (London, 1896). He concluded his work by stating: "The general result of the history of Philosophy is this: in the first place, that throughout all time there has been only one Philosophy, the contemporary differences of which constitute the necessary aspects of the one principle; in the second place, that the succession of philosophic systems is not due to chance, but represents the necessary succession of stages in the development of this science; in the third place, that the final philosophy of a period is the result of this development, and is truth in the highest form which self-consciousness of spirit affords to itself. The latest philosophy contains therefore those, which went before; it embraces in itself all the different stages thereof; it is the product and result of those that preceded it. We can now, for example, be Platonists no longer" (pp. 552-553).

One may hope that Hegel's prophecy that "we can be Platonists no longer" will be proven as incorrect as has his thesis about the continuity of philosophy in the West. There is no continuity of spirit between the Hellenic and the medieval periods of philosophy. Yet, Hegel has stated (*ibid.*, p. 553): "Our standpoint now is accordingly the knowledge of this Idea as spirit, as absolute Spirit, which in this way opposes to itself another spirit, the finite, the principle of which is to know absolute Spirit in order that absolute Spirit may become existent for it." If we substitute God for "absolute Spirit" and man for "finite spirit," we would discover the entire medieval, relational theology, under a Hegelian obfuscating phraseology. My thesis is the antithesis of this.

7. According to Aristotle, one of the outstanding practitioners of Hellenic *philosophia*, the character of this discipline is described as follows: "Evidently then we do not seek it [philosophy] for the sake of any other advantage; but as the man is free, we say, who exists for his own sake and not for another's, so we pursue this as the only free science, for it alone exists for its own sake" (*Metaphysics*, 982b 24-27).

It is doubtful whether Northern Europeans would have been able to appreciate the nobility of this Hellenic pursuit. For, during the Middle Ages, they used "philosophy" to justify religious revelations and irrational dogmas; while during modern times, they used "philosophy" to justify revolutions (political and scientific) in a greedy pursuit of power over nature and other nations. In doing so, they involved the entire globe in disastrous wars and much suffering. But technology has indeed made some progress.

8. To quote Aristotle here: "Now, passion is the quality of the soul, which begets friendship and enables us to love; notably the spirit within us is more stirred against our friends and acquaintances than against those who are unknown to us, when we are despised by them" (*Politics*, 1328a 1-4). Well, what happened? It would seem that the "pathos," the passionate love with which the Ancient Hellenes pursued "Lady Philosophy," to use Boethius' personification, has been lost in the West, where so many "philosophers" have been wasting their time in trivial pursuits of word games, whether analytical or deconstructive. If Lady Philosophy had a voice, she would address the above wise words of Aristotle to these persons, who were supposed to be her friends, but they have abandoned and despised her perhaps out of ignorance of her history rather than malice in their hearts. Hence the other meaning of the word "passion," that is, undeserved suffering, like that of Jesus Christ. But, while "The Passion of Lord" lasted less than a week in the hands of some religious fanatics, "The Passion of Lady Philosophy" has lasted for almost two millennia in the hands of the so-called "Western philosophers," Christians and Moslems, and it is not over yet. The story of this "passion" of Philosophy has not been told from the Hellenic perspective. Hence the genesis of my thesis as presented in this essay synoptically, and as it will be elaborated in the forthcoming book *The Passion of Hellenic Philosophy in Europe.*

9. The changed global conditions in the last five centuries permit the friends of Hellenic philosophy to be "cautiously optimistic" that they will have better luck than Pletho and his Florentine friends. But, as the genuine lovers of wisdom know so well, working diligently for a noble cause, like all virtuous activity, is rewarding in itself regardless of the final positive or negative outcome.

10. In this light, K.S. Murty's statement would seem optimistic and only partly correct with certain qualifications: "I think modern India and Europe can and do understand ancient India and Greece, and the West and East also can and do understand each other." See, *Philosophy in India: Traditions, Teaching and Research* (Delhi, 1991, revised edn), p. 201.

I would not like to appear to be such a pessimist as to doubt the possibility or potentiality of understanding (that is, the modality of "can"), but the historical facts (that is the modality of "do") do not support Professor Murty's claim at least in so far as it concerns Modern Europe and Ancient Hellas. For, philosophically, they are poles apart because of the intervening dogmatism and oppression of Christian and Islamic theocracies and theologies, which have affected deeply the European ethos and mind.

So, if we want to find a "kindred spirit" which resembles the philosophically free, diverse, playful, non-dogmatic, and tolerant spirit of Ancient Hellas, we should look to Ancient India rather than to Medieval Europe. That is our only hope for a better future, philosophically speaking. For Northern Europe, whether in its medieval, modern, or post-modern mental and cultural outlook, would seem more like an aberration of ancient Judaism than a legitimate offspring of Hellenism. Even within the Christendom, Western Catholicism and Northern Protestantism are seen, from the East, as heterodox revisions of the original Orthodox Christianity. The four and very different faces of Christianity (Jewish, Greek, Latin, and Teutonic), and their relation to Hellenic philosophy, constitute an interesting theme waiting for its philosophic treatment.

11. The case of Modern Greece and its "Westernization" is a very interesting but separate issue. I will say only this, to the extent that it is Christianized, like the rest of Europe, Modern Greece has lost its ancient potency for autonomous philosophic activity. In the emerging United Europe, in which tiny Greece is supposedly an equal partner, there is a real danger that the Greeks will lose their cultural and ethnic identity. Most tragic of all, they may also lose their beautiful language, which they have inherited from Homer and Plato, and were able to preserve even during the long and dark period of Turkocracy. This possibility is a nightmare for the intellectually and culturally awakened Greeks. They will have to work diligently to prevent such a disastrous outcome. We may, not only wish them good luck, but also do our best to help them in this difficult task ahead.

12. In their aggressive proselytism, utopian universalism, and the exclusive claim to the "only way" of salvation by faith (in the Bible or in the Koran respectively), Christianity and Islam, as organized religious theocracies, differ from pre-Christian and pre-Islamic Judaism from which both of them derived. With Judaism they share the monomania of monotheism on a popular level, as well as the folly of the myth of the "chosen people." In the case of Judaism, the folly of the monopoly of God and His exclusive favor, was rather innocent by reason of being ethnic and, politically, powerless at that time. But in the other two cases, it was not innocent at all, because it became super-national and soon acquired political power to the detriment of philosophy, science, reason, and free inquiry. How and whether the civilized world will be able to overcome this double calamity, this dangerous game in the "name of God," in the greedy and all-too-human pursuit of power over others, are questions which the Western world will have to face directly at the beginning of the third millennium. Whether the declared war on terror (after 9/11/01) will help or exasperate the situation remains unclear at the present time.

13. Christianity is, in A.N. Whitehead's characterization: "A thoroughgoing rationalization of the Jewish religion carried through with a boundless naivete ..." *Religion in the Making* (New York, 1926), pp. 55-56. But if Christianity is the first, then Islam would be the second, and more militant, aberration of Judaism, while the third and final would be "Marxist atheism," which was more destructive than the other two. Of course, in some parts of the West, nationalists do not even want to be reminded where Jesus Christ came from.

According to B. Russell, who knew how to say nasty things in a nice way, "If you maintain in Germany that Christ was a Jew, or in Russia that the atom has lost its substantiality and become a mere series of events, you are liable to very severe punishment." *Religion and Science* (Oxford, 1980), p. 247.

However, in fairness to the men who initiated the two religious movements, Jesus and Mohammed, a distinction should be made between what they dreamed of and what historically has happened to that dream, in the hands of men greedy for power acquired by any means, even the name of God. So, my comments would apply to Christianity and Islam as historical phenomena and as cases of theocracies. They have shaped a mentality of intolerance, which is characteristic of the societies of Western Europe, and of the Middle East. From these aberrations of Judaism the West and the East must be freed, so that the peoples of the World, with their respective gods and cultures, may learn to live together again in religious peace as in antiquity, leaving God in peace and only for philosophical speculation.

14. In contrast to Hellenic philosophers, Christian and Moslem intellectuals had found (or pretended to) all the correct answers to these difficult philosophical questions in books, such as the Bible and the Koran respectively, for whose origins and coming into being they could not dare to give a reasoned account. These religious "truths" were to be accepted on faith as "divine revelations" even by so-called "philosophers." Their servile function had thus been reduced to providing justification for the "theophanies" and the respective theocracies, which were built upon them encompassing large numbers of peoples. In this manner, the European philosophical mind acquired the "bad habit" of expecting to be provided by the ready made truth. This would come originally from the quarters of "religious revelations;" later by the authority of "scientific method;" and finally by the application of the dogma of "scientific socialism." In this sad way the degradation of the Hellenic *philosophy* or Lady Philosophy was completed in Europe.

15. To avoid confusion, I should explain that by "philosophy" is meant in this discussion all the "philosophical productions" of the Christianized and Islamized (Western or Eastern) World, whether by "systematic or edifying thinkers," to use R. Rorty's distinction. He also uses the term "philosophy" to indicate "something on the other side of the tradition." *Philosophy and the Mirror of Nature* (Princeton, 1979), p. 394. According to him, the "tradition" is supposed to extend from Plato to Nietzsche, while "on the other side" he places such thinkers as Wittgenstein, Heidegger, and Dewey (Chapter VIII, "Philosophy without Mirrors," pp. 357-394).

But this is a rather curious division, in light of the historical facts and of the gulf which separates the mentality of Christian Europe and its dogmatic and monotheistic theology from Ancient Hellas and its humanistic and pluralistic philosophy. Rorty's division may serve only what he calls "neo-pragmatism," which looks more and more like a new name for the ancient art practiced by the famous Sophists. Therefore, his project becomes virtually indistinguishable from the project of "deconstructionism."

16. According to Aristotle, *NE*, 1103a 4-10, the double sense of ethical and intellectual excellence for man is contained in the word *arete*. The Hellenes were able to produce genuine philosophy, probably because in their pre-Christian and pre-Islamic civilization the human mind was free and unfettered by religious dogmas. These were produced by Christian and Islamic intolerant monotheistic theologies with their contradictory claims to exclusivity (the chosen people myth) and universality (evangelize the whole world). For, to

quote from the wisdom of *Report* (of The Experts' Panel in Philosophy in India): "Philosophy as *seeking* of *truth* and *freedom* cannot be realized in practice without a study and analysis of alternative ideologies along with a critical assessment of their implications for action." Quoted by K.S. Murty, *ibid.*, p. 167 (emphasis is in the text).

17. It would perhaps be unfair to place Eastern or Orthodox Christianity at the same level with Western Christianity (in its Catholic, Protestant, and fundamentalist formulations). The proximity to the Ancient Hellenic world in terms of language, culture, history and geography; the marked spirituality of the Orthodox monastic life; the divided authority between the Emperor and the Patriarch and their legally constituted positions; and even the standards of living in cities like Constantinople, were most impressive. So all these factors contributed to the appearance of Platonists among the Byzantine Greeks, such as Michael Psellos in the eleventh century and Pletho in the fourteenth century. It is reasonable to assume, therefore, that the followers of Pletho in the Peloponnese might have perhaps overcome the restrictions of ecclesiastical dogma more successfully than the followers of Ficino in Florence, had there not been the replacement of the Byzantine Orthodox Theocracy by the more oppressive and brutal Ottoman Islamic Turkocracy.

Accordingly, before we blame the Modern Greeks for their philosophical lethargy, we should remember that the tiny corner of the Balkan peninsula, which became the Kingdom of Modern Greece in 1830, did not include the birthplaces of any of the great Hellenic philosophers, with the exception of Athens. Left out were Aristotle's Stagira in Macedonia, Democritus' Abdera in Thrace, Anaxagoras' Clazomenae, Anaximander's Miletus, Heraclitus' Ephesus all in Hellenic Asia Minor; Pythagoras' Samos in the Aegean, Empedocles' Acragas in Sicily, Parmenides' Elea in *Magna Graecia*, Plotinus' Alexandria in Egypt, Porphyry's Tyre in Palestine, and Proclus' Constantinople. The responsibility for this pitiful shrinkage of Hellenism must be shared equally by the incapable (as a rule) political leaders of Modern Greece and by Western Powers. These friends, in the last two centuries and at critical moments, have failed to politically support the Greek historic claims, in contrast to their advertised and emotionally charged "Philhellenism." Some psychoanalysts might see in this European failure the working of envious motives in the depths of the European *psyche* regarding the glorious Hellenic past and the possibility of its revival in those ancestral lands and islands. I, perhaps naively, see in it nothing more than the usual antagonisms of "power politics" and "the interests" of different Europeans narrowly defined.

18. According to Aristotle, "Two things are homonymous if they have in common only the name, while the essence as captured by the definition is different in each case" (*Categories*, 1a 1-2). In this sense, the so-called European "philosophies" are in fact Christian theologies, using philosophical terminology for cover-up and respectability. Hence the urgency that this theme should be properly addressed the sooner the better. For Nietzsche may be correct, in his aphorism that the Ancient Hellenic philosophers preferred "the daylight of reason," in contrast to "the dark desires" which he finds in the depths of the soul of his favorite 'blond beast,' the Teutonic knight. But he exaggerates grossly when he dogmatically asserts that: "Rationality was at that time divined as a *saviour* ..." The time to which he refers was the time of Socrates, Plato, and Aristotle; but these philosophers, unlike their Western "homonyms," had no need of saviors. Saviors had not yet become fashionable and philosophers had not yet turned into Christians or ex-Christians theologians, whether they are docile to Church (Augustine, Descartes, Pascal, Berkeley, and so on) or rebellious

against its oppressive power (Nietzsche himself, Marx, Sartre, Kirkegaard, Kazantzakis, and so on).

As for the dependence of modern "Western philosophy" on medieval dogmatic theology and "Christian philosophy," see E. Gilson, *The Spirit of Medieval Philosophy*, trans., A.H.C. Downes (New York, 1940), pp. 12ff. Gilson claims correctly, in my view, that it cannot be a coincidence that modern European thinkers, from Descartes to Kant and beyond, have tried to establish by "pure reason" the doctrines, which were taught by medieval theologians in the name of "sacred revelations," that is, "reason mediated by faith." This is exactly the central point on which ancient philosophers differ from medieval theologians as well as from modern thinkers. To Hellenic minds, "reason mediated by faith" would mean "reason falsified," while attempts to prove rationally "the truth" of revealed mysteries, as found in the Bible and the Koran, would appear as exercises in scholastic dialectic and eristic rhetoric. It is not possible for such a profound gap to be bridged by the verbal tricks of theologians and historians of "philosophy," no matter how hard they may try.

19. This statement is in need of further elaboration, which cannot be provided here. It will be the theme of my forthcoming book, *The Passion of Hellenic Philosophy in Europe*.

20. To draw, as some European scholars do, a sharp division between Platonism and Hellenic Neoplatonism is historically incorrect and unnecessary, except for the limited case of Christian Neoplatonism. Furthermore, in a sense, all Hellenic philosophy after Plato can be legitimately characterized as "footnotes to Plato." But the application of this formula to "European philosophy" is inappropriate, with all due respect to A.N. Whitehead's opinion of the contrary. On this crucial point see the second essay also.

21. Apollo and Dionysus were still beloved brothers at that time. They had not, as yet, acquired the Manichean and adversarial qualities, with which the overused Nietzschean expressions of the "Apollonian Spirit" and "Dionysian Spirit" were to be vested later.

22. It is true that the Romans did their best to imitate every aspect of Hellenic culture so that the sensitive poet Horace honestly felt that conquered *Graecia* had intellectually conquered its conquerors. The process of Hellenization of the Roman Empire continued through the second and third centuries, when we meet Roman Emperors, like Marcus Aurelius, who philosophize and write in Greek, not in Latin. It is also significant that the members of one of the last schools of Hellenic philosophy, the Neoplatonic School of Plotinus and Porphyry, which flourished in Rome in the third century, used the philosophical language of Plato and Aristotle in their writings and in their teachings. See my *Aristotle's Categories and Porphyry* (Leiden, 1996, 2nd edn), pp. 165-181.

In a serious sense, therefore, the last three centuries of the Roman Empire, before its division into Eastern and Western and the collapse of the latter, can be seen as a kind of continuous "civil war" among Hellenized intellectuals and political leaders, who were split into two opposing parties. Those who wished to Hellenize the Latin segment of the population and, thus, revitalize the whole Roman Empire, were opposed by others, who wanted to Christianize it first and Hellenize it later, by moving its center eastwards. Plotinus, Porphyry, and Julian belong to the first party, while Constantine, Eusebius, and Athanasius belong to the other party, which won the battle, to the detriment of Hellenic philosophy. For more on this, see the second essay above.

23. The schism is still holding even today, in spite of all the efforts of unification by both parties, which have invariably failed.

24. All these new and emerging political powers and peoples on the scene of world

history were the outcome of a strange fusion of two "barbarisms," the Teutonic or Gothic and the Catholic Christian. It is true that Christian Catholicism represented civilization to the conquering barbarians, whom the Popes tried hard to tame; but the fact remains that Catholic Christianity itself was perceived as a form of barbarity by educated Greco-Romans, like Celsus and Porphyry, before the fall of Rome and the barbarian invasions.

25. Ironically, Greece at that time was under the heavy yoke of the Ottoman Turks. It did not manage to liberate itself until the wars of independence in 1821-1922, which ended with a holocaust. This included the killing, expulsion, and dispersion of more than one million Greeks from their Ionian homes in Asia Minor, where Hellenic philosophy and Homeric poetry were born and thrived for millennia. Since Asia Minor, unfortunately, did not become a part of the liberated Greece, a revival of Hellenic philosophy in its birthplace has been tragically thwarted no less there than in the rest of Christian Europe.

26. What audacity, what fraud, one may be inclined to think. Yet, the trick seems to have worked well for the Northern Europeans. For at the present, multiculturalists, who rebel against "Eurocentrism," perhaps out of historical ignorance, tend to include the Hellenic philosophers in the same category as the European imperialists, which is unfair to them. This can and should be corrected in the name of justice and truth, the historical truth. For, as we have shown, there is a real gulf separating Hellenic philosophy from its many European "homonyms," whether medieval, modern, or post-modern "philosophies."

27. The case of India and its dilemma was discussed briefly in the endnotes to the third essay, "Aristotle and Western Rationality."

28. This is even worse than the monopoly of God, claimed by European Christian and Asian Islamic versions of Judaic monotheism, you may think. I would certainly agree.

29. Not surprisingly, these have been traditional or historical characteristics of the European ethos, to the extent that this has been shaped by Christian and Islamic fundamentalism. In a serious sense they still are its characteristics, and they will be intensified even more, as the Eastern European "masses" begin to search for their theistic medieval roots after the disillusionment with the false "prophecies" of atheist Marxism in its orthodox Stalinist version. In another related sense, it may seem incomprehensible to us that the European mind has, for almost two millennia, been in the service of some aberration of Judaism (Paul's "messianic mysticism," Mohammed's "militant fanaticism" or Marx's "scientific socialism"). Yet, it can harbor in its core the prejudice of "anti-Semitism." One is reminded of Nietzsche's penetrating diagnosis of this malady, a very strange "phenomenon" of European culture: "The Jews are the most remarkable nation of world history because, faced with the question of being or not being, they preferred, with a perfectly uncanny conviction, being *at any price*: the price they had to pay was the radical *falsification* of all nature, all naturalness, all reality, the entire inner world as well as the outer ... We encounter the same phenomenon again and in unutterably vaster proportions, although only as a copy—the Christian Church, in contrast to the 'nation of saints', renounces all claim to originality. For precisely this reason the Jews are the *fateful* nation in world history: their after-effect has falsified mankind to such an extent that today the Christian is able to feel anti-Jewish without recognizing he is the *ultimate consequence of the Jews*" (the emphasis is in the text), quoted from "*Antichrist*," in *A Nietzsche Reader*, R.J. Hollingdale, tr. (London, 1977), p. 188.

30. This could be a valuable and needed lesson for the fanatical fundamentalists of all kinds (Christians, Jews, or Muslims). Even in the dawning of the third millennium, they are

set to exterminate each other in the name of their respective One and only true God (as we see in Bosnia, Palestine, Iraq, Chechnya and so on). What a pity and shame! What a degradation of humanity, you may think. But, I suspect, this is only the prelude of a renewed and religiously colored conflict that may be coming with terrific force (in Eastern and Western Europe, in Central and South Asia, and even in Northern Africa).

31. In the opening lines of *Metaphysics* (980a 22-28) we read: "All men by nature desire to know. An indication of this is the delight we take in our senses; for even apart from their usefulness they are loved by themselves; and above all others the sense of sight. For not only with a view to action, but even when we are not going to do anything, we prefer seeing (one might say) to everything else. The reason is that this, most of all the sense, makes us know and brings to light many differences between things."

32. In this light, it would seem that the natural fanaticism, which has historically characterized the dogmatically monotheistic religions of Christianity and Islam, would be revived with greater force now. Since the common threat of atheist communism, which had kept them quiet for a while, has been removed, these two old rivals will ready themselves to battle again over the foolish question of which of them has the most exclusive revelation of the saving truth as the only and truly "chosen people" of God! As usual, Judaism would not resist the temptation of playing the one fool against the other and of siding with the victorious party at the end of the bloody day to come. To prevent such a horrific outcome, humanity will need all the help it can get from every source, including Hellenic philosophy and its everlasting enlightening power. Hence the problematic, the genesis, the passion and the urgency of my present thesis.

33. In the *Republic*, genuine philosopher is described and distinguished from the sophists and the politicians of that time. Consider the following and compare it with the *Sophist*: "Then the nature which we assumed in the philosopher, if it receives the proper teaching, must needs grow and attain a consummate excellence, but, if it be sown and planted and grown in the wrong environment, the outcome will be quite the contrary unless some god comes to the rescue. Or are you too one of the multitude who believe that there are young men who are corrupted by the Sophists, and that there are Sophists in private life who corrupt to any extent worth mentioning, and that it is not rather the very men who talk in this strain who are the chief Sophists and educate most effectively and mold to their heart's desire young and old, men and women? ... Each of these private teachers who work for pay, whom the politicians call Sophists and regard as their rivals, inculcates nothing else than these opinions of the multitude which they opine when they are assembled and calls this knowledge wisdom. It is as if a man were acquiring the knowledge of the humors and desires of a great strong beast which he had in his keeping, how it is to be approached and touched, and when and by what things it is made most savage or gentle ... Do you not think, by heaven, that such a one would be a strange educator? I do, he said" (492a-493c).

What a good mirror has the Platonic Socrates provided for post-modernity to look at and see its (philosophically speaking) unattractive image, at least to Hellenic eyes!

34. The Platonic Stranger describes the Sophist as follows in *Sophist*, 268b-d:

"Stranger: And with whom shall we identify the more long-winded type—with the statesman or with the demagogue?

Theaetetus: The Demagogue.

Stranger: And what shall we call the other—wise man or Sophist?

Theaetetus: We cannot surely call him wise, because we set him down as ignorant, but as a mimic of the wise man he will clearly assume a title derived from his, and I now see that here at last is the man who must be truly described as the real and genuine Sophist.

Stranger: Shall we, then, as before collect all the elements of his description, from the end to the beginning, and draw our threads together in a knot?

Theaetetus: By all means.

Stranger: The art of contradiction making, descended from an insincere kind of conceited mimicry, of the semblance-making breed, derived from image making, distinguished as a portion, not divine but human, of production, that presents a shadow play of words—such are the blood and lineage which can, with perfect truth, be assigned to the authentic Sophist.

Theaetetus: I entirely agree."

In this Socratic light, it is clear that people who do not devote their energies to the finding the truth about the cosmos, the *polis*, and their own *psyche*; and do not take Socratic care to improve and perfect their souls, cannot be called philosophers. If they waste their time in trivial games of words, like the post-modern practitioners of the art of "deconstruction," they do not deserve the honorable Hellenic name of philosopher. Yet, in the European and the Western world in general, these people pass undetected, as "philosophers" and grow rich by selling their cheap "wares" to the dupes they can find.

35. In this sense, every healthy and normal human being, by its very nature and its potential, can become a lover of excellence, depending on specific natural endowments, cultural environment, and above all, appropriate *paideia*. Aristotle has diagnosed this: "There are three things which make men good and virtuous; these are nature, habit, rational principle. In the first place, every one must be born a man and not some other animal; so, too, he must have a certain character, both of body and soul ... Animals lead for the most part a life of nature, although in lesser particulars some are influenced by habit as well. Man has rational principle, in addition, and man only. Wherefore, nature, habit, rational principle must be in harmony with one another; for they do not always agree; men do many things against habit and nature, if rational principle persuades them that they ought. We have already determined what natures are likely to be most easily molded by the hands of the legislator. All else is the work of education; we learn some things by habit and some by instruction" (*Politics*, 1332a 39-b 10).

36. "Now virtue also is differentiated in correspondence with this division of the soul. Some forms of virtue are called intellectual virtues, others moral virtues. Wisdom or Intelligence and Prudence are intellectual, Liberality and Temperance are moral virtues." *NE*, 1103a 4-7 (H. Rackham's translation and capitalization of virtues).

37. When, for convenience, I use "he," the disjunctive "he or she" is understood here. As on the issue of erotic sexuality, so on the issue of generic equality, the Hellenic democracies were more open minded and tolerant than the Christian and the Islamic theocracies. From the Mantinean Diotima to the Alexandrian Hypatia, many female philosophers flourished in the land of Hellas, especially in the Pythagorean tradition. I doubt that such a phenomenon could have appeared in the theocratic West, or in the theocratic East, during the Middle Ages or even in modern times. Post-modernity is a different case, but it is too soon to be able to foresee and foretell its future outcome.

38. Both during his short life on earth and, especially, after his death, when his wisdom would perhaps gain a sort of "immortality" by being present in the minds of other philosophers and other mortals as Socrates argues in the *Symposium*. See my "Eros and

Immortality in the *Symposium* of Plato," *Diotima* 14 (1985): 200-211.

39. Or, one may add, the ancient Indian and the ancient Chinese philosophers, whose speculations were free from theocratic dogmas, in ways in which no Western "philosophers" could have been until recently. What will happen in the future time will reveal. We can only hope and work for the better, that is, the revival of the lost spirit of Hellenic philosophy in post-modern Europe and the World at large.

40. Once again, I would like to make it clear that I am talking only about philosophy here. The arts are a different story. Many artists can be commissioned to produce works of art which are masterpieces. Philosophy, as the queen of arts and sciences, needs its freedom absolutely in order to thrive. For genuine philosophers accept no masters other than human reason and virtue to guide their pursuits. With God and the gods, they are always in good terms, if they are of the gentle Hellenic kind. For Plato and Aristotle, the genuine Hellenic philosopher is "most beloved" to their gods (*theophilestatos*). It is a sign of the Christianized and changed European mentality that Modern Greeks use the same Hellenic and beautiful word "*theophilestatos*" to address their Bishops, many of whom have nothing to do with philosophy. They avoid it, as Devil avoids the incense!

41. Not that such practices are useless to the "*hoi polloi*" for practical or political purposes, whether theocratic or otherwise, but they are certainly unworthy of philosophers with some sense of self-respect.

42. In my view, this was the core of the conflict, which developed between Hellenic and Christian Platonism, as typified by Porphyry and Augustine. See also the second essay.

43. The prevailing climate, religious, political, intellectual and so forth, was not conducive to the growth of the spirit of Hellenic philosophy in Europe, because such a spirit is in need not only of bright light and unclouded skies, but also of religious tolerance, democratic institutions, freedom, and much, much more.

44. However, we should not forget what happened to those who dared to think and speak freely and without respect for the established dogma or against the power of the Church. When they were not burned at the stake, like Bruno, they were publicly humiliated, like Galileo, or driven to insanity prematurely, like Nietzsche. The Islamic theocracies also had their free spirits (Al-Ashari and Al- Hallaz, and so on), whose fates were similar.

45. As I have emphasized, this is a preliminary account of my thesis, which will be further developed in a book, tentatively titled: *The Passion of Hellenic Philosophy in Europe*.

46. Even Hume and Kant would be included in this group. Those who might object to including in the list even "the skeptical" Hume and "the critical" Kant, (that is, the most critical and skeptical minds which "Western philosophy" has produced), may consider the following quotations to see how "philosophy" makes room for faith: "There is only one occasion, when philosophy will think it necessary and even honorable to justify herself, and that is, when religion may seem to be the least offended; whose rights are as dear to her as her own, are indeed the same. If any one, therefore, should imagine that the foregoing arguments are any ways dangerous to religion, I hope the following apology will remove his apprehensions ... If my philosophy, therefore, makes no addition to the arguments for religion, I have at least the satisfaction to think it takes nothing from them, but that every thing remains precisely as before." *A Treatise of Human Nature* (Oxford, 1973), pp. 250-251. I do not think that Hume is "ironic" here because even Kant, who learned from him and had no taste for irony, makes essentially the same point in *The Critique of Pure Reason*,

p. 651: "The only point that may seem questionable is the basing of this rational belief on the assumption of moral sentiments ... If we leave these aside, and take a man who is completely indifferent with regard to moral laws, the question propounded by reason becomes merely a problem for speculation, and can, indeed, be supported by strong grounds of analogy, but not by such as must compel the most stubborn skepticism to give way. But in these questions no man is free from all interest. For although, through lack of good sentiments, he may be cut off from moral interest, still even in this case enough remains to make him *fear* the existence of a God and a future life. Nothing more is required for this than that he at least cannot pretend that there is any *certainty* that there in <u>no</u> such being and <u>no</u> such life." The underlining is in the text. So much of fear, faith, and "Western philosophy" as practiced in the enlightened Europe. One can imagine what this "philosophy" was like during the "darker times" of the Middle Ages.

47. I emphasize the adverbial "philosophically" in contrast to scientifically and artistically, which are different cases lying outside our strictly limited concern with philosophy.

48. This came at the critical time after Constantinople, the capital of the Eastern Roman Empire, had fallen to the Turks in 1453. This tragedy cut short the process of a general Hellenic revival, including Hellenic philosophy, which had begun with Pletho and his friends in Mistra and the Peloponnese.

49. The difference was that Protestantism replaced Catholicism this time, with Hegel assuming the role of Thomas Aquinas. See *Hegel's Lectures on the Philosophy of Religion*, P.C. Hodgson, ed. (Berkeley, 1988), Part III, "The Consummate Religion."

50. In this light, the verdict of E. Gilson, as noted, seems perfectly justified. But the conclusions which he draws from this historical fact are very different that mine. He wants to silence those historians of "Western philosophy" who have raised doubt whether there was any philosophy in the Middle Ages. He claims that, given the dependence of Modern European philosophy, (from Descartes to Leibniz, Kant, and beyond), on the Medieval Christian theology, it is unfair to apply the glorious name of "philosophy" only to the former and not to the latter. The truth of the matter is that, precisely because of that affinity, neither Medieval theology nor European "philosophy" deserve the name of *philosophia*, in the same sense as the Ancient Hellenic philosophers used this beautiful word. To make clear to the reading and reasoning public this simple, but forgotten, truth has been the purpose of my thesis.

51. Because of the old tradition of their role in the West and the popularity of these movements, especially existentialism, this group of thinkers would be the most familiar to philosophy students.

52. These are the so-called "tough minded" logicians who have made up their (tough but narrow) minds, out of intellectual honesty, we are told, to serve only the needs of science by providing "logical analysis" of the concepts and the language in which "the truth," to be discovered by the scientific method, will have to be wrapped. Never mind that no scientist worth of his name would pay much attention to what these men say or write. Yet, Ayer and his peers are held highly as great contemporary "philosophers."

53. This group has been responsible to a large extent for the mindless destruction of valuable cultural traditions of great countries such as Russia, with its centuries old mystical spirituality, and China with its millennia old philosophical traditions of Lao Tse and Confucius. While we may be heartened by the collapse of communism in Russia, we would

have to wait and wonder about the philosophical direction, which the New Russia will take. Will it turn back to its Eastern Orthodox past and its deeper Hellenic roots, or to "Western philosophies" of the recent past, which even post-modern Europe is trying to by-pass? We would also have to wait and wonder how much longer it would take for the Chinese people to wake up, set Marx and Mao aside, rediscover their ancestral roots, and move forward to a brighter future in freedom and democracy.

54. Among the characteristics of a Sophist, the Platonic Socrates include: "a hired hunter of rich young men;" "a sort of merchant of learning;" "a retail dealer in the same wares;" "a player in a shadow play of words;" and "an athlete in debate appropriating that subdivision of contention which consists in the art of eristic" (*Sophist*, 231d-268d).

But there is an important difference between the ancient Sophists and their post-modern imitators. For, unlike the latter, the former had a Hellenic refinement in their polished use of language. For example, Protagoras could make up a meaningful myth to explain human imperfections with lucidity and humor. Prodicus, when he was not working in mathematics, could tell beautiful and edifying stories like that of Hercules facing the choice between "Virtue and Vice." Gorgias could say in three aphorisms, "Nothing is; and if it is, it cannot be known; and if it can be known, it cannot be said," what Heidegger, Rorty, and Derrida would not be able to say in three large volumes on "negativity!" Derrida especially (God rest his soul) suffers from such acute "logorrhea" that he repeats himself (even the same long footnotes verbatim!). See notes 10 and 22 of his essay, "The Ends of Man," in *After Philosophy: End or Transformation*? K. Bayness, et al., eds (Cambridge, MA, 1987, pp. 119-58). As for lucidity consider the following passage which is typical of de-constructive style: "Being in-itself and Being for-itself were *of Being*; and this totality of beings, in which they were effected, itself was linked up to itself, relating and appearing to itself, by means of the essential project of human reality" (p. 131). Here, of course, he tries to interpret "hermeneutically" the "phenomenological ontology" of Sartre's *Being and Nothingness*, which is another sample of foggy (theistic or a-theistic) "European philosophy." But the comic irony reaches its climax, when Richard Rorty talks about "A Post-Philosophical Culture" in "Pragmatism and Philosophy" (*ibid.*, pp. 21-66). For he assumes, uncritically, that there has been "genuine philosophy" and a continuity of the philosophical ethos in the Western World all along from Plato to Nietzsche. My thesis has shown that the exact opposite of this assertion is and has been the case.

55. Hardly any of the representatives of these movements would have met the specified criteria of genuine philosophy, especially the second criterion of "lived philosophy" as a model of human excellence and virtue of the type which Socrates has exemplified. The sad fact is that the so-called "philosophy," in the West and in the last four hundred years has assumed the role of handmaid or *ancilla* (that is, *ancilla technologiae* and *ancilla ideologiae*), in addition to its medieval role of *ancilla theologiae*, as we have stressed. That is a sad state of affairs.

56. Hence also, we may add, our responsibility, as free persons and as lovers of wisdom and truth, to do our duty to enlighten, if we can, our Christian and Muslim friends, in Europe, Asia, Africa, and America, that it is unwise to try to monopolize God. Such an unholy monopoly, as the Hellenic philosophers knew so well, will inevitably lead to fanaticism and intolerance. Since, in the last millennia, Christians and Muslims in their monomania of monotheism, did not succeed in exterminating each other in the name of the "One True God," whose "chosen people" each of them claim to be "exclusively," it would

be unwise to be allowed to do so in the new third millennium. So they must learn to see that Christ, (as he has been historically understood by Orthodox, Catholic, Protestant, and fundamentalist Christians), would appear so different from his historical self, as the many Hellenic gods appear from each other. Similarly, the Koran, as it has been read and interpreted by Sunni, Shiite, and Sufi Muslims, to an outsider at least, looks like a different Book. So, one may hope that the "devout brethren" will learn at last to tolerate each other in the name of the One God with many names and masks, the poly-morphic and poly-onymous God. This enlightening lesson they can learn from Hellenic *philosophia*.

　　May they listen to the gentle voice of reason! May Athena, the Hellenic Goddess of wisdom, guide their minds to the light of philosophic freedom!

Glossary

agathos, -on	good, the good
aeikinetos	moving constantly, all the time
aidios	everlasting, unchangeable, eternal
Aigyptos (-us)	Ancient Egypt, the Nile
aischros, -on	ugly, bad, shameful
aesthesis	activity of the senses, sensation
aither	ether, Aristotle's fifth element
aitios, -a, -on	cause, causality
akinetos	immobile, unmoved, unmovable
akoinonesia	lack of community, lack of communion
alius, -um (pl. alia)	other, different
amor	eros, erotic love, love
anamnesis	recollection
anathema	curse, accursed, anathema
ancilla	handmaiden, servant, subordinate
anthropos	human being, man
apotheosis	deification, making a god out of a human being
arche (pl. archai)	source, principle
archegos	leader, initiator
arbor, -oris	tree
arete (pl. aretai)	excellence, virtue, good quality
Aristotelikus, -um	Aristotelian, belonging to Aristotle
aristokratia	aristocracy, rule of the best citizens
aristotechnes	excellent artisan, artificer, craftsman
arithmos	number
a quo	from that point in time
askesis	exercise, practice
asymbletos	incompatible, incommensurable
atman	the self, self-conscience in Hinduism
Brahman	the Supreme Self or Being in Hinduism
Christianus, -a	Christian
chronos	time

civitas, -atis	city, state
corruptio, -onis	corruption
cosmos (kosmos)	world, ordered universe
cosmopolis	large city, the cosmos considered as one city
corpus	body, collected works of an author
deus, -a	God, Goddess
demokratia	democracy, rule of the many, the people
dialectica	dialectic
dialektike	dialectic, dialectical
diaspora	dispersion of a people
differentia (pl. –ai)	difference
dogma	doctrine dogmatically held
doxa	opinion
eidos (pl. eide)	look, shape, form, idea
eikon	image, picture
eikos	likely, probable, reasonable
einai	to be, being, essence
elan vital	vital force, energy
empeiria	experience, sense experience
eros	erotic love, love
eudaimonia	well being, flourishing, happiness
evangelica	pertaining to the gospel
evangelium	good news, the gospel
genesis	generation, coming into being
generatio, -onis	generation
gnosis	knowledge, sacred or revealed doctrine
Graicia	Ancient Greece, Hellas
hedone	pleasure
hegieia	health
hegieinos, -on	healthy
Hellas	Ancient Greece, the country of Ancient Hellenes
Homo	human being
homo sapiens	the intelligent human being, our proximate ancestor
homonymia	homonymy, having the same name, equivocation
homonymos, -on	homonymous, having the same name
homoousios	of the same ousia or substance
hypostasis	subsisting entity, independent existence or essence

idea	look, idea
ideologia	ideology, a set of political beliefs
kainotomia	novelty, innovation
kalos, -on	beautiful, good
kalos kai agathos	beautiful and good
kallistos, -on	most beautiful, best
katharsis	purification
kenos, -on	empty, void
kinesis	motion, movement
kosmos	cosmos
Kronos	Cronus, Saturn
legomenos, -on	said, that which is said
legomenon pollachos	said in many ways, having many meanings, polysemantic
logos	word, reason, proportion, cause, analogy
Logos	the Second Person of the Holy Trinity, Son of God, Christ
makrobios, -on	having a long life, living long
Magna Graicia	Great (or Greater) Greece, South Italy and Sicily
magnus, -a, -um	great, big
magnum opus	major work
mania	madness, the condition of the maniac person
mesotes	mean as opposed to extreme, middle state, moderation
metempsychosis	transmigration of the soul
mochtheria	wickedness, viciousness, badness
mochtheros	bad, vicious, wicked
moria	folly, foolishness
mousike	music, the art of music
mythos	myth, fable, opposite to logos
natura	nature
naturalis	natural
nihil	nothing, zero, void
noein	to think, to conceive intuitively
noetic	pertaining to nous, intelligent, intellective
noesis	the activity of nous, mental energy
nomos	law, convention
Nomos	the Mosaic Law, the Decalogue, the revealed will of God
nous	human mind, intellect
Nous	the divine Mind, Intellect, Intelligence
on (pl. onta)	being, that which has reality, opp. painomenon

ontologia	theory of being and reality
organon	tool, instrument
orthos, -on	straight, right
opus	work, written work
ousia	substance, substantial being, opp. accident, quality
ousiologia	theory of ousia or substance
paideia	education, cultivation, culture
paliggenesia	rebirth, reincarnation
pammochtheros	all bad, very wicked
paradeigma	model, specimen, paradigm
pecatum	error, sin
phainomenon	appearance, phenomenon
pharmakon	medicine, drug
philosophia	philosophy, love of wisdom
physis	nature
pollachos	in many ways
polis	city, state, ancient Hellenic city-state
praxis	act, action, practice, opp. theory
preparation	preparation
principium (pl. -a)	principle
proson (pl. prosonta)	present traits, characteristics
psyche	soul, principle of life
raison d'etre	reason of being, reason of existence
ratio, -onis	reason, the rational faculty
religio, -onis	religion
scientia, -ae	science, scientific knowledge
scholion (-um)	note, comment
sophia	wisdom, philosophy, love of wisdom
synodos	coming together, convergence
synonyma	synonyms, synonymous terms
tat tvam asi	thou art that, you are that, the *atman* in you is Brahman
techne	craft, skill, art
telos	end, aim, goal, purpose
terminus	limit, boundary, terminal
theologia	theology, theory of the divine
theoria	theory, opp. practice
to hen	the one, one
toioutos, toiaute	of such type, kind or character
to on (pl. ta onta)	being, the being of something

tyche	luck, fortune
via universalis	universal way
vita	life
zeitgeist	spirit of the times

Bibliography

Aeschylus, *Septem quae supersunt tragodiae*, G. Murray, ed., (Oxford: University Press, 1937).

Allen, R.E. *Greek Philosophy: Thales to Aristotle* (London: The Free Press, 1985, 2nd edn).

Altaner, B. *Partology*, H.C. Graef, tr. (New York: Herder, 1961, 2nd edn).

Anastos, M. "Porphyry's Attack on the Bible," in *The Classical Tradition, L. Wallach*, ed. (Ithaca, NY: Cornell University Press, 1966).

Anton, J.P. and Kustas G. eds, *Essays in Ancient Greek Philosophy* (Albany, NY: SUNY Press, 1972).

Anton, J.P. and Preus A. eds, *Essays in Ancient Greek Philosophy*, vol. 3, *Plato* (New York: SUNY Press, 1989).

Anton, J.P. "The Aristotelian Doctrine of *Homonyma* in the *Categories* and its Platonic Antecedents", *JHP* 6 (1969): 315-326.

Armstrong, A.H. ed., *The Cambridge History of Later Greek and Early Medieval Philosophy* (Cambridge: Cambridge University Press, 1967).

———. *The Architecture of the Intelligible Universe in the Philosophy of Plotinus* (Cambridge: Cambridge University Press, 1940).

———. *Plotinus: Enneads, Armstrong, A.H., ed.,* (7 vols, Cambridge, Mass.: Harvard University Press, 1978-1988).

———. "Some Advantages of Polytheism," *Dionysius* 5 (1981): 181-188.

Augustine, *Confessions.* R.S. Pine-Coffin, tr. (New York: Dorset Press, 1986).

———. *The City of God.* M. Dods, tr. (New York: The Modern Library, 1950).

Ayer, A.J. *Language, Truth and Logic* (Great Britain: Penguin Books, 1972).

Bargeliotes, L. "Pletho as Forerunner of the Neo-Hellenic and Modern European Consciousness," *Diotima* 1 (1973): 33-60.

———. *The Revised Subjectivism of A.N. Whitehead* (Athens, Greece: The University Press, 1984).

———. ed., *Platonism and Aristotelianism in Pletho* (Athens, Gr: Erevna, 1987).

Baumgarten, I.A. *The Phoenician History of Philo of Byblus: A Commentary* (Leiden: E.J. Brill, 1981).

Bayness, K. et al., eds, *After Philosophy: End or Transformation?* (Cambridge, Mass.: MIT Press, 1987).

Beierwaltes, W., ed., *Platonismus in der Philosophie des Mittelalters* (Darmstadt: Wissenschaftliche Buchges, 1969).

Benakis, L. "Πλήθωνος προς ηρωτημένα άττα απόκρισις," *Philosophia* 4 (1974): 348-9.

Bernal, M. *Black Athena*, vol. I (New Brunswick, NJ: Rutgers University Press, 1991).

Berstein, R. *Philosophical Profiles* (Philadelphia: University of Pennsylvania Press, 1986).

———. "Why Hegel Now?" in *Hegel*, Ch. Taylor, ed. (Cambridge: Cambridge University Press, 1975).

Bidez, J. Vie de Porphyre (Hildesheim: Olm, 1961).

Bigg, Ch. *The Christian Platonists of Alexandria* (Oxford: Clarendon Press, 1968).

Boethius, *The Consolation of Philosophy*, R. Green, tr. (Indianapolis: Bobbs-Merrill, 1975).

Boardman, J. et al., eds, *The Oxford History of the Classical World* (Oxford: Oxford University Press, 1987).

———. *The Greeks Overseas* (Baltimore, MD: Penguin Books, 1964).

Boudouris, K., ed., *Aristotle's Political Philosophy* (Athens, Gr: Kardamitsa Press, 1995).

———. ed., *The Ionian Philosophy* (Athens: Kardamitsa Press, 1991).

———. ed., On *Justice* (Athens: Kardamitsa Press, 1988).

Broadie, S. *Ethics with Aristotle* (Oxford: Oxford University Press, 1991).

Burkert, W. *Lore and Science in Ancient Pythagoreanism* (Cambridge, Mass: Harvard University Press, 1972).

Burnet, J. *Greek Philosophy: Thales to Plato* (New York: St. Martin's Press, 1968).

———. *Early Greek Philosophy* (London: Adam and Charles Black, 1948).

Bury, J.B., et al. eds, *A History of Greece: To the Death of Alexander the Great* (New York: St. Martin's Press, 1978, 4th edn).

Busse, A., ed., *Commentaria in Aristotelem Graeca*, IV, 1 (Berlin: Reimer, 1887).

Burtt, E.A. *The Metaphysical Foundations of Modern Science* (Garden City, NY: Doubleday, 1954).

Cavafy, C. *The Collected Poems*, R. Dalven, tr. (New York: Hardcourt, 1976).

Chadwick, H. *Early Christian Thought and the Classical Tradition* (Oxford: University Press, 1996).

Chadwick, J. *The Decipherment of Linear B* (Cambridge: University Press, 1967, 2nd edn).

Clark, G. *Iamblichus: On the Pythagorean Life* (Liverpool: Liverpool University Press, 1989).

Clement of Alexandria: *Stromata,* in *Greek and Roman Philosophy after Aristotle*, J.L. Saunders, ed. (New York: The Free Press, 1966).

Cook, S.A. et al., eds, *The Cambridge Ancient History*, XII (London: Cambridge University Press, 1961).

Cornford, F.M. *Principium Sapientiae: A Study of the Origins of Greek Philosophical Thought* (New York: Harper Torchbooks, 1965).

Cooper, J. *Reason and Human Good in Aristotle* (Cambridge, Mass.: Harvard University Press, 1975).

———. "Contemplation and Happiness: A Reconsideration," *Synthese*, 72 (1987): 187-216.

Derrida, J. "The Ends of Man," in *After Philosophy: End or Transformation?* K. Bayness, et al., eds (Cambridge, MA: MIT Press, 1987).

Diogenes Laertius. *Lives of Eminent Philosophers*, R.D. Hicks, ed. and tr. (Cambridge, Mass.: Harvard University Press, 1980).

Dodds, E.R. *The Greeks and the Irrational* (Berkeley: University of California Press, 1951).

———. *Pagan and Christian in an Age of Anxiety: Some Aspects of Religious Experience from Marcus Aurelius to Constantine* (Cambridge: University Press, 1965; and New York: Norton, 1970).

Emmett, D. "Theoria and the Way of Life," *Journal of Theological Studies*, n. s., 17 (1966): 38-52.

Erasmus, *The Praise of Folly*, C. H. Miller, tr. (New Haven: Yale University Press, 1979).

Euripides, Helen, R. Lattimore, tr., vol. 2 (Chicago: The University of Chicago Press, 1969).

Evangeliou, Ch. *Aristotle's Categories and Porphyry* (Leiden: E.J. Brill, 1988; 2nd edn, 1996).

———. *The Meaning of the Mean in the Nicomachean Ethics* (MA Thesis, Emory University, 1976).

———. "The Ontological Basis of Plotinus' Criticism of Aristotle's Theory of Categories," in *The Structure of Being: A Neoplatonic Approach*, R. Baine Harris, ed. (Albany, N.Y.: SUNY Press, 1982).

———. "Porphyry's Criticism of Christianity and the Problem of Augustine's Platonism," *Dionysius* XIII (1989): 51-70.

———. "Plotinus' Anti-Gnostic Polemic and Porphyry's Against the Christians," in *Neoplatonism and Gnosticism*, Wallis, R. and Bregman, J., eds (Albany, NY: SUNY Press, 1992).

———. "The Aristotelian Tradition of Virtue: The Case of Justice," *On Justice*, K. Boudouris, ed., (Athens: Kardamitsa Press, 1988).

———. "The Plotinian Reduction of Aristotle's Categories," *Ancient Philosophy 7* (1988): 147-161.

———. "Vlastos, *Socrates: Ironist and Moral Philosopher*," *Journal of Neoplatonic Studies* 1 (1992): 133-141.

———. "Ancient Hellenic Philosophy and the African Connection," *Skepsis 4* (1994): 14-76.

———. "MacIntyre, *After Virtue*," *The Review of Metaphysics 37*, no, 1 (1983): 132-134.

———. "O'Meara, *Pythagoras Revived*," *Skepsis* 2 (1991): 162-165.

———. "O'Meara, *Neoplatonism and Christian Thought*," *Journal of the History of Philosophy 21*, no. 4 (1983): 565-568.

———. "Eros and Immortality in Plato's Symposium," *Diotima* 13 (1985): 200-211.

———. "Pletho's Critique of Aristotle and the Revival of Platonism in the Italian Renaissance," *Skepsis 8* (1997): 146-170.

———. "Philosophy, Human Wonder and Hellenic Logos," *Skepsis* 2 (1991): 29-41.

———. "Dangerous Deviations from Judaism: Islamic and Christian Fanaticism," *Mediterranean Quarterly* 14 (2003): 86-111.

———. "Bargeliotes: The Revised Subjectivism of A.N. Whitehead," *The Greek Philosophical Review* 3 (1986): 195-197.

———. "Nehamas: Nietzsche: Life as Literature," *The Review of Metaphysics*, 40, no. 3 (1987): 592-594.

———. "Nussbaum, *The Fragility of Goodness: Luck and Ethics in Greek Tragedy and Philosophy*," *Skepsis* I (1990): 210-216.

———. "Harris, ed., *The Significance of Neoplatonism*," *Philosophy and Phenomenological Research* 38, no. 4 (1978): 593-594.

Ferejohn, M. "Aristotle on Focal Meaning and the Unity of Science," *Phronesis* 25 (1980): 117-128.

Finley, M.I., ed., The *Legacy of Greece* (Oxford: University Press, 1984).

Findlay, J.N. "The Neoplatonism of Plato," in *The Significance of Neoplatonism*, Harris, R.B., ed., (Albany, NY: SUNY Press, 1976).

Fukuyama, F. *The End of History and the Last Man* (New York: The Free Press, 1992).

Gadamer, H.G. *The Idea of the Good in Platonic and Aristotelian Philosophy*, P.Ch. Smith, tr. (New Haven: Yale University Press, 1986).

Garraty, J.A. and P. Gay, eds, *The Columbia History of the World* (New York: Harper and Row, 1894).

Gibbon, E. *The Decline and Fall of Rome* (London and New York: Dent, 1911).

Gilson, E. *History of Christian Philosophy in the Middle Ages* (New York: Randon House, 1955).

———. *The Spirit of Medieval Philosophy*, A.H.C. Downes, tr. (New York: C. Scribner's, 1940).

Golding, M. "Towards a Theory of Human Rights," *The Monist* 52 (1968): 521-48.

Griswold, Ch. *Platonic Writings and Platonic Readings* (New York: Routledge, 1988).

Grube, G.M.A. *Plato's Thought* (Indianapolis: Hackett, 1980).

Guthrie, W.K.C. *A History of Greek Philosophy* (6 vols, Cambridge: Cambridge University Press, 1962-1981).

———. *Orpheus and Greek Religion* (New York: W. Norton, 1966).

Hadot, P. *What is Ancient Philosophy?* M. Chase, tr. (Cambridge, Mass.: The Belknap Press, 2002).

————. "Citacion de Porphyre chez Augustine," *Revue des etudes augustiniennes* (1960): 205-244.

Hamlyn, D.W. "Focal Meaning," *PAS* 78 (1978): 1-18.

Hankins, J. *Plato in the Italian Renaissance* (Leiden: E.J. Brill, 1991).

Harris, R.B., ed., *The Significance of Neoplatonism* (Albany, NY: SUNY Press, 1976).

Havelock, E. *Preface to Plato* (Cambridge, Mass: Harvard University Press, 1982).

Hegel, G.W.F. *Lecture on the Philosophy of Religion: The Lectures of 1827*, P.C. Hodgson, ed. (Berkeley: University of California Press, 1988).

————. *The Phenomenology of the Mind*, J.B. Baillie, tr. (New York: Harper, 1967).

————. *Hegel's Lectures on the History of Philosophy*, E.S. Handale, ed. (3 vols, London: Routledge and Kegan Paul, 1896).

Herodotus. G.P. Goold, ed. and tr. (4 vols, Cambridge, Mass.: Harvard University Press, 1920).

————. *The Histories*, Selincourt, A. tr. (New York: Penguin Books, 1954).

Hollingdale, R.J., ed. and tr., *A Nietzsche Reader* (London: Penguin Books, 1977).

Homer. *Iliad*, A.T. Murray, tr. (2 vols, Cambridge, Mass.: Harvard University Press, 1988).

————. *Odyssey*, A.T. Murray, tr. (2 vols, Cambridge, Mass.: Harvard University Press, 1984).

Huffman, C.A. *Philolaus of Croton: Pythagorean and Presocratic* (Cambridge: University Press, 1993).

Hulen, A. *Porphyry's Work against the Christians* (Scottdale: Mennonite Press, 1933).

Hume, D. *A Treatise of Human Nature* (Oxford: Clarendon Press, 1973).

Iamblichus. *On the Pythagorean Life*, Gillian Clark, tr. (Liverpool: Liverpool University Press, 1989).

Inge, W.R. "Religion," in *The Legacy of Greece*, R. Livingstone, ed. (Oxford: University Press, 1969).

Isocrates. *Busiris*. Larue Van Hook, tr. (Cambridge, Mass.: Harvard University Press, 1986).

Irwin, T. "Aristotle's Defense of Private Property," in *A Companion to Aristotle's Politics*, D. Keyt and F. Miller, eds (Oxford: Blackwell, 1990).

————. "Generosity and Property in Aristotle's *Politics*," in *Beneficence, Philanthropy and the Common Good*, E. Paul et al., eds (Oxford: Blackwell, 1987).

Ivanka, E von. *Plato Christianus: Uebernahme und Umgestaltung des Platonismus durch die Vaeter* (Einsiedeln: Johannes Verlag, 1964).

Jaeger, W. *Paideia: The Ideals of Greek Culture*, G. Highet, tr. (3 vols, New York: (Oxford University Press, 1943).

————. *Aristotle: Fundamentals of the History of his Development*, Robinson, R., tr. (Oxford: Clarendon Press, 1934).

————. "*Altertum und Gegenwart,*" in *Humanistische Reden und Vortaege* (Berlin: De Gruyter, 1937).

James, G.M. *Stolen Legacy: Greek Philosophy is Stolen Egyptian Philosophy* (Trenton, NJ: African World Press, 1992).

Jonas, H. *The Gnostic Religion* (Boston: Beacon Press, 1963).

Kant, I. *The Critique of Pure Reason,* N.K. Smith, tr. (New York: St. Martin's Press, 1965).

Kazantzakis, N. *Odyssey: A Modern Sequel,* K. Friar, tr. (New York: Simon & Schuster, 1958).

Keith, A.B. "Pythagoras and the Doctrine of Transmigration," *The Journal of Royal Asiatic Society* (1909): 569-606.

Keyt, D. "Intellectualism in Aristotle," *Paideia* (1978): 138-157.

————. and F. Miller, eds, *A Companion to Aristotle's Politics* (Oxford: B. Blackwell, 1990).

Kirk, G.S. and Raven, J.E. *The Presocratic Philosophers* (Cambridge: University Press, 1975).

Klibansky, R. *The Continuity of the Platonic Tradition during the Middle Ages* (London: The Warburg Institute, 1939).

Kraemer, H.J. *Plato and the Foundations of Metaphysics,* J.R. Catan, tr. (New York: SUNY, 1990).

Kraut, R. *Aristotle: Political Philosophy* (Oxford: Oxford University Press, 2002).

Kristeller, P.O. *Renaissance Thought* (New York: Harper, 1961).

————. *Eight Philosophers of the Italian Renaissance* (Stanford: Stanford University Press, 1965).

————. "Renaissance Aristotelianism," GRBS 6 (1965): 157-174.

Kroeber, A.L. and Kluckhorn, C., *Culture: A Critical Review of Concepts and Definitions* (New York: Vintage Books, 1981).

Lagarde, B., ed., "*La 'De differentiis' de Plethon,*" *Byzantium* 43 (1973): 312-343.

Lamberton, R. *Homer the Theologian: Neoplatonist Allegorical Readings and the Growth of the Epic Tradition* (Berkeley: University of California Press, 1989).

Leclerc, I. *Whitehead's Metaphysics: An Introductory Exposition* (Bloomington: Indiana University Press, 1975).

————. *The Nature of Physical Existence* (New York: The Humanities Press, 1972).

Lefkowitz, M. *Not Out of Africa* (New York: Basic Books, 1996).

————. and Rogers, G.M., eds, *Black Athena Revisited* (Chapel Hill: The University of North Carolina Press, 1996).

Lewis, W.H. "History Restored: The Return of Empire," *The Mediterranean Quarterly* 6, no. 3 (1995): 1-13.

Lindberg, D. *The Beginnings of Western Science* (Chicago: The University of Chicago Press, 1992).

Locke, J. *An Essay Concerning Human Understanding* (2 vols, London: Everyman's Library, 1972).

Lord, C. *Education and Culture in the Politics of Aristotle* (Ithaca: Cornell University Press, 1982).

Lovejoy, A.O. *The Great Chain of Being: A Study of the History of an Idea* (Cambridge, Mass: Harvard University Press, 1964, 2nd edn).

Manetho. *Fragmenta*, W.G. Waddell, ed. (Cambridge, Mass.: Harvard University Press, 1956).

Masai, F. *Plethon et le platonisme de Mistra* (Paris: Les Belles Lettres, 1956).

———. "Le probleme des infuences byzantines sur le platonisme italien de la Renaissance," *Bulletin de l'Association G. Bude* 12 (1953): 82-90.

Mayhew, R. "Aristotle on Property," *Review of Metaphysics* 46, no. 4 (1993) 803-831.

McKeon, R., ed., *The Basic Works of Aristotle,* (New York: Random House, 1941).

McManners, J., ed., *The Oxford Illustrated History of Christianity* (Oxford: Oxford University Press, 1990).

Mencius. *The Wisdom of Confucius* (New York: The Modern Library, 1966).

Merlan, P. *From Platonism to Neoplatonism* (The Hague: M. Nijhoff, 1960).

Miles, J. *John Colet and the Platonic Tradition* (La Salle, Ill: Open Court, 1961).

Miller, F.D. *Nature, Justice and Rights in Aristotle's Politics* (Oxford: Clarendon Press, 1995).

———. "Aristotle on Property Rights," in *Aristotle's Ethics*, J.P. Anton and A. Preus, eds (Albany, NY: SUNY Press, 1991).

Moutsopoulos, E. "Byzance et l'hellenisme medieval," *Bulletin de l'association G. Bude* 19 (1960): 389-396.

Mukund, L., "Aristotle and the Roots of Western Rationality," *Journal of Indian Council of Philosophical Research* 9, no. 2 (1992): 55-68.

Murty, K.S. *Philosophy in India: Traditions, Teaching and Research* (Delhi: Motilal Banarsidass, 1991).

———. *The Teaching of Philosophy* (Paris: UNESCO, 1952).

Navia, L.E. *Pythagoras: An Annotated Bibliography* (New York: Garland Publishing, 1990).

Nehamas, A. *Nietzsche: Life as Literature* (Cambridge, Mass.: Harvard University Press, 1985).

Nietzsche, F. *Twilight of the Idols and The Antichrist*, R.J. Hollingdale, tr. (New York: Penguin Books, 1985).

Nozick, R. *The Nature of Rationality* (Princeton, NJ: Princeton University Press, 1993).

Nussbaum, M. *The Fragility of Goodness: Luck and Ethics in Greek Tragedy and Philosophy* (London: Cambridge University Press, 1986).

Oehler, K. "Aristotle in Byzantium," GRBS 5 (1964): 113-146.

Oldfather, C. H., ed. and tr., *Diodorus of Sicily* (12 vols, Cambridge: Harvard University Press, 1933).

O'Meara, D. *Neoplatonism and Christian Thought* (Albany, NY: SUNY Press, 1982).

————. *Pythagoras Revived* (Oxford: Clarendon Press, 1989).

O'Meara, J. *Porphyry's Philosophy from Oracles in Augustine* (Paris: Etudes Augustiniennes, 1959).

Ostrogorsky, G. *History of the Byzantine State* (New Brunswick: Rutgers University Press, 1957).

Owen, G.E.L. "Τιθέναι τα φαινόμενα," in *Logic, Science and Dialectic*, M. Nussbaum, ed. (Ithaca, N.Y.: Cornell University Press, 1986).

Owens, J. *The Doctrine of Being in the Aristotelian Metaphysics* (Toronto: The Pontifical Institute of Medieval Studies, 1963, 2nd edn).

Patrides, C.A., ed., *The Cambridge Platonists* (London: Edward Arnold, 1969).

Pirenne, H. *A History of Europe: From the Invasions to XVI Century* (New York: University Books, 1965).

Pindar. *Pindari carmina cum fragmentis*, C.M. Bowra, ed., (Oxford: Clarendon Press, 1947).

————. *The Odes of Pindar*, J Sandys, tr. (Cambridge Mass.: Harvard University Press, 1937).

Plato. *The Collected Dialogues of Plato*, Hamilton, E. and Cairns, H. eds (Princeton: Princeton University Press, 1971).

Plutarch. *De Iside et Osiride*, J.G. Griffiths, ed. (Wales: University of Wales Press, 1970).

Popper, K. *The Open Society and Its Enemies*, vol. 1, *The Spell of Plato* (2 vols Princeton: Princeton University Press, 1971).

Porphyry, A. Nauck, ed., *Porphyrii philosophi Platonici: Opuscula selecta* (Lipsiae: Teubner, 1886).

————. Sententiae ad intellegibiles ducentes, E. Lambart, ed. (Leipzig: Teubner, 1975).

————. *Selected Works of Porphyry*, Th. Taylor, tr. (London: Th. Rodd, 1823).

————. *Porphyry Against the Christians: The Literary Remains*, R.J. Hoffmann, ed. and tr. (Oxford: Oxford University Press, 1994).

Preus, A. "Greek Philosophy: Egyptian Origins," *in Research Papers on the Humanities and Social Sciences* (SUNY at Binghamton: Institute of Global Cultural Studies, 1992).

Preus, A. and Anton, J.P., eds, *Aristotle's Ontology* (Albany, NY: SUNY Press, 1992).

Proclus. *A Commentary on the First Book of Euclid's Elements*, G.R. Morrow, ed. (Princeton, NJ: Princeton University Press, 1970).

Ptolemy. *Tetrabiblos*, F.E. Robbins, ed. and tr. (Cambridge, Mass.: Harvard University Press, 1956).

Radhakrishnan, S. and Ch. Moore, eds, *Indian Philosophy* (Princeton, NJ.: Princeton University Press, 1973).

Raju, P.T. *Structural Depths of Indian Thought* (Albany, NY: SUNY Press, 1985).

Randall, J. *The Dramatist of the Life of Reason* (New York: Columbia University Press, 1970).

Robb, N.A. *Neoplatonism of the Italian Renaissance* (New York: Octagon Books, 1968).

Rorty, R. *Philosophy and the Mirror of Nature* (Princeton, NJ: Princeton University Press, 1979).

Runciman, S. *The Last Byzantine Renaissance* (Cambridge: Cambridge University Press, 1970).

Russell, B. *Wisdom of the West* (New York: Crescent Books, 1989).

Sibree, J. *The Philosophy of History* (New York: Dover Publications, 1956).

Strabo. *The Geography of Strabo*, H.C. Jones, tr. (8 vols, Cambridge Mass.: Harvard University Press, 1917).

Saunders, J.L., ed., *Greek and Roman Philosophy after Aristotle* (New York: The Free Press, 1966).

Stevenson, L. *Seven Theories of Human Nature* (Oxford: University Press, 1974).

Tatakis, B. *La Philosophie Byzantine* (Paris: Presses Universitaires de France, 1949).

Taylor, A.E. *Plato: The Man and His Work* (London: Methuen, 1926).

Tejera, V. *Plato's Dialogues One by One* (New York: Irvington Publishers, 1984).

Thomas, I., ed. and tr., *Greek Mathematical Works: Thales to Euclid* (Cambridge: Harvard University Press, 1980).

Tigerstedt, E.N. *The Decline and Fall of the Neoplatonic Interpretation of Plato: An Outline and Some Observations* (Helsinki: Societas Scientariarum Fennica, 1974).

Tomadakis, N. "Georgios-Gemistos Plethon," *SBMK* 2 (1966): 151-159.

Toynbee, A. *The Greeks and their Heritages* (Oxford: Oxford University Press, 1981).

———. *Hellenism: The History of a Civilization* (Oxford: Oxford University Press, 1959).

Tozer, H.F. "A Byzantine Reformer (Gemistus Plethon)," *JHS* 7 (1886): 353-380.

Vernant, J.-P. *The Origins of Greek Thought* (Ithaca, NY: Cornell University Press, 1982).

Vlastos, G., ed., *Plato* (2 vols, Garden City, NY: Doubleday, 1971).

———. Socrates: *Ironist and Moral Philosopher* (Ithaca, N.Y.: Cornell University Press, 1991).

———. "The Third Man Argument in *Parmenides*," *Philosophical Review* 63 (1969) 182-301.

Vourveris, K. *Plato and the Barbarians* (Athens, Gr: Gregoris, 1966).

Vryonis, S. and Birnbaum, H., eds, *Aspects of the Balkans: Continuity and Change* (The Hague: Mouton, 1972).

Waldron, J. ed., *Theories of Rights* (Oxford: University Press, 1984).

Wallis, R.T. *Neoplatonism* (New York: Scribner's, 1972).

———. and Bregman, J., eds, *Neoplatonism and Gnosticism* (Albany, NY: SUNY Press, 1992).

Webster, H. *Early European History* (Boston: Heath, 1920).

Werner, M. *The Meaning of Aristotle's Ontology* (The Hague: M. Nijhoff, 1954).

White, M. *The Age of Analysis: Twentieth Century Philosophers* (Boston: Houghton Mifflin, 1955).

Whitehead, A.N. *Process and Reality: An Essay in Cosmology*, D.R. Griffin and D.W. Sherburne, eds (New York: The Free Press, 1978).

———. and Russell, B. *Principia Mathematica* (Cambridge: University Press, 1927).

———. *Science and the Modern World* (New York: The Free Press, 1967).

———. *Religion and Science* (Oxford: Oxford University Press, 1980).

———. *Religion in the Making* (New York: New American Library, 1926).

Whittaker, T. *The Neoplatonists: A Study in the History of Hellenism* (Cambridge: University Press, 1928, 2nd edn).

Wilken, R.L. *The Christians as the Romans Saw Them* (New Heaven: Yale University Press, 1984).

Williams, B. "Philosophy," in *The Legacy of Greece*, M.I. Finley, ed. (Oxford: Oxford University Press, 1984).

Wittgenstein, L. *Tractatus Logico-Philosophicus*, D.F. Pears and B.F. McGuiness, trs, (London: Routledge, 1961).

———. *Philosophical Investigations*, G.E.M. Anscombe, tr. (New York: McMillan, 1968, 3rd edn).

Woodhouse, C.M. *George Gemistos Plethon: The Last of the Hellenes* (Oxford: Oxford University Press, 1986).

Yutang, L., ed., *The Wisdom of China and India* (New York: Modern Library, 1942).

Zeller, E. *A History of Greek Philosophy*, S.E. Alleyne, tr. (London: Longmans, 1881).

Index

Pausanias, 43
peccatum, 90, 94
Peloponnese, 74, 186, 192
people, -s, 1, 7, 8, 10, 11, 13, 15-17, 19-
		25, 29, 31-2, 34-5, 30, 40, 41, 45,
		51, 53-4, 68, 71, 74, 83, 86-7, 91,
		94, 112, 114-6, 119, 127, 130,
		133-4, 139, 143, 144, 146, 148,
		165, 174-5, 177, 184-5, 187, 189,
		190, 193
perception, 40, 46, 53, 90, 103, 195,
		106,117, 126, 158
perfection, 25, 99, 120, 127, 145, 149,
		158, 171, 178
	perfected, 28, 33, 67, 70, 87, 99, 100,
		104, 115, 127, 141, 148
Peripatetics, 77, 100, 118, 129, 131, 162
perplexity, 131
Persia, 20, 43, 50
Persians, 7, 14, 20, 41, 43, 49, 50, 114,
		146
person, 8, 17, 29, 31, 37, 41, 71, 72, 77,
		82, 91, 91, 103, 105, 114, 118,
		124, 143, 168, 173, 183, 193
personality, 110
personification, 183
perspective, 19, 23, 39, 124, 146, 180
phenomenon, 3, 10, 84, 188, 190
	Phenomenology, 126, 179
phil-Egyptian, 27
philhellenism, 186
philosophia, 15, 25, 42, 47, 77, 83, 89,
		93, 98, 107, 118, 123, 166,171,
		173-180, 183, 192, 194;
	philosophy, 7-10;and throughout
		Ancient, 22, 37, 42, 93, 131, 167
		Christian, 84, 187
		European, 1-3, 29, 59, 61, 63-65,
			67, 69, 73-77, 79, 81, 83, 85,
			87, 89, 90-94, 120, 172, 178,
			181, 187, 192, 193
		Hellenic, 1-4, 7-10; throughout
		Indian, 52, 55, 123, 128
		Medieval, 34, 84, 166, 187
		Post-modern, 100
		Western, 8, 97, 102, 118, 121,
			126, 130, 171, 174-180, 197,
			191- 192
Phoenicia, 11, 32
	Phoenicians, 41

phronesis, 21, 93, 134, 167
Phthiotis, 40
physics, 78, 95, 103, 127, 131, 147, 162,
		169, 171
picture, 10, 11, 48, 50, 54, 101, 107, 133,
		156
piety, 21, 87, 91
Pindar, 37, 41, 42, 104, 162, 169
Pirenne, H., 51, 56
plan, 50, 139
planet, 54
plant, 39, 76, 105, 106
Plato, 1, 2, 7, 9, 10, 15-6, 18-9, 20, 24-5,
		26-7, 29, 32-3, 35-9, 41-2, 44-56,
		59-79, 81-83, 84-94, 97, 101,
		107-8, 117-125, 127-134, 139-
		143, 145-149, 150-156, 158-166,
		169, 180-187, 191, 193
Platonism, 2, 3, 7, 29, 34, 36, 56-70, 72-
		76, 81-88, 90, 94, 119, 123-125,
		147, 153-4, 158, 164-167, 172-3,
		180-181, 187, 191
	Platonists, 2, 34-5, 37, 64-69, 70, 72-
		74, 84, 90-91, 95, 104, 122-
		4, 129, 156-9, 160, 164, 171,
		172-4, 180, 182-3, 186
Platonopolis, 86
Pletho, 2, 29, 35-6, 64, 74-5, 77, 84,
		89,92, 119, 153-159, 160-170,
		181-2, 186, 192
Plotinus, 29, 34, 36, 44-5, 61, 65, 68-9,
		73-4, 77, 86-7, 97, 99, 153, 162,
		166-9, 181, 186-7
pluralism, 36, 101, 153
	plurality, 104
Plutarch, 9, 32, 39, 44, 50, 55, 97
poem, 40, 128, 133
	poet, 1, 10, 11, 12, 13, 33-4, 37-9,
		40, 45, 50, 104, 113, 127,
		129, 187
	poetics, 8
	poetry, 9, 45, 50, 188
point, 1-3, 12, 15-17, 19-22, 26, 28, 33,
		37, 39, 45, 47, 50-57, 65-69, 72,
		79, 81, 83, 86, 90, 01, 95-97,
		100, 103, 105, 114, 119, 121-
		124, 129, 142-143, 147, 149,
		150, 154, 156, 158, 161, 163-4,
		166, 168, 169, 172, 174, 178,
		181, 187, 191, 192